Dialogic Approaches to TESOL

Where the Ginkgo Tree Grows

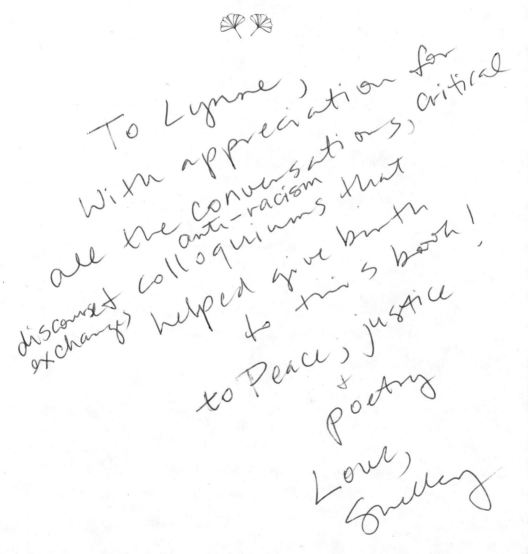

To Lynne,
With appreciation for all the conversations, critical discourse & exchanges, anti-racism colloquiums that helped give birth to this book!
to Peace, justice & poetry
Love,
Shelley

Dialogic Approaches to TESOL

Where the Ginkgo Tree Grows

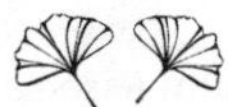

Shelley Wong
George Mason University

2006
LAWRENCE ERLBAUM ASSOCIATES, PUBLISHERS
Mahwah, New Jersey London

Lawrence Erlbaum Associates, Inc., Publishers
10 Industrial Avenue
Mahwah, New Jersey 07430
www.erlbaum.com

Cover design by Tomai Maridou
Cover photo by Patricia Lay-Dorsey. Used with permission.

Library of Congress Cataloging-in-Publication Data

Wong, Shelley. Dialogic approaches to TESOL : where the ginkgo tree grows / Shelley Wong.

p. cm.

Includes bibliographical references and index.
ISBN 0-8058-5597-1 (cloth : alk. paper)
ISBN 0-8058-3901-1 (pbk. : alk. paper)
1. English language—Study and teaching—Foreign speakers. 2. Multicultural education. 3. Critical pedagogy. 4. Dialogue. I. Title.
PE1128.A2W655 2005
428'.0071—dc22 2005047315
CIP

Books published by Lawrence Erlbaum Associates are printed on acid-free paper, and their bindings are chosen for strength and durability.

Printed in the United States of America
10 9 8 7 6 5 4 3 2 1

To Tyrone

Contents

Foreword

A ginkgo seedling sits on my veranda, another trace of the Chinese diaspora in the Malay peninsula. Because it's not native to Singapore, I'm watching to see if it manages to survive the tropical sun and heat. Ginkgo trees sit in parks and gardens around the world - from the famous ginkgo that survived Hiroshima, to those planted as symbols of peace, wealth and health in India, North America, Europe, to those in bonsai gardens in Japan where they have been cultivated since the 15th century. Considered a "living fossil" by scientists, the ginkgo's survival and spread has depended on its unique and multiple ways of regeneration.

The ginkgo, Shelley Wong reminds us, is a powerful metaphor in Chinese history and folk culture. Its naming in Western science by Linnaeus in the 18th century was proceeded in the Sung Dynasty (960 BC). Ginkgo Biloba, the "silver apricot" (gin = silver; kyo = apricot), is a source of shade, protection and food. It is also a bearer of cultural continuity, kinship and sustainability—symbolizing through its longevity, cultural continuity and knowledge. It is taken as a tonic to stimulate mental acuity and memory. Shelley Wong here uses the metaphor of the ginkgo tree to ask perennial educational questions about whose knowledge and language counts, whose cultural wisdom and symbols matter, and which discourses work for whom and to what ends.

Like the ginkgo, when relocated, transplanted and domesticated - languages and cultures are transformed in use and value. When they are, literally, re/placed in western, English-dominant locales they take on new practices and functions. They are reshaped, blended, and their symbolic and practical "places" in their new homes change: in the case of the ginkgo from medicinal to the decorative, from a source of sustenance to an aesthetic object. But how they are recognized and misrecognized, valued and ignored in their new, non-indigenous contexts is a crucial matter.

What becomes of bodies and identities, languages and cultures, when they are transplanted across space and time—whether through migration or slavery, through a search for work or escape from political or religious oppression, through the whims and accidents of history and kinship? This is a question of contemporary social and cultural studies of cosmopolitanism and of the great postcolonial novels of our time (e.g., Ghosh, 2000). It also is at the heart of second language education in the "advanced" educational economies of the North and West.

Shelley Wong's response is to argue for a dialogic approach to second language and minority language education that values students' linguistic and cultural resources, engaging with histories and legacies in ways that realize their cultural and political potential. She questions the social foundations and consequences of dominant models for second language teaching, tracing them back to their psycholinguistic, cognitivist and sociolinguistic roots. At the same time, this volume traces Shelley Wong's own history as nomadic scholar and educational activist, a history that has taken her to ESL classrooms in the US and Asia, to work with Chinese students studying in American universities, to her current work with teacher trainees in midwestern and eastern American "heartlands."

Shelley Wong and I grew up together. Our families left LA Chinatown about the same time in the 1950s, we lived about a mile from each other, our parents were and are dear friends, we played together at Sunday school, went to weekend Chinese school together, read Dick and Jane in primary school together, swapped homework and shared school projects—I played in rock 'n roll bands with her brother. We cared for each other as friends and kids.

We also received our somewhat unusual political educations together. Our parents were a rare breed in the Chinese community then, politically left of center, continually calling our attention to social and community issues. Some of the parents of kids we grew up with, Shelley recently reminded me, were blacklisted writers and artists. Our pastor in the 60s, George Cole, introduced us to a social gospel, and we marched together for civil rights, including our own and our community's, and later against the Vietnam War. For what it's worth, we got a "critical" education from back as far as I can remember. Our schooling was that odd blend of American meritocracy and progressivism of the Los Angeles School District, circa 1955. It was *this* postwar blend of cultural history, institutional context, intercultural engagement that politicized us, an alchemy of mainstream but prototypical multicultural schooling, Chinese community organizations, the church, exposure to the burgeoning media and popular culture of the 60s and 70s.

The commitment you see in this book thus comes from our fathers and mothers, brothers and sisters, from our communities, and indeed, from that historical context. It could be recounted as another "model minority" story, as some kind of "Asian-American" essentialist tale, as yet another migrant "home/school" narrative—but it was and is so much more complex than that, as are those of the African American, Latino, Chinese and other minority students that Shelley Wong writes about here.

If there is an insight here it is an indirect one: that as much as it can be taught or viewed as an educational responsibility, the "critical" is constituted by position and disposition, by history and by agency, by the interaction of all those fields and forms of life that make us what we are (Luke, 2003). It can be generated from the experience of having been "other," when and if that "otherness" can find its dialogic and institutional locations and places where it can be called into play, realized into both capital value and ideological/intellectual power. This can occur, Shelley Wong argues, when we move past the convergent approaches of the school or university that tend to read off "deficit" and "lack" (or, inversely, expectation: as young Chinese-American kids, we both were expected by our teachers to be wizards at mathematics; neither of us were).

That we would succeed, become professionals, work like mad to get to university, marry other Chinese—was part of the folk wisdom of that postwar minority community. What wasn't part was that narrative is that people like Shelley would remain so steadfast in their political orientation, that some would cross many, many national and racial boundaries again and again across their lives, and remain committed to marginalized communities. For throughout this book, there is that keen sense of the other, of the struggles not just of her life, but that of her partner Tyrone's and her other families and children in the African-American community. The roots and branches of this particular tree, then, take us not just back to Guangzhou, but as well to Martin Luther King and DuBois, to the American South and the ongoing struggles of African American and Asian American communities.

True to its title, *Dialogic Approaches to Teaching English to Speakers of Other Languages* offers a dialogue with a teacher, teacher–educator and scholar who has "lived" these politics across diasporas, in several languages, to Asia and back, and taught them to colleagues and, indeed, to our racial and linguistic "others." It reflects a rare tenacity, an abiding commitment, and an absolute, resolute refusal of inequality in education.

—Allan Luke
Jurong, Singapore
October 2004

REFERENCES

Ghosh, A. (2000). *The crystal palace.* New York: Harper-Collins.

Luke, A. (2003). Two takes on the critical. In B. Norton & K. Toohey (Eds.), *Language learning and critical pedagogy* (pp. 54—76). Cambridge: Cambridge University Press.

Preface

The ginkgo is considered to be one of the toughest of all cultivated trees, a belief borne out by a famous specimen growing near the hypocenter of the 1945 atom bomb blast over Hiroshima, Japan. According to Michel and Hosford, the tree that still grows there today survived the bomb by sprouting from its base after its trunk was completely destroyed.

Another indication of ginkgo's exceptional power of survival is its long life span. Throughout Asia there are many large and ancient specimens that are in excess of a thousand years old. According to Professor Ling of the Zhejiang Forestry Department, the largest and perhaps oldest ginkgo in China is a specimen growing in Folaishan in Ju County, Shandong Province. It is an ovulate (female) tree, approximately three thousand years old, with a diameter at breast height (DBH) greater than 4 meters and a height of 26.5 meters (del Tredici, 1991; p. 4).

Like the ancient ginkgo tree, the roots of dialogic pedagogy can be traced to Chinese soil. In tracing the origins of dialogic inquiry, many draw only from Western foundations such the Socratic dialogues. However, rich sources of dialogic pedagogy can be found in Asia, Africa, Australia, and the Americas. Dialogic inquiry in the form of storytelling, oral histories, and knowledge from the ground up and from the margins has much to offer to the field of teaching English to speakers of other languages (TESOL) (Mama & Romney, 2001). This book locates dialogic pedagogy within the history of TESOL approaches and methods in which the communicative approach has been the dominant paradigm (Richards & Rogers, 1986).

Introducing newer critical, feminist, and racial, linguistic and cultural minority voices that have been historically underrepresented within TESOL, dialogic approaches to TESOL draw upon diverse theoretical sources from traditional philosophy such as Socrates and Confucius and from 20th-century pedagogies of liberation such as those of Paolo Freire and Mao Zedong, and the cultural historical psychology of Lev Vygotsky and dialogic translinguistic theories of Mikhail Bakhtin. In dialogic approaches to TESOL, the teacher and students learn in community, and the students' home languages and cultures, families, and communities are seen as resources.

The book explores the significance of feminist and womanist theories and women's ways of knowing for dialogic approaches in the field of TESOL, and calls for the integration of antiracist, feminist, and critical perspectives. It discusses teacher research, feminist contributions to voice, social identity and dialogic pedagogy, and ESOL teachers, students, families, and communities as advocates and change agents.

INTENDED AUDIENCE

In the pages of this book I make the distinction between English as a second language (ESL) and English as a foreign language (EFL) (Ellis, 1994). ESL refers to teaching in English to nonnative speakers of English in English-speaking countries such as the United States or Australia, and also in countries such as Singapore and Kenya, in which English is an official language. EFL refers to teaching English to speakers of other languages in countries where English is not an official language, such as Thailand, Turkey, or Burkina Faso. However, I hope not to dichotomize but to draw the connections and unity of and between ESL and EFL experiences. I believe that many of the best second/foreign language teachers are those who have experienced being "foreigners" themselves (Rivers, 1983; Tinker Sachs, 2002).

I hope that *Dialogic Approaches to TESOL* provides questions, frameworks, and resources for those who are just beginning in the field and for United States based educators who want to bring critical multicultural and multilingual perspectives into language arts, reading, and literacy education. I hope that the ginkgo tree provides a shady place for dialogue and reflection on the prospects for transforming educational institutions to serve those who have historically been excluded and marginalized.

OVERVIEW OF CONTENT AND PLAN FOR THE BOOK

The ginkgo tree metaphor I present in the Personal Prologue is relevant to the structure of the book. Two kinds of text are included. One is the main chapter text, which, like the main trunk of the tree, considers a single topic related to the concept of dialogic pedagogy. The other texts, set off from the main text, are the branches of the tree. Like trees that line a country road, some of these branches intertwine between trees, forming a connection between those trees, especially when it is summer. The trees shade the road, forming a leafy tunnel with their intertwined branches. Branches allow for these all-important digressions without allowing the reader to forget the main point of the chapter. This structure allows readers to become well rooted in each component of dialogic pedagogy and to "branch out" into deeper philosophic understandings as well as actual practices across a range of contexts.

The book begins with a history of TESOL methods, from grammar translation to the direct method, the reading approach, audiolingualism, and communicative approaches. It includes a brief introduction to dialogic pedagogy, the newest approach discussed. In chapters 2–5 I identify and discuss four features of dialogic approaches to TESOL that I have found to be most important in my teaching:

- *Learning in community* encourages teachers to learn with and from their students, and to encourage a diversity of voices within the classroom. This is in contrast to what Paolo Freire (1970) called a "banking pedagogy," in which teachers "deposit" knowledge into students as if they were empty receptacles.
- *A problem-posing* approach to curriculum identifies meaningful, important questions involving students' lives and the purposes for which they want to learn English. It encourages students to reflect on their learning strategies and to draw on their own linguistic and cultural awareness as resources.
- *Learning by doing* embodies the principle that the best way to learn English is through classroom activities, assignments, and evaluation that encourage students to actively use English for real-world communicative purposes. Similarly for us as teachers, the best way to learn to teach is by actually teaching and reflecting on our practices.
- The fourth feature of dialogic pedagogy is to pose the question, *"Knowledge for whom? Or whom does knowledge serve?"* in order to understand and oppose inequities for working-class students, girls and women, racial and ethnic minorities, and indigenous people, who have traditionally been excluded from education.

In chapter 6, the conclusion returns to the roots of TESOL methodology, dialogic interpretations of the nature of language and the learner, in light of challenges from "postmethodology." It also revisits a reoccurring debate in TESOL methodology: Is language teaching an art or a science? The appendix includes an excerpt from the dialogic Pilgrimage Curriculum I developed for three theological students from the People's Republic of China to prepare them for graduate school in the United States. The Pilgrimage Curriculum is available on my web site at www.http://mason.gmu.edu/~swongl/. The appendix is followed by a glossary of Chinese characters used in the book, for TESOL professionals who like me are beginning students of Chinese. It includes characters like *ren* (*jen*) which are difficult to translate into English, as well as Cantonese dialect expressions.

Personal Prologue

My journey in teaching English to speakers of other languages (TESOL) began in Hong Kong in the early 1970s. I had gone to Hong Kong not to teach English, but to study Cantonese. As a fifth-generation Chinese American who had grown up outside of a Chinese-speaking community, I was searching for my roots.

Hong Kong, of course, was a British colony. Although 98% of the people spoke Cantonese, English was the language of the government officials, the courts, and the schools. It was literally the language of power. "Foreigners" (which conveyed a negative connotation in England or the United States) were referred to as "expatriates," a term that was positive in the Hong Kong context. The "ex-pats" earned higher salaries than local Chinese with similar qualifications. Ex-pats had special housing allowances that were not provided to local people. Many who had lived with modest means in England were members of exclusive country clubs and had Chinese servants in Hong Kong.

There were numerous privileges attached to the British and, by extension, English speakers in general. If you ordered a telephone in English (whether British or American dialect), it would be installed immediately. But if you ordered it in Chinese, you could wait for months. The "best" schools were those in which English was the medium of instruction for all subjects except Chinese language and history.

I was offered a position at Tak Nga Middle School, a Catholic girl's school in Kowloon, as a teacher of English language and literature. My only credentials were that I had graduated from an American university and I was a native speaker of English.

Being a native speaker didn't help me answer my students' questions. I frantically read *A Midsummer Night's Dream* one scene ahead of my students and relied, as they did, on *Cliff* notes. When the students asked me the difference between the "simple past tense" and "the present perfect," I had *no* idea.

As a novice teacher, I depended on my Chinese colleagues at the school and my friends—tutors at the Chinese University of Hong Kong—to interpret my students' second-language writing. My friends' knowledge of Chinese enabled them to understand what my students wanted to express, for example, when student writers translated Chinese idioms literally into English. My friends and colleagues clued me in on how to correct what was a new genre for me—the précis, a brief summary of an article.

The educational system in Hong Kong was like a pyramid, with many students at the bottom and few at the top. Each year students were evaluated and weeded out so that only the best graduated. Tak Nga Middle School's good reputation was based on a moderately successful pass rate of its students for the British school leaving exams; only its best students were allowed to continue from Form 1 all the way to Form 5.

In the 1970s, Hong Kong had only two universities. Admission, which was based on examination scores, was extremely competitive. Examinations also played a critical role in determining prospects for employment in a colonial economy. Students with better scores in English would be hired for white-collar jobs as clerks, as opposed to factory jobs in electronics.

But there were also harsh consequences to the weeding out process. During my first year of teaching at Tak Nga middle school, there was a Form 2 girl who failed the examination that would allow her to continue in Form 3 and who was therefore asked to leave the school. She committed suicide.

The experience of beginning to teach English under British colonialism shaped my view of education in profound ways. I came to understand that education could be literally a matter of life and death.

The Form 2 student's suicide caused me to look at the problem of examinations, language teaching, and power. Suicide was her response to academic failure, her inability to accept the reality of failing a school examination and the consequences of not being promoted to the next form. Not being promoted to Form 3 reflected the closing of life chances, not just for the girl but for her family. She and the vast majority of students would fail not because they were lazy or not sufficiently motivated, but because only a small minority of the 12-year-olds would be promoted up the pyramid from Form 1 to Form 5 and then take the most important examination, the British School Leaving Certificate Exam.

The girl's suicide raised questions for me: What did it mean to be a good ESOL teacher in the context of the examination system? How can one help students take a meaning-centered approach to learning a language when the examination system promotes a focus on memorization of vocabulary and grammatical structures? How might one teach not just to but beyond the test?

At a broader level, I wondered: Why couldn't everyone who studied hard succeed? Why was there such a disparity between educational opportunities for the rich and the poor, between the first world and the third world? Given that English is a language of colonialism, is it possible to teach it in a non- or even anticolonialistic manner? What, if anything, could a single ESOL teacher do to address systemic oppression?

At that point, I felt helpless. Because of my ignorance of formal English grammar, the standard interpretations of Shakespeare, and other items that would appear on their tests, I had failed as a teacher and my failure could have serious consequences for my students. Yet they were the ones facing the examination that determined the shapes of their lives, not I. The only consequences I faced for being an inadequate teacher were those of my own making, those of my own conscience.

Those questions about teaching have continued to shape my teaching and thinking for the 30 years since my stay in Hong Kong. I have undertaken research and planned classes around my growing understanding of some of the possibilities for answering those questions. I have attempted to find avenues around that sense of helplessness in the face of seemingly immutable institutions. I have used my thinking and my research so that I could become a successful teacher, not only one who helps students to succeed within a given system, but one who enables students to take a critical stance regarding that system and possibly even to contribute to changing the system. This book is the fruit of those 30 years of teaching, researching, and thinking.

ABOUT THIS BOOK

As I have explored nonoppressive approaches to teaching, a metaphor has arisen, a metaphor that not only connects my own Chinese American culture to my teaching, but that illuminates how that teaching can work. The metaphor takes the form of the ginkgo tree, an ancient, tenacious, generous tree—a tree that survived the atomic bomb blast in Hiroshima, a tree that can live longer than a thousand years, a tree that is considered a source of food to some and a source of a rotten smell to others, depending on culture.

English as second or foreign language learning has existed across history and cultural contexts, from efforts to erase children's home language and culture through enforced English speaking in schools to the hopeful potential graduate student passing the TOEFL exam and gaining admittance to an educational opportunity that will benefit him or her as well as family and community, from the overcrowded, underappreciated ESL program in the basement room of an American urban school to the well-funded university program teaching English to business executives. An individual classroom, or a multinational effort, like the ginkgo tree, can be seen as something desirable or something to be avoided, depending on the perspective of the observer.

The ginkgo tree can be as old as a thousand years or as young as last week's sprout. Dialogic pedagogy, like the ginkgo tree, has roots in ancient philosophies of both East and West. It also incorporates modern Eastern and Western pedagogies of liberation and recent approaches to understanding oppression.

Whatever the context, teachers have a limited set of choices about teaching. Some teachers have a great deal of latitude, whereas others have few choices about what and how to teach. Dialogic pedagogy helps teachers to maximize their own choices in the interest of student learning and empowerment. Where choice exists, dialogic pedagogy guides teachers into helping students learn how to use language to achieve their own goals—to be flexible and thoughtful users of a new language.

Dialogic pedagogy also helps teachers to recognize where, how, and why they are limited and to make it known to the students that the limitations of the system are not the fault of the students. Not only can students then potentially become part of a grass-roots effort for change, but also they can recognize how their own performance is influenced by the institutions in which they learn and work. By stepping outside of their immediate situation, students and teachers can identify the forces that create teaching and assessment practices that cause harm. After all, the Form 2 girl who committed suicide thought that her failure was personal when, in fact, it was systemic.

In the summer, the leaves of the ginkgo create a cool green shade, just right for long philosophical conversations or a short lesson on how to accomplish grocery shopping in English. This book is a long philosophical conversation between voices as disparate (and similar) as Socrates and Mao, Vygotsky and Confucius. It is a long conversation about how to teach something as practical as grocery shopping as well as why and how we teach it. In the shade of the ginkgo tree, those who love to teach can have the pleasure of discussing the "whys and wherefores" of teaching in the interest of doing the best job we possibly can.

Acknowledgments

My deepest appreciation to Naomi Silverman. I could not have had a more politically conscious and supportive editor. Her many years of experience in academic publishing in the areas of language, literacy and culture and her lifelong commitment to grassroots movements for social justice are a rare and unique combination. Naomi Silverman was truly a midwife. If not for her, I would have been one of the thousands of women who never finished, simply being overwhelmed by what Tillie Olsen (1977) termed the "abnormal silences." Naomi Silverman played a special role in the "growing" of this book. She helped me re-conceptualize and restructure the contents of this book, most dramatically from the first to the second draft.

My two reviewers Suzanne Wong Scollon and Brian Morgan provided feedback that was both generous and specific. Both have spent many years themselves being students of Chinese cultures and communities throughout the Diaspora and were attuned to issues that less knowledgeable readers might not have been aware of. Suzanne read the first draft of this book when she was doing research in China. She brought insights from a lifetime of work that has bridged culture, semiotics and education throughout the Pacific Rim from Hawaii, Alaska, Korea, Taiwan, Hong Kong and other parts of China. Both reviewers were well read in critical literacy and applied linguistics. Brian is a long-time activist for social justice and brings his own teaching experiences in critical pedagogy. While having the benefit of expert reviewers, I did not always follow their advice. Errors in perspectives and interpretation are my own.

The dialogic pedagogy about which I theorize in this book has been shaped by my own learning and life experiences as a fifth-generation Chinese-American woman. I was blessed with grandparents who lived long lives, had good memories and were willing to talk about their lives in great detail. As I was growing up, I was told many stories from my grandmother who was born in Weaverville, a gold-mining town in Northern California and my grandfather who came over from China at age 15 to work as a houseboy in Sonoma, California.

To the extent that this book is feminist/womanist I owe to the strong women in my life, especially my mother Dolores Wing Wong. She was a pioneer in progressive child-rearing practices, having four children by natural childbirth, and breast-feeding all four in Los Angeles in the 1950s during a time when most of her generation thought bottle feeding was "scientific" and breast feeding "primitive." She sought out progressive co-op nursery schools such as the Hollywood Los Feliz Jewish Community Center for my brothers Pudgy (Duane), Kent and Marshall and bought us United Nations and inter-racial, inter-faith children's books and records. She promoted bilingualism by speaking Cantonese at home with me and my brother Pudgy (although being American-born herself, English was her strongest language). She set up Saturday heritage Chinese language classes at our church. She sent us and dozens of her friends' children to Brotherhood Camp an interracial, intereligious camp for high school students sponsored by the National Conference of Christians and Jews. She and my father, Judge Delbert E. Wong supported us in attending alternative and progressive schools—Kent and Marshall attended L.A. Unified School District alternative high schools, Kent was a graduate of the People's College of Law, founded by the National Lawyer's Guild and our parents supported us to study abroad—Hong Kong for me and Cuernavaca, Mexico for my brother Marshall.

My mother was born in 1921 in Vallejo, California a U.S. Navy town near San Francisco. The oldest daughter and first in her family to attend college, in the 1930's she picketed at U.C.–Berkeley's Sather Gate to protest the Japanese invasion of China and the United States sending scrap metal to Japan. In 1943 she joined the National Association for the Advancement of Colored People (NAACP). She never understood how anyone who had experienced discrimination for their race or ethnicity could then turn around and discriminate against another group. Throughout her whole life she has always been willing to take up the cause of the underdog. I want to thank my parents, Dolores and Delbert E. Wong for their love, encouragement and support. As my first teachers, from my very first steps, they supported my learning through doing.

The book is anti-racist and anti-imperialist because I was a part of the Asian American student movement during the period of the Third World Strikes at San Francisco State and U.C.–Berkeley in 1968–1969 and the movement against the War in Vietnam. I want to particularly thank U.C.–Santa Cruz professors Herman Blake, Bill Domhoff, Wally Goldfrank, Arlie Hochschild, Leonard Kunin, Barry McGlaughlin, Ruth Needleman, and

Alan Sable for setting an example with their own critical scholarship. This book is stamped with a deeply anti-colonial perspective because I first began my career in Teaching English to Speakers of Other Languages/Bilingual Education (TESOL/BE) in Hong Kong in the early 70s. I want to express gratitude to the many unnamed movement friends and extended family from U.C.–Santa Cruz and the Bay Area, Hong Kong, Los Angeles, New York, Washington, DC, and North Carolina for lessons and insights throughout the years.

Throughout this book are the voices of my own teachers, my professors in Teaching English as a Second Language and Applied linguistics at UCLA: Clifford Prator, Russ Campbell, Marianne Celce-Murcia, Evelyn Hatch, Donna Brinton, Diane Larsen-Freeman, Mary McGroarty. The framework for dialogic pedagogy was suggested by my dissertation advisor at Columbia Teachers College, Clifford Hill, who first guided me towards the philosophical orientation of teacher-as-researcher. He helped me frame my dissertation using the lens of the dialogic mode and encouraged me to write it as a narrative description. Professor Frank Horowitz introduced me to Saussure and the Prague School. Professor Jo Anne Kleifgen introduced me to the world of applied linguistics and ethnographic research in computer mediated language learning. Professor Maria Torres-Guzman provided ethnographic methods in cross-cultural, bilingual research and the culture of the classroom. Professor Maxine Greene inspired me to take an explicitly political stance in looking at my research methodology and introduced me to the dialogic imagination of Mikhail Bakhtin, the aesthetic and cultural dimension of politics and education and John Dewey. Her voice makes its way throughout the pages of this book. My struggle to articulate dialogic pedagogical approaches was also influenced by professors Ray McDermott, Lucy Calkins and Heidi Jacobs.

Deepest respect and gratitude go to Rev. Gao Ying, Li Yading and Zhang Xian yong without whom this book would never have been written. In 1986–1987 these three Chinese theological students were the very first to be sent from the churches in the People's Republic of China for graduate study in the United States. I was their English language tutor employing a dialogic approach to introduce them to the many voices in New York City. Describing the students' orientation in preparation for graduate studies in theology became the basis of my dissertation. As a study of three people entering a new culture, it's important to note that I was observing the students in a particularly limited context, during a time of "strangeness" when they were not themselves, not at home living their "normal" highly capable lives. I observed them in their "foolishness" as Li Yading termed it, when they felt home-sick, ill-at-ease, child-like, and moody. Their efforts to learn English and adjust to their new environment were quite extraordinary and heroic.

The students' journey was a joint project of the China Christian Council in the People's Republic of China and the China Program of the National Council of the Churches of Christ in the United States of America. Clearly it is difficult for those of us who have never suffered for our religious beliefs to be able to understand, let alone write about the faith experiences of Chinese Christians. Gao Ying, Li Yading and Zhang Xianyong shared their stories and hopes and inspired me with the strength of their convictions.

On the Chinese side, the president of the China Christian Council, Bishop K. H. Ting, personally played an active role as mentor, advisor, and pastor for the students through his many visits, letters and calls. On the American side, Rev. Dr. Franklin Woo, director of the China Program of the national Council of Churches and his wife Jean played the key role of advisors for the students in the United States. Jean and Franklin served as bilingual bicultural role models for the students and for me. My friend Marion Yuen has lent advice and encouragement throughout the years from the initial preparation of the Pilgrimage Curriculum to the present manuscript. Dr. Brenda Sansom, a staff person for the China Program, applied her knowledge of Chinese language and history from her own dissertation to working with the Chinese students. Appreciation to Father Paul Woodrum for his talk with the students, Ken Guest, Hu Yang, Asian Americans for Equality and Rev. Dr. Wyatt T. Walker of Canaan Baptist Church for welcoming the students and participating in dialogue with them. Thanks go to Mary Jerome, Patrick Aquilina and Polly Medinger of the American Language Program at Columbia University, where they were full time students, President Donal Shriver, Dean Milton Gatch, Professor Christopher Morse, Augustine Masopola and Kathryn Pething of Union Theological Seminary for welcoming the students into the Union community. Professor Morse graciously allowed us to audit and videotape each of his lectures for Foundations of Christian Thought which provided the basis for our English language tutorials.

Thanks to my former students from the University of Maryland: especially Suhanthie (Su) Motha, Dana Frye, Will Roberts and Charlie Wang. The genesis of chapter three comes from a collaborative research project conducted when Dana, Will and Charlie were doing their student teaching and Su was their university supervisor. Other research projects which make their way into this book include a National Reading Research Project a joint project between the University of Maryland and Arlington, Virginia ESL specialists Etta Johnson, Emma Violand Sanchez, ESL teachers Marty Maher, Ruth Sedei and Grace Avis, Reading and 1st and 2nd grade classroom teachers, a Prince George County literacy project including William

De Lorenzo, Karen Spezio, Ruby Best-Lewis, Lisa Malaev, Sharon Teuben-Rowe and a parental involvement project with Dana Frye, Soyini Janice Harden and Rachel Grant in Fairfax, Virginia.

Thank you to Yvonne Gentzler for introducing me to Sadker and Sadker and Carol Gilligan when we taught at the University of Maryland together. Special appreciation to Rachel Grant for moral support and the 673+ various survival strategies throughout the years that it has taken to write this book. Angel Lin graciously read the manuscript and lent support. And special thanks to Carolyn Cutler, my writing teacher, editor and coach.

Thank you to Jim Lantolf, Gabriela Appel and the many L2 Sociocultural colleagues for the stimulating talks over the years about Vygotsky and second language research. I want to especially thank Steve McCafferty, Maria de Guerrero, and Elizabeth Platt, for conversations and articles concerning the zone of proximal development and i + 1.

Deep appreciation to Allan Luke for sharing his critical discourse analysis assignments he developed at James Cook University. Many of the ideas in this book were worked out through a series of TESOL colloquiums on critical discourse analysis with Lynne Diaz Rico, Helmut Vollmer, Suhanthie Motha, Dana Frye, Anne Marie Foerster Luu, Jennifer Binckes Lee, Yen YuhYun, and one memorable session in New York in 1999 with Allan Luke, when former students reflected on his critical discourse analysis assignments as beginning teachers in the field. I want to thank Theresa Austin for organizing a session on challenging monolingual norms at the American Association of Applied Linguistics, providing an opportunity for critical appraisal of the contributions of Clifford Prator.

The Ohio State University has been a fertile place for the "growing" of this book. I want to thank my mentor Charles Hancock for encouraging me to write this book. The Zambian proverb he quotes, "Start where you are, but don't stay there" has been a source of daily support, as has the friendship of colleagues Keiko Samimy, Alan Hirvela, Vickie Ellison, Khadar Bashir-Ali and Mari Haneda. Anna Soter generously shared her book proposals with me and gave feedback to me on my proposal. Mollie Blackburn read and commented on chapter two. I want to thank the many students at Ohio State University who read various drafts of the book and gave feedback. Thanks to my colleagues Brenda Custodio, Carmen Chacon, and Khadar Bashir-Ali who used the book when they taught EDU T & L 640 TESOL Methods. Thank you to Mary Armentrout for helping with the book proposal and the first 3 drafts of this book and Emily Malor for her assistance with draft four and six. Thank you for computer support from Jan Dow's office of capable staff: Jon Lehman, Ryan Stocker and William Strucke. Yen Yuh-Yun helped to research the Ginkgo tree and was an able research assistant in the early stages of this book. Hyungmi Joo helped in the subsequent stages with careful reading and editorial support and references. Her wise counsel and her blessing of the Conclusion enabled me to "let go" of this book. Ko Yi-fang helped with the Chinese Glossary. The core of the Chinese Glossary came from the glossary from my dissertation which was done with the help of Li Yading and my friends from the Chinese Community Church in Washington, DC. Yee Yat-bing and Mina Chan. Support of an International Travel Grant from the Ohio State University enabled me to meet with Michelle Kwan who translated characters throughout the book and prepared the Glossary. GMU student Betty Chan Dailly and OSU students helped with research and the final additions to the Chinese characters and glossary: Fu-Chun Chen, I-Chia Chou, Yen-Hui Ho, Chiung-Tzu Hou, Hyunju Lee, Ming-Ching Li, Hsin-Mei Lin, Jeng-Jia Lou, Charm Moreto, Hiroshi Shima, Ivan Stefano, Mei-Hsing Tsai, Maggie Wu, Yan Xun, , Hyunsook Yoon, Eunjyu Yu, and Yang Yu. Francis Bangou, Anita Bright, Betty Chan Dailly, Rachel Grant, Soyini Harden, Marilyn Morales, Suhanthie Motha, Yang Yu, and Yen Yuh-Yun read chapters from the final proofs. Suzanne Sheppard was a dialogic relational production editor who exemplified *ren*. I want to thank my friend Donna Vanderhoff and research assistant Anna Safi from George Mason University who helped with editorial advice and perspectives from their own teaching, references and indexing in the final production stage. Thank you to Maggie Gonzales for all her kind and generous assistance. Thanks to artist, writer and peace activist Patricia Lay-Dorsey who photographed the picture taken in the Detroit Zoo of the ginkgo tree that appears on the cover of this book.

Finally, I want to thank the Wong family and the Pitts family and my extended family—including my sister scholars—without whose love and support this book would never have been written. Last but not least deepest gratitude and love to my husband Tyrone Pitts who read every chapter through its successive drafts and for unbelievable encouragement throughout the years.

1

Political and Philosophical Roots of TESOL

Taproot, n. *the main root of a plant, which grows directly downward with small branch roots spreading out from it.*

—Webster's 20th Century Dictionary Unabridged, 2nd ed., 1983

The roots of the ginkgo provide a foundation for the tree. Each tree has numerous roots, ranging from large to microscopic. Some roots are not essential for the life of the tree; if you cut them, others will grow back to provide nourishment and support. But each tree has taproots that enable the tree to get water, minerals, and nutrients from deep in the soil and to position itself vertically to grow towards sunlight. If you cut a taproot, the tree will not survive.

The roots of pedagogy lie in larger social and historical forces such as political and economic structures, and they center around the question, "What purpose does education serve?" This question can be divided into two possibilities, which in any classroom in actual schools become mixed up with one another: Should education replicate hierarchical social structures, as they currently exist? Or should education seek to change these structures to allow every person to participate fully in a democratic society with liberty and justice for all (Edelsky, 1991; Wiley, 1996)?

History includes many examples of education that reproduced oppressive social structures (Baugh, 1999; Collins & Blot, 2003). Before emancipation in the United States, it was against the law to teach enslaved people to read. Indigenous people such as the Alaska Eskimos, Indians and Aleuts, Lakota and the Navajo in the United States and Canada, the Sami in Norway, and the Aborigines in Australia were put in English-speaking boarding schools and were beaten or had their mouths washed with soap for speaking their native languages (Crawford, 1998; Jordan, 1988; McClanahan, 1986). Most universities did not admit women in equal numbers to men until well into the 20th century; at the beginning of the 21st century, women remain underrepresented in positions of academic leadership in university, professional, and graduate programs around the world (Balderrama, Texeira, & Valdez, 2004). In middle schools and high schools in which there are equal numbers of girls and boys, what is privileged as "natural," "normal," and "right" in the classroom and curriculum silences, shadows, and hides certain voices with respect to class, race, and gender (Weis & Fine, 1993).

The replication of unequal social structures through education continues (Apple, 1982; Chomsky & Macedo, 2000). Although university personnel recognize the cultural bias of entrance examinations (e.g., SAT and GRE), these test scores nonetheless remain significant to admissions processes (Haney, 1993). Kozol (1991) pointed out that in the United States, within the same district there are different schools for the rich and the poor. In predominantly European American middle- and upper-middle-class neighborhoods there are attractive, well-maintained public schools, with well-lit classrooms, state-of-the-art libraries and computer labs, manicured lawns, and well-equipped gymnasiums with clean locker rooms. Public schools in poor and racial minority neighborhoods have metal detectors, unsanitary and smelly toilets with no doors, leaky roofs and unsafe structures, outdated books, and no computers. Even within the same school, tracking and sorting of students into ability levels produces disparities between the quality of education provided to the children of upper-middle-class families and those of poor and working-class and racial minority families (Oakes, 1985; Harklau, 1994).

Drawing from the U.S. Bureau of the Census data, Sorlorzano and Ornelas (2002) showed that out of every 100 Chicana/Latina[1] students who begin elementary school, 56 will drop out before graduating from high school:

- Only 44 will go on to graduate from high school.
- Only 24 will pursue some form of postsecondary education; 13 continue on to community colleges and 11 will go to a 4-year institution.
- Of the 13 who enter a community college, only 1 will transfer to a 4-year institution.
- Only 6 Chicana students will graduate with a baccalaureate degree.

[1]Solorzano and Ornelas used *Chicana/Latina* as a gender-neutral term to be applied to both women and men. Chicanas/Latinas are defined as female and male persons of Mexican and Latin American ancestry living in the United States, irrespective of immigration or generation status.

- Less than 1 will receive a doctorate degree.

Differences in the treatment of rich and poor children result in dramatic differences in incarceration rates for drug-related offenses. Although the majority of drug users are White, a disproportionate number of minorities are arrested and put in jail. In the United States there are more African American young men in prison than in college. Differences with respect to race and class background are reflected in who gets elected to public office. In the entire history of the United States there have been only two African American senators.[2]

What does it mean for education to help people gain access to economic success and political influence? To do so would mean realizing the dream of framers of the U.S. Constitution, wherein all people—who are created equal—have the opportunity to make for themselves a life of liberty, in which they can pursue happiness rather than remain at the margins, scraping for survival.[3] This sounds like an educational ideal with which everyone can agree, and yet since the institutionalization of this ideal through the French and American revolutions more than two centuries ago, serious discrepancies remain. French sociologists Pierre Bourdieu and Claude Passeron found that more French university students came from the middle- and upper-class families than from working-class families and that students from rural areas were underrepresented (Bourdieu & Passeron, 1977). The patterns they found in France exist around the world (Heller & Martin-Jones, 2001; Lin, 2001b). The democratic ideal of education for all is not easily attained, for complex reasons that become apparent in this chapter and throughout this book.

How do we understand the role of language in the creation and maintenance of institutions as well as what it means to teach another language, particularly the "power language," English? How do we understand the forces within and among our educational institutions that replicate injustice as well as the possibilities for ending oppression? How do we understand the possibilities for action that can be taken by individuals, especially teachers? This chapter and the succeeding chapters address TESOL in the broadest way, drawing from a variety of perspectives, includ-

---

[2]There are different theories to account for the differential incarceration rates and differences in who goes to the university. For critiques of biological determinism, see Gould (1981) and Selden (1999).

[3]The ideals of the American Revolution for freedom from tyranny and "no taxation without representation" did not include the indigenous people, the Native American Indians. Women were excluded from the democratic rights, as well as African slaves and their descendants. Similarly, the French Revolution ideals of "liberty, equality, and fraternity" were limited to men with property. Excluded were women, landless peasants, and the emerging urban proletariat, who did not own property.

ing political and philosophical theories (e.g., Marx, Freire, and Mao) that account for teaching and learning in the context of social and political liberation; dialogic perspectives on language, literature, and linguistics (e.g., Bakhtin); sociocultural psychology (Vygotsky); critical race and postcolonial approaches that question racism and differential treatment with respect to the historical legacies of the descendants of slaves, plantation workers, and colonized and indigenous people whose language and accents are respected or discriminated against (Canagarajah, 1999; Lippi-Green, 1997; Matsuda, 1991; Vandrick, 2002); and feminist and poststructural perspectives on gender, race, language, and identity (Collins, 1991; Greene, 1986, hooks, 1981, 1994; Lather, 1991; Lin, 2001a; Luke & Gore, 1992; Norton, 2000; Pavlenko, 2001, 2004).

TEACHING METHODOLOGY

Teaching begins with methodology, which has roots in philosophy, politics, psychology, and various understandings of the nature of language. Although we may think of method as a series of steps taken within a given class session, we find that these steps can change drastically (or even not so drastically, but with a greater deliberation) based on which roots are identified as the taproots.

Methodology in TESOL includes the theory and practice of "curriculum *and* instruction," "teaching *and* learning" at several levels, from the everyday planning of classes to understanding how one's own teaching fits into the larger context of linguistic, psychological, social, and political constructs. It includes study of syllabus design, activities and assignments, selecting, adapting and creating appropriate teaching materials, and evaluating and assessing student progress, as well as raising teachers' awareness of our own learning, as we reflect on how to better meet the needs of our students.

Clifford Prator (1979) provided three questions or "cornerstones" (Fig. 1.1) to consider in developing TESOL methodology.[4] These three questions are *taproots* in preparing to teach ESOL students in both EFL and ESL contexts:

1. What is known about the nature of the language?
2. What is known about the nature of the learner?
3. What are the aims of instruction?

[4]Dr. Prator wrote "Cornerstones of Method" in 1964–1965 when he was on sabbatical leave from UCLA. It appeared as a chapter in Celce-Murcia and McIntosh (1979).

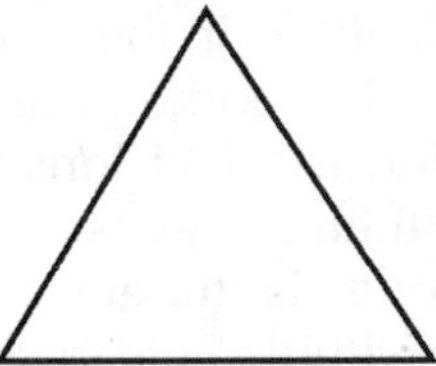

FIG.1.1. Prator's three cornerstones of method.

For Prator, the field of linguistics was related to his first question, "What is known about the nature of language?" and the field of psychology was related to the second question, "What is known about the nature of the learner?" As we show later, the emphasis on psychology was in keeping with Prator's time. Today we would point to the value of interdisciplinary perspectives from anthropology, sociology, political economy, and history to help us understand the nature of the learner. Although the answers and the fields of study relevant to Prator's questions might have changed with time, his *questions* remain central to TESOL methodology.

As a teacher educator, Prator trained his students to determine how to teach EFL or ESL by inquiring into the nature of their students and the purposes for which they needed to learn the language. He encouraged teachers to use a flexible and pragmatic approach to language teaching by asking, "What is the aim of instruction?" This question was *student* centered. Like the Council of Europe (Wilkins, 1976), which developed notional functional approaches to the teaching of foreign languages, Prator's cornerstones of method was rooted in *needs analysis*, a careful, systematic account of the purposes for which students were studying a foreign language.

In surveying the history of foreign and second language methods, Prator observed a tendency toward "violent swings in the pendulum," citing examples such as the role of rules, the use of phonetic symbols, and vocabulary control:

> A first dip into the literature on methods ... is likely to be a puzzling, even a disheartening, experience. In fact one highly touted "method" or "approach" has succeeded another in the favor of educators, and the proponents of each have tended to deny the validity of all that preceded. The use of the mother tongue in the foreign language classroom has been successively emphasized, banned, required, and barely tolerated. (p. 5)

Prator wanted teachers to know about the history of teaching approaches, and to not get caught up in the passing fad of the moment. He thought that teachers should become familiar with many approaches and methods and make informed decisions concerning which methods to utilize for the benefit of their students. In that respect, he fostered a professional discourse among his students. This enabled his students to locate themselves critically within a field that had contending paradigms, schools of thought, and various charismatic leaders in its history. However, his own approach to foreign language teaching was more "apolitical." It could be characterized as an "autonomous" rather than an "ideological" model of literacy, which would link language teaching to a critical analysis of unequal political and economic relations in the world (Street, 1984).

Across the history of the TESOL field, there have been paradigm shifts in psychology and linguistics that have led from traditional "transmission" models—teacher-centered methods that focus on conveying knowledge to students, as if students were passive receptacles—to interactive and communicative models—which begin to take into account student perspectives because they center on making meaning—and finally to dialogic perspectives on language learning—which account for the sociopolitical aspects of language learning (Auerbach, 1989; Darder, 1991; Skutnabb-Kangas, 1988). Broadly, the shift has moved from teacher-centered to learner-centered to dialogic, interactive, participatory language learning as social practice situated within the educational institution and community contexts.

BRANCH 1-1: TEACH TO THE NEEDS OF STUDENTS, NOT TO A BOOK! REEXAMINING PRATOR'S CONTRIBUTIONS

I remember 30 years ago, as a graduate student in the Teaching English as a Second Language program at the University of California–Los Angeles (UCLA), when Dr. Clifford Prator (1911–1993) advised us that methodology should be based on the needs of our students. To plan lessons around what the students needed, rather than to allow a book to dictate the syllabus, was timely advice for me and became a taproot for my own teaching. As a new teaching assistant I was rushing my ESL 33B class through the textbook, attempting to "cover" all the grammatical points in the syllabus. Over the years as I've taught in different contexts, I've heard Prator's voice admonishing me to "Teach to the needs of the students, *not* to a book!" I have imagined his voice each time I have tried to study what students need, learn about their life experiences, or analyze the purposes for which they were studying English. His questions have become a cornerstone of my teaching methodologies.

Yet the passage of time has brought new understandings that Prator and other TESOL theorists of that time had never considered. For example, psychology as a purely cognitive field devoid of concern for cultural and social contexts has been supplemented by anthropological and sociological insights (Bruner, 1990). In these new lights we must reexamine Prator's contributions, and in so doing we will find that Prator asked vital questions but, perhaps because of the time and place of his birth, was not able to allow those to be answered in fully egalitarian ways.

What Is the Nature of the Learner?

Is there any reason to assume that a Third-World learner of English is less of a person, from a lesser culture, than a First-World learner of another language? Poststructural and critical perspectives in women's studies and ethnic studies suggest that we be more inclusive rather than automatically adopt Eurocentric, upper-middle-class or male-as-norm answers to the "nature of the learner" (Ladson-Billings, 2004). Sociohistorical and dialogic approaches stress the complex and contested, hybrid, and heteroglossic nature of any learner. The individual learner is seen as a site of struggle, through membership in overlapping, heterogeneous, and sometimes conflicting social groups. The nature of the self is dynamic and fluid, rather than fixed and static. As Cynthia Nelson put it:

> Identities began to be theorized not as facts but as acts ... not attributes but positionings ... not essences but strategies ... not "museum pieces or clinical specimens" but "works in progress." (Nelson, 1999, p. 374)

Prator was criticized by Braj Kachru (1986), Sandra McKay (1991), Arjama Parakrama (1995), and others for his position on which dialects or varieties of English were acceptable models for the classroom.

In "The British Heresy in TESL," Prator (1968) argued against using local varieties of English, such as Indian or West African English, and argued that only "mother-tongue" English (British or American) should be used as a model. His stance was based on the French model of foreign language teaching in which Parisian French was unquestioned as the standard. The French government defined and set the standards for the national language, and a suggestion to emulate "deviant" pronunciation would be dismissed as absurd. Prator criticized a position advanced by M. A. K. Halliday, A. McIntosh, and P. Strevens (1964). Writing from the standpoint of teaching English in newly independent countries, Halliday et al. had come to question British Received Pronunciation as the only appropriate model. They argued for using local educated varieties as the standard. Prator disagreed with Halliday, McIntosh, and Stevens.

He warned that using diverse models would lower instructional standards:

> The doctrine of establishing local models for TESL seems to lead inevitably in practice to a deliberate lowering of instructional standards. In the minds of many students it becomes a convenient, officially sanctioned justification for avoiding the strenuous effort entailed in upgrading their own pronunciation. It weakens any sense of obligation a teacher may feel to improve his own speech and makes it impossible for him to put any real conviction into his attempts to encourage or impel his students in the same direction. (p. 474)

He was particularly critical of Indian English:

> After 20 years of testing the English of hundreds of incoming foreign students semester after semester at the University of California, I am firmly convinced that for the rest of the English-speaking world the most unintelligible educated variety is Indian English. The national group that profits least from the University's efforts to improve their intelligibility by classroom instruction also seems to be the Indians; *they can almost never be brought to believe that there is any reason for trying to change their pronunciation.* It is hard to doubt that there is a direct connection between these conclusions and the fact that the doctrine of local models of English is championed more often and more vehemently in India than anywhere else. (p. 473, italics added)

Prator's comments reflect limitations in his own ability to understand the implications of colonialism for English language teaching. Prator acknowledged that proposals for the acceptance of local varieties inevitably occurred in former colonies:

> In fact, such proposals seem to arise spontaneously and inevitably in every formerly colonial area where English as been the principal medium of instruction long enough for the people to begin to feel somewhat possessive about the language. (p. 460)

But Prator's comment on "possessiveness" shows that he was not able to understand the implications of colonialism from the standpoint of the colonized. Who owns English? Why is it that American English, which also is derived from the descendants of a British colony, is considered "native English" but the language of the "natives" is not?[5]

While Prator's "The British Heresy in TESL"[6] was published in 1968, it was written before the Civil Rights Movement became the Black Liberation Movement, and before there was a resurgence of the women's movement in the

[5]Prator acknowledged that the area where second language varieties of English would be needed would be at the lexical rather than the phonological level: "New words are certainly needed to identify things and processes for which there is no name in British or American society."

[6]1968–1969 was the year of the Third World Liberation Strike at San Francisco State University.

United States. After World War II, which devastated the former European powers, the United States emerged as the top imperialist power in the world. However, many U.S. academics possessed little awareness of colonialism or imperialism.[7] During the McCarthy period, some of the leading African American and progressive intellectuals like W. E. B. DuBois and Paul Robeson were fired, blacklisted, imprisoned, exiled, and, in the case of Paul Robeson, refused passports (Robeson, 1958). It was not until the "natives" themselves began to write from their own perspectives that the legitimacy of varieties of English such as Black English, African American Vernacular English, or Ebonics became an issue in the public discourse (Smitherman-Donaldson & van Dijk, 1988). Although linguists like Braj B. Kachru began conceptualizing a theoretical framework for Indian English as early as 1965, organized efforts to discuss the concept of World Englishes occurred with the convening of conferences at the East-West Culture Learning Institute in Honolulu, Hawaii, and the University of Illinois at Urbana Champaign in 1978 (Kachru, 1995).

Linguists say that all languages are equal, but educational institutions teach only the language of the elite. We must work as language teachers to educate the public on the myths of the superiority of one language over another. We must dispel linguistic stereotypes (Luke, 1986).

This includes making sure that the voices of language-minority speakers are included in the curriculum (Perry & Delpit, 1998). It is also critical that language minorities be hired at all levels of the educational system, from elementary schools to the university, and in all capacities from teachers, counselors, and social workers to administrators, professors, educational researchers, and technical and educational support staff (Grant & Wong, 2003). Recognition of multiple languages is a struggle over language policy. We seek to teach English as an *additional* language, not to replace the home language or dialect with standard (White) English. To produce curriculum in the home languages of all the students is a struggle for linguistic equality.

What Are the Aims of Instruction?

What is the fine line between helping our students become intelligible to other speakers of English and psychologically colonizing our students by insisting that their rendition of English match as much as possible British or "standard" American speech? At some level, accent is of a part of identity:

> Your accent carries the story of who you are—who first held you and talked to you when you were a child, where you have lived, your age, the schools you attended,

[7]For this reason, the courage of Noam Chomsky who was willing to use his position as a university scholar to speak out against U.S. involvement in Vietnam and oppose U.S. imperialism is particularly noteworthy. See Rai (1995).

> the languages you know, your ethnicity, whom you admire, your loyalties, your profession, your class position: traces of your life and identity are woven into your pronunciation, your phrasing your choice of words. Your self is inseparable from your accent. Someone who tells you they don't like the way you speak is quite likely telling you that they don't like you. (Matsuda, 1991, p. 1329)

When I was a student in Dr. Prator's phonology class, "native speakers" of English were paired with "nonnative speakers" to work with a diagnostic passage in Dr. Prator's *An American Manual of Pronunciation*. I was paired with a classmate from Japan, and the pairing worked to our mutual advantage. Looking back critically I would today still encourage students from the United States and students from Japan to work in pairs and would encourage tutorials for pronunciation, stress, and intonation, as well as listening. Although these pairings are helpful, in my opinion, I also encourage my graduate students to read Professor Mari Matsuda's (1991) article on accent discrimination in the *Yale Law Review*.

My own consciousness has been raised through two former graduate students from the University of Maryland, experienced ESOL teachers with whom I have worked collaboratively in TESOL presentations and on publications. Ruby Best Lewis is a teacher originally from Trinidad. Henry Amador is Puerto Rican, a former Young Lord in New York City in the 1960s.[8] Both Best Lewis and Amador have said, "My accent is a part of me. If you try to change my accent you are trying to change me."

Best Lewis and Amador challenge us to ask the definition of native speaker. Does native speaker mean "White?" Why is it that White New Zealanders or Canadians or South Africans whose accents evolved from British English are considered "native speakers" and Blacks from the former colonies of Rhodesia (now Zimbabwe) or Trinidad are not? Why are Indian and Singapore English varieties or Native Hawaiian pidgin seen as being "incomprehensible?" TESOL scholarship on World Englishes, Black English or African American Vernacular, and nonnative English language professionals raises the need to address racism in language teaching. Unlike the field of bilingual education, the field of TESOL has had a blind spot when it came to accent discrimination; this discrimination has prevented language-minority teachers from entering our profession. Instead, they went to bilingual programs because there, their knowledge of two languages was valued. Too often in TESOL only "native speaker" competence has been valued (Braine, 1999; Brutt-Griffler & Samimy, 1999):

---

[8]In the 1960s the Young Lords like the Black Panther Party and the Red Guards in Chinatown organized youth to "Serve the People." For example, college students at UC Santa Cruz supported the Black Panther Party in developing a Breakfast for Children Program. Advocates of self-determination and self-defense and against police brutality, these organizations were targeted by the police and FBI. The Black Panther Party leadership was systematically attacked through the COINTELPRO program of the FBI.

> The term *accent reduction* comes from a particular paradigm in which ESL teachers feel responsible for changing the speech habits of learners of English. Why not consider another term that could possibly come from the perspective of those who teach and do research in the ESL world: *accent addition*? English-knowing bilinguals are often capable of demonstrating convergence in their speech acts by approximating the accent of monolingual English speakers while being deeply aware of and proud of their own distinguishable accents.... It is perhaps time to rethink the identity and intelligibility issue because the English that English-knowing bilinguals will use will be inextricably intertwined with who their interlocutors will be. (Pakir, 1999, p. 110)

All people internalize oppression. People at all levels in oppressive hierarchies are deeply affected and divided by these ideologies. They are so deep that they seem "normal" to us. Unexamined racist ideology hurts our profession and drives away the very students we should be attracting to our profession. We need to find fresh and imaginative ways to address all forms of discrimination in our field. Cultural studies and critical discourse analysis provide tools for the critique of racist and gender-biased textbooks. They help us to support those who are victimized by racism, religious intolerance, and homophobia and to develop proactive responses to prevent violence. Multicultural, ethnic studies and women's literature, especially postcolonial literature, provide fertile soil for the ginkgo nut (Ngũgĩ, 2003; Pennycook, 1994b).

The Role of the Teacher: Prator's Empowerment of Teachers as Researchers

Who determines the needs of the students? Prator respected the language teacher. He placed the teacher at the center of decision making. For example, his three questions from "Cornerstones of Method" led me to view teachers' concerns, such as "When did my adult ESL students who worked in Chinatown actually use English? How could I prepare lessons that addressed their needs? Could there be a closer fit between their communicative needs and the classroom?" as legitimate questions for scientific investigation (Wong, 1985). In that respect his work as a teacher educator encouraged my own development as a teacher researcher. Prator believed that ESOL teachers were both capable and the best people to conduct this research.

Prator often asked the right questions, and he placed proper emphasis on the role and the ability of the teacher in making informed decisions about teaching methods and strategies (e.g., in contrast to instructional methods so highly scripted that teachers become mere technicians). In contrast to his thought-provoking questions, his answers to them were elitist and limiting. He was not able to give the full, rich answers that we can give to these questions today, yet his questions and his perspective on the role of the teacher continue to provide a taproot for today's ESOL teachers.

HISTORY OF TESOL METHODS

During the 20th century, TESOL methods used in the United States, such as grammar translation, the direct method, the reading approach, the audiolingual method,[9] and the communicative approach,[10] evolved considerably. Early on, TESOL was dominated by structural approaches to language; that is, primary attention was paid to the phonological, morphological, and syntactic structures of English. Yet structural approaches emphasize structures at the expense of developing communication skills, which may impede second language students' abilities to use the language they are learning. They may become self-conscious about mistakes, and they have not been encouraged to develop strategies for cobbling together meaning from what they know.

The second problem that both structural and communicative methods ignore is the sociopolitical context for learning a second language, particularly for learning English (Hall & Eggington, 2000; McKay, 1993; Morgan, 1998). English is the language of colonization—and not only the literal colonization that reached its height in the 19th century, but also mental colonization, as children, for example, learn English in American schools and forget their native languages and heritages (Wong-Fillmore, 2000). The learning of English opens some doors that run contrary to people's native cultures, even while it opens the doors of educational and economic opportunity. Because English has become a worldwide language, many native speakers of English have never learned a second (much less a third) language, and this limits their understandings of other cultures. Frequently, learning English is a one-way door: Outsiders come in but insiders less often venture out. These sociopolitical realities are significant in the classroom. Students (and their parents) may have mixed feelings about learning the culture of English, and these concerns may profoundly affect their motivation. Further, if we want to keep students and their desires to communicate at the center of classroom teaching, then the social identities of the students—who they are, who their friends and families are, and

[9]The British counterparts to the audiolingual method (ALM), the oral approach and situational language teaching, were developed by linguists Harold Palmer and A. S. Hornby from the 1920s and firmly established as the major British paradigm through the 1950s and 1960s. Like the ALM, there were vocabulary control, a structural syllabus, and behaviorist habit formations. Unlike the ALM, due to the influence of British linguists J. R. Firth and M. A. K. Halliday, there was an emphasis on context, hence the term "situational approach" (Richards & Rogers, 1986).

[10]Celce-Murcia and Prator's (1979) outline of teaching approaches in the 20th century listed the "cognitive approach," rather than "the communicative approach," after the audiolingual approach. The cognitive revolution in psychology had been so thorough that the audiolingual method was discredited, but what would become the new paradigm in the field in the 1980s, the communicative approach, was not yet established.

the communities to which they belong—become important subjects about which to communicate (Norton, 1997, 2000; Hansen & Liu, 1997; McNamara, 1997). As teachers, we need to get to know the many contexts of our students, their histories and realities, so we can provide them with the language to communicate about them. This is a central purpose of dialogic pedagogy, as shown later.

The Grammar Translation Approach

The oldest structural approach, which remains popular in teaching English in Asia and many parts of the world, is the grammar translation approach, sometimes called the "Prussian approach." An example of this approach still in use in the United States would be the teaching of a Classic "dead" language such as Latin. In this approach, sentences are translated from the foreign language into English. The mother tongue is used as the medium of instruction, and speaking the target language is not a major aim of instruction:

> Language learning had become grammar recitation and dictionary thumbing. Students defined the parts of speech, memorized conjugations, declensions, and grammar rules; and translated selections, using a bilingual dictionary or glossary. (Lado, 1964, p. 4)

The goal of grammar translation is to read classic texts so as "to benefit from the mental discipline and intellectual development that result from foreign-language study" (Richards & Rogers, 1986, p. 3). Grammar translation is a *structural* approach to language teaching because the focus is on linguistic structures, including syntax or word order (e.g., how to form the passive construction) and morphology or word formation (e.g., roots, prefixes, and suffixes). However, the structures selected for study are not necessarily sequenced according to difficulty or frequency of use. The grammar translation approach has been criticized because it taught students to recite rules and to translate written passages, but not to speak the language.

The Direct Method

In response to the grammar translation approach, modern language professors in Europe created a reform movement. For example, in 1886, Dr. Otto Jespersen, professor of English from the University of Copenhagen in Denmark, Prof. Western from Norway, and Prof. Lundell in Sweden "struck a blow for reform" (Jesperson & Bertelsen, 1912, p. 1) The reformers sought to teach modern languages such as German or English differently from the way that classical languages such as Greek or Latin were taught. The reformers taught *structures* of the foreign language, and also emphasized oral language. Dr. Jespersen thought that spoken language was essential to foreign language teaching. He wrote during the time the international phonetic alphabet was developed, and he advocated the scientific use of phonetics in teaching modern languages.

Another early reformer was Henry Sweet. His book *The Practical Study of Languages,* first published in 1899 and reprinted in 1964, emphasizes sensible and comprehensive principles of language teaching that remain applicable today. Like Jespersen, he advocated the use of phonetics and he emphasized oral language:

> All study of language, whether theoretical or practical, ought to be based on the spoken language. In European languages, where the difference [between written and spoken language] is much less, most grammarians tacitly assume that the spoken is a mere corruption of the literary language. But the exact contrary is the case: it is the spoken which is the real source of the literary language. (p. 49)

Like Jespersen, Sweet was opposed to the elitist view that classical languages were superior to modern languages or that written language was superior to oral language:

> Even such forms as *thou hast, he hath* were ordinary colloquialisms a few centuries ago, though they now survive only as fossil, dead colloquialisms side by side with the living colloquialism *you have, he has*. Every literary language was a mixture of colloquialisms of different periods. (p. 49)

Critical of studying word lists or language out of context, Sweet supported the judicious use of translation, rather than translation as the only classroom activity. He also supported the use of grammatical rules through teaching patterns.

This reform movement included the founder of the Berlitz schools and exists today. It was referred to as "new method, reform method, natural method, and even oral method, but they can all be referred to as direct methods or the direct method" (Lado, 1964, p. 4) The direct method was used to teach modern languages. The object was to enable the student to speak the language, by using the language. Harold and Dorothy Palmer developed oral drills so students could have direct contact with the foreign language. A typical example of the direct method was for the teacher to issue commands to create a situation for language use in the classroom, for example: "Go to the door. Open the door. What are you doing?" "I'm going to the door. I'm opening the door."

The direct method, like the grammar translation approach, was also a structural approach. However, the structures for study were selected with regard to frequency of occurrence in modern languages, rather than being selected from classical texts. Englishman T. Prendergast (1806–1886) proposed the first "structural syllabus" (Richards & Rogers, 1986, p. 5). The direct method focused on basic patterns with a pedagogical principle of moving from more simple to more complex. Like Asher's total physical response of today, which is associated with a natural approach to learning languages, advocates of the direct method looked to child language learning and naturalistic principles of language learning for inspiration. Rather than tie language learning to the first language, they used the second language to actively promote speaking and using the language in the classroom. Although the reform movement and the direct method were promulgated throughout Europe, the direct method never become the dominant method of teaching in the United States.[11] Instead, it gave way to the reading approach.

The Reading Approach

The reading approach—which was prominent in the United States in the 1930s and 1940s until World War II, stressed reading. The Coleman Report of 1929 set reading as the major goal for foreign language instruction in the United States, based on a number of factors. A study of foreign language teaching in the United States had revealed that there was a lack of sufficiently trained foreign language teachers. Few teachers had native-like competency to utilize the target language almost exclusively in instruction without a textbook. The direct method required that teachers be fluent in the foreign language. The Coleman Report also argued that it was not important for secondary and college students who might never go abroad to study conversation. These students could benefit from reading and learning about the history of other countries. Unlike the grammar translation and the direct method, the reading approach did not emphasize the teaching of grammatical structures. Students were introduced only to grammar that was needed for reading comprehension. The reading approach was the only dominant approach in the United States that was not structural in nature.

---

[11]A recent sample text item for the TESOL Praxis Exam asked, "Which of the following approaches to language learning makes *the greatest use* of active participation, including gestures and bodily movement? (a) Cognitive Code Learning, (b) Total Physical Response, (c) Natural Approach, (d) Direct Method" (italics added). One may speculate the "correct" answer, Total Physical Response (TPR), is a language teaching method built around the coordination of speech and action; it attempts to teach language through physical (motor) activity. Therefore, B is the correct answer." The item reflected the test makers' U.S.-centric or ahistorical lack of knowledge of the direct method.

The Audiolingual Approach

The audiolingual approach (sometimes in the U.S. called the Army Method) got a boost in World War II when the United States needed to train military personnel for active communication, including intercepting messages and interrogating prisoners. The reading approach, which did not prepare students to speak, was inadequate. With the expansion of the war to Asia and the Pacific there was also a need to train personnel in non-European languages. The Army Specialized Training Program (ASTP) enlisted linguists such as Leonard Bloomfield at Yale, who designed the methodology and materials to train the military (Richards & Rogers, 1986).

The first center of teaching English as a foreign language was established at the University of Michigan in 1939 by Charles Fries, a structural linguist and innovator of the audio-lingual approach. The audiolingual method became the dominant approach in foreign language teaching in the United States. It was at its height of popularity in the 1950s and 1960s.

A typical audiolingual textbook, such as the Lado 900 series, began with a conversational dialogue. Students listened to audio tapes of the dialogue and repeated the phrases until they had memorized it. The dialogue had key sentence structures or grammatical points. Another feature of the audiolingual textbook and lessons was "pattern practice" drills. Students practiced linguistic structures through substitution drills in which they repeated a pattern, substituting a noun or a verb to memorize vocabulary and grammatical structures.

Audiolingualism stressed "mim-mem" (mimicry and memorization). Behaviorist theories of learning stressed that "language learning was a habit," learned through imitation and repetition. Errors were corrected immediately, so that they wouldn't become bad habits and "fossilize." Emphasis was placed on oral proficiency with native-like pronunciation, stress, and intonation. Teachers taught listening and speaking before reading and writing. From structural linguistics, a contrastive analysis was made between the native language (L1) and the target language (L2). The analysis was used to predict difficulties and to train students to have more native-like pronunciation. For example, Spanish speakers may have difficulty in distinguishing English /b/ and /v/ sounds. Minimal pair drills were developed to assist Spanish speakers in distinguishing and pronouncing the sounds. The teacher would put words in two columns:

(1)	(2)
ban	van
berry	very
best	vest

The teacher would then say a word and ask students to put up one finger if the word was from column 1 and two fingers to indicate that they heard a word from column 2. The teacher would also call on students to pronounce the sounds.

The Cognitive Revolution

The audiolingual approach was discredited by the "cognitive revolution," a paradigm shift in linguistics and psychology. The linguist Noam Chomsky (1957) led the assault on the two theoretical foundations of audiolingualism—behaviorism and structural linguistics—through his scathing critique of Skinner's stimulus-response theories that equated human language learning with laboratory rats going through mazes.

Chomsky rejected the behaviorist view that "language learning was habit formation" and that the best way to learn language was through drill and pattern practice. To Chomsky, language learning was a creative and cognitive process. Chomsky stressed the innate ability for human beings to communicate through language, a biological inheritance. He pointed to the fact that children would say unique or novel utterances that could not be the result of parroting adult speech, such as an English-speaking young child saying "two feets." This example was cited as evidence of the child's cognitive ability to apply rules. The child understood the rule that "s" signaled plurals and overgeneralized that rule with an irregular plural. This example showed that the child was not imitating adult speech around her or him, but was applying rules. To Chomsky, the example illustrated that language acquisition is "rule-governed." The child's error had a rational basis to it and demonstrated that language acquisition is a cognitive process.

Any speaker of English would recognize the first of these two sentences to be a grammatical sentence in English (Chomsky, 1957, p. 15):

1. Colorless green ideas sleep furiously.
2. Furiously sleep ideas green colorless.

Sentence 1 was meaningless from a semantic point of view—how could something "colorless" be green? Despite its being nonsensical, a native speaker of English would recognize the sentence as a grammatical English sentence. Chomsky's view of grammatical competence was formal knowledge of the rules of a language (i.e., syntactic structures or word order), which was *independent of meaning.*

Chomsky distinguished between "competence" and "performance." To Chomsky, a native speaker would make errors in performance due to fatigue, memory limitation, shifts of attention or interest, or other factors that were not a reflection of that person's actual competence or knowledge of what was grammatical. Chomsky's linguistics was based on an idealized speaker/hearer's knowledge of grammar as word order or syntax.

Using ambiguous sentences, Chomsky demonstrated problems with the behaviorist argument that knowledge of structures was learned inductively through stimulus response and pattern practice. For example:

> Visiting relatives can be boring.

This sentence could have two interpretations, two deep structure meanings:

> It can be boring (for someone) to visit relatives.
>
> Or
>
> Relatives (who visit) can be boring.

Similarly Chomsky (1972, p. 166) contrasted the following two sentences:

> John is eager to leave.
>
> John is easy to leave.

Although the two sentences are identical in surface structure, they have different deep structures. In the first, John is eager to leave someone or someplace. In the second, it is easy (for someone) to leave John. Chomsky's transformational grammar posited that there were deep structures that went through transformations until they reached the surface forms. The "someone" in "John is eager to leave someone" and "It is easy for someone to leave John" is deleted in the surface forms. Chomsky used these examples of syntactic structures to discredit the behaviorist views that language learning was a question of substitution drills, habit formation and stimulus response. To Chomsky,

> one can describe the child's acquisition of knowledge of language as a kind of theory construction. Presented with highly restricted data, s/he constructs a theory of the language of which this data is a sample (and in fact, a highly degenerate sample, in the sense that much of it much be excluded as irrelevant and incorrect—the child learns rules of grammar that identify much of what s/he has heard as ill-formed, inaccurate and inappropriate). The child's ultimate knowledge of language obviously extends far beyond the data presented to her/him.... Furthermore, the task of constructing this system is carried out in a remarkably similar way by all normal language learners, despite wide differences in experience and ability. (Chomsky, 1972, p. 171)

Rather than viewing language acquisition as mimicry and parroting, Chomsky saw it as cognition or "a theory of human intelligence that has a distinctively rationalist flavor" (Chomsky, 1972, p. 171).

Linguists and psychologists were not the only ones to be dissatisfied by the behaviorism of the audiolingual method. Teachers questioned whether memorization of dialogues helped their students use the language. Students could rattle off native-like renditions of a dialogue to ask for directions, but were unable to understand responses that varied from the memorized dialogue. Pedagogically, many teachers questioned the efficacy of drilling students. The drills were boring, and rather than being habit-forming they were turning students off. Teachers wanted students to be able to *use* the language.

The Communicative Approach

The communicative approach emphasized that foreign and second language teachers should help students to be able to *use* the target language. Widdowson (1978) pointed out the distinction between "usage" and "use." Although "usage" is a learner's ability to demonstrate his or her knowledge of the properties of formal linguistic rules, "use" is the learner's ability to apply knowledge of linguistic rules in effective communication. Communicative language teachers were interested in the latter. The communicative approach shifted emphasis from structural to *functional* perspectives on language, which in the United States was influenced by the work of sociolinguists such as Del Hymes, who coined the term *communicative competence.*

For language teachers, communicative competence implies performance, the ability to use the knowledge of what is grammatical in actual communication. Language educators who were inspired by Chomsky's critique of behaviorism and influenced by sociolinguistic perspectives were concerned with developing *both* competence and performance (Savignon, 1983, 2002). Second and foreign language teachers didn't want students who could recite rules, or parse sentences, but couldn't use the grammar in action. They wanted students to be able to perform, to understand and speak, to read and to write.

Some communicative methods modified audiolingual features to make that approach more creative, dynamic, and imaginative. An example would be the John Rassias or Dartmouth approach, which uses role playing rather than strict memorization of dialogues. The Rassias approach is structural and incorporates drills from the audiolingual approach. By using finger snapping, surprise, and timing, the Rassias approach makes sure that students concentrate during the drills. The unpredictable finger snapping (you never know when you may be called on)—and the small size of the group—four or five students with a tutor—ensures that students remain alert during drilling.

The Natural Approach

Another communicative approach which was influenced by Chomsky's cognitive revolution was the natural approach,[12] which incorporated first-language acquisition studies in the teaching of second languages. Stephen Krashen found it significant that babies have a long period of listening before they utter their first words. Krashen and Terrell (1985) argued that second language learners could benefit from a period of time in which they listen to the sounds, vocabulary, and structures of the new language before they were expected to speak. They referred to this as the "silent period." In total physical response, students are not required to speak during the first 21 hours of instruction (Asher, 1969, 1982). They listen to commands in the L2 and indicate their understanding through their actions (stand up, go to the door ...). Learners have less anxiety and are more receptive to acquiring a second language naturally. Krashen and Asher believed that languages were best acquired when the learner's "affective filter" was lowered. If the filter was "high" and students were fearful about making mistakes, it would be more difficult to learn the new language.

Krashen formulated his understanding of the process of student learning as: "i + 1," where "i" refers to "input" and "+ 1" refers to grammatical structures that are somewhat above what the student has already acquired. Krashen's model of language acquisition focused on the importance of comprehension (which can take the form of listening or reading). He believed that the best input was meaningful (rather than boring to the student) and slightly above the student's level. This slightly higher level provided students something to which they could aspire and at the same time, something that students could achieve.[13]

Whole Language and Other Language Arts Methods

TESOL has been influenced by revolutions in first-language language arts and English education, notably whole language approaches to reading

[12]Richards and Rogers (1986) pointed out that 20th century communicative approaches have their parallels in 18th and 19th century language teaching reformers such as Gauguin and Sweet, who also looked to first language acquisition as a source of inspiration in teaching foreign languages.

[13]For an in-depth critique of Krashen's theories, see deBeaugrande (1997).

and writing (Freeman & Freeman, 1992), as well as process approaches to writing (Flower & Hayes, 1981; Reid, 1993; Zamel, 1983). Although the audiolingual approach sequenced the four skills (of listening, speaking, reading, and writing) and delayed reading and writing, contemporary communicative approaches stress reading and writing connections (Belcher & Hirvela, 2001). Some of the newer approaches in language arts and English education that can contribute to an understanding of our work in TESOL have also included readers and writers workshops (Atwell, 1987; Calkins, 1986) and journal writing (Peyton, 1990, 1993), which overlap with dialogic approaches to TESOL. Rather than delaying literacy until there is a strong oral foundation, reading and writing begin immediately. Bilingual whole language approaches have stressed the importance of biliterate development (Franklin, 1999; Goodman, Goodman, & Flores, 1979; Perez & Torres-Guzmán, 1992).

Communicative Competence and the Communicative Approach

Canale and Swain (1980) suggested that communicative competence is actually composed of several types of competencies:

> Grammatical competence (which is similar to Chomsky's linguistic competence).
>
> Sociolinguistic competence (appropriate politeness or register according to social status, roles of the speakers within a specific social context).
>
> Discourse competence (the connections and relationship between various elements in a text, which includes both spoken, signed and written modes).
>
> Strategic competence (use of coping strategies to initiate, terminate, maintain, repair and redirect the conversation).

Del Hymes (1974, p. 206) put forth seven themes that are relevant to communicative competence and communicative approaches to language teaching:

1. Linguistic theory as theory of language, entailing the organization of speech (not just of grammar).
2. Foundations of theory and methodology as entailing questions of function (not just of structure).
3. Speech communities as organizations of ways of speaking (not just equivalent to the distribution of the grammar of a language).

4. Competence as personal ability (not just grammatical knowledge, systemic potential of a grammar, superorganic property of a society, or indeed irrelevant to persons in any other way).
5. Performance as accomplishment and responsibility, investiture, and emergence (not just psycholinguistic processing and impediment).
6. Languages as what their users have made of them (not just what human nature has given).
7. *Liberté, égalite, fraternité* of speech as something achieved in social life (not just postulated as given as a consequence of language).

If language education is to actualize the ideals of the French revolution for *liberté, égalité, fraternité* (and one might add sisterhood and racial and economic equality) it must be seen as an ongoing project, a work in progress or social practice, requiring ongoing analysis, reflection, and further transformation.

Hymes's seven themes contrast with formal, structural approaches of language teaching in the concern for the social and political dimensions of communication. Hymes's second theme, which emphasizes *function*, not just structure, is a linguistic foundation to the communicative approach. Functional approaches to language learning emphasize the teaching of language to express meaning and to communicate. Wilkins's notional syllabus (1976) in Europe was an attempt to organize the class syllabus around notions (i.e., ideas such as time or measurement) and functions of language (i.e., to compliment, to apologize). The idea was to teach the types of language an adult would need to function effectively in any of the countries in Europe. This contrasted with previous structural syllabi, which organized the syllabus to introduce grammatical structures in order of complexity (i.e., in English first the copula "be," then present continuous).

In Europe and Australia, impetus for functional approaches has come from the work of linguist Michael Halliday (1973, 1985), who developed an understanding of language based on why people use it (its function) in social settings, "social semiotic," or how language makes meaning in the context of relationships between people. For Halliday and Hasan, social context influences meaning as much as grammatical structures, which is why they used the phrase: "functional-systematic grammar as a social semiotic" (Halliday & Hasan, 1985).

For Halliday there are three functional components of the semantic system of language: the ideational, subdivided into logical and experiential; the interpersonal; and the textual. In a study of first-language acquisition in baby Nigil, Halliday (1975) identified seven functions that emerged:

1. The instrumental function: using language to get things.
2. The regulatory function: using language to control the behavior of others.
3. The interactional function: using language to create interaction with others.
4. The personal function: using language to express personal feelings and meanings.
5. The heuristic function: using language to learn and to discover.
6. The imaginative function: using language to create a world of the imagination.
7. The representational function: using language to communicate information.

The seven functions that Halliday identified in baby Nigel's language are a good point of departure for us as we think about the functions of talk in school. Baby Nigel developed the representational function after he developed other functions of language. In contrast, in classroom talk we often begin with the representational function of language and emphasize it to exclusion of other functions:

Where is the book? It's on the table.

What's the capital of Iran? Tehran.

It might be more engaging if instead, from the beginning we emphasized all seven functions of language.

Halliday's functions of language have also been applied to literacy instruction. In analyzing the act of reading, Wells (1990) posed a framework of five modes of engagement with text:

1. The performative mode—related to decoding text.
2. The functional mode—uses text as a means to get things done. For example, a deposit slip for a bank or note to a family member with instructions to put a casserole in the oven—(similar to Halliday's instrumental and regulatory function combined).
3. The information mode—text is a medium to communicate from one person to another such as filling out a questionnaire or consulting an atlas.
4. The re-creational mode—text is created "for the pleasure of constructing and exploring a world with words" (Wells, 1990, p. 373)—examples include imaginary literature, a letter to a friend, a personal journal.
5. The epistemic mode—text is created by the writer to capture through writing a provisional, or partial understanding—the text is then

used for further interrogation. Examples are: works of philosophy, poetry, a legal brief, a scientific report.

Wells argued that only the 5th mode—epistemic—fully exploits the power of literacy to develop thought or higher order thinking. Serpell (1991) cautioned against viewing Well's five modes of engagement as a well-ordered taxonomy. The modes overlap—reading a text usually involves more than one mode of engagement. A productive focus for us as teachers is to explore how the literacy activities we construct with our students involve a range of meaningful talk about texts—imaginative, exploratory, analytical, satirical, and so on.

Halliday's work is significant because his grammar is *meaningful* and it is *discourse based.* Halliday's work is also significant because it is contextualized within a culture and is a way to link ideology and power with the everyday workings of face to face communication (Luke, 1995–96). His students and others influenced by him took functional linguistics in an explicitly political direction through critical discourse analysis (Fairclough, 1989; Kress, 1985; Kress & Hodge, 1979).

BRANCH 1-2: STRUCTURAL AND FUNCTIONAL APPROACHES TO UNDERSTANDING LANGUAGE

Prator's question, "What is the nature of the language?" leads us to two different views of language, and two different kinds of linguistics: structural and functional. Along with suggesting significantly different answers for the question about the nature of language, each of these views has profound implications for Prator's other questions about the nature of the learner and the aims of instruction.

Structural Linguistics

Ferdinand de Saussure (1966), the founder of modern linguistics and the structural perspective, saw language and grammar as a set of formal rules. He distinguished between *langue*, the rules of language, and *parole*, actual speech with its variations; Saussure's division of language is similar to that of Chomsky's "competence" and "performance." As structural linguists, Saussure and Chomsky were concerned with discovering rules of language as an "internalized system." Chomsky and his school of linguistics utilized a speaker's knowledge or intuition of language to develop grammar.

Implications of Structural and Functional Linguistics for TESOL

A structural approach to language is the building-block approach to language. There are phonemes or phonology, morphemes—the smallest unit of meaning—or the study of morphology, syntax or word order, and inflections including adverbial phrases of time and place, tense and aspect, modality, and so on. Larger than a sentence are discourse rules—including cohesion—rhetorical patterns, and genre analysis. A structural approach requires one to teach the phrase structure rules of the language, the forms and patterns of the language, and to build up from the smallest parts to the largest stretches of discourse including essays, business letters or lab reports.

A functional approach to language asks, "Why do people use language?" There is the *interpersonal* aspect of language: We use language to compliment, to cajole, scold, to woe, to complain, to amuse, to reprimand. Some speech acts, "performatives," have consequences. The act of pronouncing certain words may have legal consequences or involve a change of state. These are often formulaic or fixed expressions, such as "I now pronounce you husband and wife." When a minister, magistrate, or rabbi utters these words, they have consequences for taxes, inheritance, and financial responsibility.

The notional functional syllabus of the Council of Europe is an example of an implementation of the functional perspective of language development in foreign language teaching. The applied linguists in the Council of Europe developed a taxonomy across the various situations in which adults would use language, which included such notions as time or measurements and functions such as various survival transactions such as taking a bus or finding lodging.

Structural approaches have been criticized because a focus on form separate from meaning, as in substitution drills, may not help the student to communicate and may be taught in a way that is boring. Similar criticisms could be made of functional approaches if the syllabus or textbook becomes a meaningless laundry list of materials. This is why most textbooks today incorporate both structural and notional/functional aspects into the design. An example would be Molinsky and Bliss' *Side by Side,* which begins with a structural outline (present continuous before simple present) and also features at the end of each chapter functions such as "apologies, greetings" from the dialogues.

Foreign language teachers need to help people *use* the language in grammatically appropriate ways, not to recite rules of usage (unless they are language teachers themselves) (Celce-Murcia, 1998). Students need enough knowledge about grammar to manage the rules of language and not so much that they become tongue-tied. They need use their knowledge of the rules effectively in real communication.

Through the communicative and dialogic approaches to language, we see a shift from focus at the sentence level to larger stretches of discourse in language teaching. Teaching at the sentence level may be superior to learning isolated words (i.e., word lists), but it is only a slight improvement. Authentic communication consists of language use that employs multiple structural and functional dimensions. It can be oral or written. In oral work, this may be utterances—meaningful phrases, not necessarily complete sentences. In written discourse, the genre of the work may be more significant to the work's meaning than any given sentence contained within. There has been a lot of work in Australia among Halliday's colleagues and students to use genre as an approach to language education (Martin, 1993; Christie, 1999). In teaching writing we look at various genres such as a short story, haiku poems, or lab reports. Examination of various genres enables us to become better writers because we are looking at form or structures, in relation to function and use within a text (Lemke, 1995; Luke 1996).

Saussure and Chomsky take a formal approach to language. Halliday and Bakhtin take a functional and textual and dialogic approach to language, recognizing that language is culturally constituted and historically situated. Saussure and Chomsky look at rules as if there is an ideal speech community, whereas Halliday and Bakhtin look at the language of social groups. There are patterns in and across groups—but the patterns may be overlapping and there may be conflict between various rules of different social groups. For Bakhtin, this notion of dialogic comes into his very view of language (Marchenkova, 2005).

The cognitive approach is the sender–receiver model of language, implying that language is a neutral medium to convey thoughts from A to B. In contrast, Bakhtin pointed out that within an utterance, each word has a history associated with it. Because any two people have different histories, there are multiple messages conveyed. Some are unconscious and have double meanings. We do not use a neutral medium, but instead we use a value-laden language that has consequences both intended and not intended. Teaching a foreign language, therefore, involves engaging with both structural and functional approaches to language, and helping students to engage with the complexities of language across the range of its use.

Anthropological Linguistics

Robert de Beaugrande (1997) contrasted the "homework" methodology of generative or transformational grammar, in which linguists use their own intuition of language sitting in their office, with "fieldwork" linguistics, in which linguists don't study what people *say* they know about language, but what they actually *do*. Unlike Saussure and Chomsky, anthropological linguists such as Franz Boas, Bronislaw Malinowski, Benjamin Whorf, John Sapir, and Leonard Bloomfield worked in the field to record and describe non-European languages. This entailed describing not only a different language from the linguist's mother tongue or language of education, but a different culture and language use in different situations from which the anthropologist was familiar. Field linguists such as Elinor Ochs (1988) teach us that it was not possible to merely tell their linguistic informants to "be themselves" in trying to get samples of informal as opposed to more formal registers. Sociolinguists need to observe, hypothesize, and work with a variety of informants within various cultural, economic, and social roles to be able to recognize kinship patterns and characterize various registers of language from polite to informal, or how language is gendered. This is an interpretive problem as the distinction between description and explanation is never clear cut (van Lier, 1994). Transcription itself is a political question (Roberts, 1997; Green, Franquiz, & Dixon, 1997). The anthropological tradition is concerned with meaning *in use.*

Prator's question, "What is the nature of language," is therefore best answered not by a linguistics that is informed only by British or North American English, but by a cross-culturally informed or anthropological linguistics. For this reason and because of the social nature of communication, language teachers in TESOL should study other languages themselves, and like anthropological linguists, learn more about language in the field. Examples of contemporary work in TESOL in this anthropological tradition, which falls broadly under "communicative approaches," are the work in cross-cultural literacies (Dubin & Kuhlman, 1992) and the development of work that sees linguistic difference as resources, rather than deficits (Murray, 1992). In addressing Protor's question concerning the nature of language it is also important to pay attention to dialect issues in classrooms (Lucas & Borders, 1994). Language diversity reflects differences in political and economic relations between speakers of different groups (McDermott, 1987). In both EFL and ESL contexts as teachers we need to be aware of unconscious linguistic stereotypes that may affect our attitudes, assessment and expectations towards students from poor and working class families who may speak rural, village, or other dialects not valued as "the educated standard."

Dialogic Pedagogy and Prator's Questions

Cultural psychology or sociocultural or sociohistorical psychology accounts for the human ability to think and to interact socially within a cultural context or a web of cultural, social, and historical meanings (Wertsch, 1985). Psychology was the discipline that Prator pointed to as being most able to answer his question, "What is the nature of the learner?" Table 1.1 shows approaches to answering this.

Educational psychology includes the study of learning and the development of thought, or cognition. Cultural psychology looks at the development of thought, language, and mind not only through what is as a

TABLE 1.1
Theories of Psychology

	Audiolingual Approach	*Communicative Approach*	*Dialogic Approach*
What is the nature of the student/learner?	Behaviorism (i.e., Skinner)	Cognitive psychology	Sociocultural, cultural psychology (i.e., Vygotsky, Bruner, Cole & Scribner, Moll, Ochs, Rogoff)

"universal" for human beings as opposed to other species, but at thought and language as a culturally specific or historically constituted cultural heritage. To the cultural psychologists who follow in the tradition of John Sapir and Benjamin Whorf, cognition cannot be separated from language and culture (Hall, 2002).

Lev Vygotsky on the Nature of Learning

A major breakthrough for the establishment of a social and cultural theory of mental functioning was laid in 1924 when Lev. S. Vygotsky presented his first major study at the Second Russian Neuropsychological Congress in Leningrad. Vygotsky's paper challenged the relevance of reflexes for understanding the nature of human thinking.[14] Vygotsky considered human thought to be more than reflexes, or responses to stimuli. In contrast to empiricists such as Pavlov and Skinner, who were suspicious of invisible mental phenomena such as consciousness, introspection, and subjectivity, Vygotsky thought that psychology should study human consciousness.

To Vygotsky, consciousness separates humans from other living beings. It is a self-regulatory mechanism that humans deploy in their problem-solving activities. It is akin to meta-cognition, or higher order thinking processes. Vygotsky set out to develop a set of theoretical principles to explain the formation and functioning of consciousness, an appropriate unit of analysis for its study, and a methodological paradigm to carry out the necessary research (Lantolf & Appel, 1994).

[14]Vygotsky's critique of Pavlov took place a generation before Chomsky's (1957) critique of Skinner, but Vygotsky was unknown in the United States. Many who participated in the cognitive revolution in the United States were later introduced to Vygotsky's work through cultural psychologists such as Jerome Bruner, who wrote the preface to Vygotsky's *Thought and Language* (1962), and Michael Cole, Sylvia Scribner, Ellen Souberman, and Vera John Steiner, who translated and introduced Vygotsky's *Mind in Society* (1978).

In child development, lower order, biologically specified mental functions (i.e., vision, hearing, tactile and olfactory systems, natural memory, involuntary attention systems) are retained, but develop into more complex or higher order, socioculturally determined mental functioning. Higher order mental processes include logical memory, voluntary attention, conceptual thought, planning, perception, problem solving, and voluntary inhibitory and disinhibitory functions. All of these mental functions are a part of and represented by people's use of language. Although the structural perspective suggests that language is somehow static in meaning (structure determines meaning), the functional perspective suggests that meaning lies not simply in structure but also in the reasons why and the contexts in which language is used.

Within the communicative approach in the United States the dominant psychological paradigm was cognitive. Although Vygotsky wrote long before Chomsky, his work was not introduced in the United States until the 1970s and 1980s. Within the field of second and foreign language education and TESOL, Vygotsky's sociocultural perspectives have been introduced though the work of Ochs (1988),Tharp and Gallimore (1988) Richard-Amato (1988), Moll (1990), *Lantoff and Appel (1994)*, Lantolf (2000), Ohta (2001), Hall (2000), Haneda (2000), Wink and Putney (2002), Haley and Austin (2004), Hawkins (2004), and others.

BRANCH 1-3: CONTRASTING KRASHEN'S (i + 1) AND VYGOTSKY'S ZONE OF PROXIMAL DEVELOPMENT

It has been debated whether Krashen's i + 1 and Vygotsky's concept of the "zone of proximal development" are commensurate or compatible concepts (De Guerrero, 1996; Dunn & Lantolf, 1998; Kinginger, 2001). It has been argued that both can be seen as teaching slightly above the student's level (Richard-Amato, 1996) or challenging the student to achieve collaboratively what s/he could not do alone. The *zone of proximal development* (ZPD) is defined as the difference between what a child (or student of any age) can do independently and what the child can do with the assistance of a more capable peer or adult (teacher). One difference between the two concepts is that although Krashen focused on "input" for language acquisition, Vygotsky focused on concept formation or problem solving, which involved any kind of learning. The latter is more comprehensive and includes all aspects of complex mental functioning—not only within the field of language learning, but math, science, history, music, and so on. Vygotsky (1978) was concerned with the development of mind or human consciousness, not only language. He thought that language played a crucial *mediating* role in the development of thought.

Krashen's i + 1 was concerned with second-language acquisition, not the broader concern of complex mental functioning. According to Krashen, we acquire language when we concentrate on meaning and understand what is being said. He distinguished between "acquisition," which was "picking up" a language the way that children subconsciously acquire the first language, and "learning," the formal knowledge of rules of the language. "Acquisition" is implicit, whereas "learning" is conscious and explicit knowledge (Krashen, 1985). To Krashen and Terrell (1985) second-language acquisition for adults should approximate first-language acquisition, focusing on meaning, rather than form.

The acquisition and learning distinction has been criticized by Barry McLaughlin (1987) and others who questioned the dichotomy between "subconscious" and "conscious" and suggested that there may be a continuum, rather than a rigid distinction. Interactive models of language learning such as those of Merrill Swain (1985) and others have pointed out that learning a language involves not only "input" but "output" as well. Language learners listen or read, but also speak and write. Teresa Pica (1987) and others have focused on interlanguage adjustments that language learners make as a result of negotiation with native speakers of the language. Coughlan and Duff (1994) pointed out that even if we give students the same task, different students may come up with very different activities. Sociocultural perspectives on interaction move away from "input–output" models, which are seen as predictable or having one possible correct answer. When we observe that the talk students construct collaboratively in classroom tasks results in different possibilities, "output" starts to be *redefined* and "extended to include its operation as a socially-constructed cognitive tool. As a tool, dialogue serves second language learning by mediating its own construction, and the construction of knowledge about itself. Internalization of process and knowledge is facilitated by their initial appearance in external speech … verbalization has important consequences for learning" (Swain, 2000, p. 112).

Further, Krashen's "input" model (as well as the "input–output" model of language, which is also a computer metaphor) is based on the cognitive "conduit" or "container" metaphor of language (Platt, 1995). The sender–receiver model of language presumes that the message is encoded and decoded. This metaphor, although very powerful, can be misleading when it comes to learning a second language—this becomes even more obvious when the two languages are linguistically, culturally, and historically unrelated.

First, the cognitive input–output model is flawed because it does not reflect the complexity of natural human language. In a computer program, something is either "0" or "1." But human language is messy and ambiguous. Learning another language is not like learning an algebraic formula, or a mathematical code, in which $a = 1$.

Setting aside syntactic differences between languages, if we look at vocabulary, even of historically related languages, translating a word from one language to another language is not a precise mathematical equation. Another characteristic of natural languages is that although they are "rule governed" with respect to phonology, morphology, and syntax, there are always exceptions. From a semiotic perspective, there is always more than one system operating. For example, various languages have different rules with respect to how close or far away interlocutors of different status should stand when speaking. Pragmatics includes the study of gestures, body language, stress, and overlapping. Communication breakdowns can arise due to difficulties with various levels of language, from pronunciation and stress to word choice, and from syntax to pragmatics.

What Difference Does It Make if We Equate the Two Concepts?

As a language teacher, I find that the metaphor "comprehensible input" can be a good starting point. One part of the dialogic process is to check to see if students understand and to accommodate our speech to enable students to be exposed to and understand utterances in the L2 as soon as possible (Wong-Fillmore, 1985). Structuring activities to make lessons comprehensible is important. I have also found that beginning language learners benefit from being able to show their comprehension through gestures and other nonverbal means. However, there are limitations to Krashen's i + 1 as a model for second-language acquisition (Platt & Brooks, 1994).

Although Krashen's i + 1 superficially seems to be similar to the ZPD because the +1 is beyond the current level, the current level that Krashen refers to is the interlanguage of the language learner, the next step in a universal order of acquisition, a path that is linear and predictable (Table 1.2).

TABLE 1.2

Krashen's i + 1	*Vygotsky' s ZPD*
Interlanguage of the learner is linear and predictable and fixed.	Development is complex and open.
An individual receives input. One can theoretically acquire language without talking.	Development is socially and historically situated. All learning occurs on the social (interpsychological) plane before it develops on the individual (intrapsychological) plane.
Questionable whether formal instruction of a structure far above the current level will help.	Instruction "blazes a trail" for development.
Conduit metaphor of language acquisition.	Participation metaphor.

Vygotsky saw all development as complex and open, rather than predictable and fixed. Krashen saw language acquisition in terms of an individual who receives input. Vygotsky saw development as a social and historically situated activity. To Krashen, it was questionable whether formal instruction of a structure that is far above the current developmental level will help. But Vygotsky suggested that instruction can precede development and can "blaze a trail." For example, a mentally retarded child can be taught abstract concepts with assistance through the concept of the zone of proximal development (Vygotsky, 1978). Through the zone of proximal development, teachers can develop activities and pose problems that provide opportunities for students not only to react to what they understand through gestures or other nonverbal means but to also engage in dialogue, and to participate in shared and guided reading and writing activities. The zone of proximal development enables us to work between students' current independent level of performance and their future level of performance through social assistance so that control is transferred to the individual student. As Aljaafreh and Lantolf (1994, p. 468) pointed out:

> The ZPD is the framework, par excellence, which brings all of the pieces of the learning setting together—the teacher, the learner, their social and cultural history, their goals and motives, as well as the resources available to them, including those that are *dialogically* constructed together. (emphasis added)

Communicative and Dialogic Approaches to Prator's Question: What Is the Nature of the Language?

In TESOL we can contrast the communicative approach with the dialogic approach not only with respect to psychology, but also with respect to the theories of language (see Table 1.3).

Within the communicative approach, rather than having a unified theory of the nature of language, there were actually two competing schools of linguistics. The theories of the two major linguists Noam Chomsky and Del Hymes that provided impetus for the communicative approach are actually in opposition to each other. One way of looking at the contrast is to see their work in relation to that of the founder of modern linguistics, Ferdinand Saussure. Chomsky was interested in competence, similar to Saussure's *langue*, whereas Hymes and other anthropological linguists and sociolinguists looked at performance, similar to Saussure's *parole*. Chomsky (in the tradition of Saussure's *langue*) looked at syntactic structures from the perspective of forms separate from actual use. Hymes and other anthropological linguists and sociolinguists were not concerned with what people said was "grammatical," but wanted to analyze what people actually said in the

TABLE 1.3
Theories of Linguistics

	Audiolingual	*Communicative*	*Dialogic Approach*
What is the nature of language?	Structural linguistics (i.e., Leonard Bloomfield, Charles Fries)	Generative, transformational grammar (i.e., Noam Chomsky) Sociolinguistics: Functional–systemic grammar (i.e., Del Hymes) or language as a social semiotic (i.e., Michael Halliday & Raquia Hasan)	Sociolinguistics and anthropological linguistics (Michael Halliday, Mikhail Bakhtin)

field. Chomsky relied on rationalism, intuition, and selected strings of sentences to analyze what native speakers of English would say were grammatical syntactic structures. What was grammatical for Chomsky did not depend on social context, or even meaning (as we saw earlier from the "Colorless green ideas sleep furiously" example).

In contrast, sociolinguists utilized empirical, observable data gained in the field and working with linguistic informants. Social context and meaning is critical to sociolinguistics and functional linguistics. The dialogic approach overlaps with the communicative approach in sharing sociolinguistics and anthropological linguistics and functional systemic linguistics such as Halliday and Hasan's language as a social semiotics. In addition, a major theorist who contributes to a dialogic approach concerning the nature of language is Mikhael Bakhtin.

Bakhtin on Prator's Question, "What Is the Nature of Language?"

For Bakhtin, the dialogical principle is central to understanding the nature of language. He first discussed his revolutionary concept of "dialogism" in *Problems of Dostoevsky's Art*, published in 1929. To Bakhtin, there are two forces operating simultaneously not only in literature, such as the novel, but in all language. These are centripetal forces that "unify and centralize the verbal–ideological world" and "centrifugal stratifying forces of historical heteroglossia":

> Every utterance participates in the "unitary language" (in its centripetal forces and tendencies) and at the same time partakes of social and historical heteroglossia (the centrifugal, stratifying forces).

> Such is the fleeting language of a day, of an epoch, a social group, a genre, a school and so forth. It is possible to give a concrete and detailed analysis of any utterance, once having exposed it as a contradiction-ridden, tension-filled unity of two embattled tendencies in the life of language. (Bakhtin & Holquist, 1981, p. 272)

Unlike Saussure or Chomsky or the Russian formalists who saw language as an ideal formal system (Saussure's *langue*, not *parole*), Bakhtin saw the *utterance* as the unit of analysis. Clark and Holquist explained the significance of the *utterance* as follows:

> This is the basic building block in his dialogic conception. An utterance, spoken or written, is always expressed from a point of view, which for Bakhtin is a process rather than a location. Utterance is an activity that enacts differences in values. On an elementary level, for instance, the same words can mean different things depending on the particular intonation with which they are uttered in a specific context: intonation is the sound that value makes. (Clark & Holquist, 1984, p. 10)

Clark and Holquist further explained that the ways that values are expressed is "authoring":

> All of us who make utterances so understood, whether spoken or written, are thus authors. We operate out of a point of view and shape values into forms. How we do so is the means by which we articulate who we are amid the heteroglossia of ideological possibilities open to us at any given moment. Bakhtin treats values not as an abstract axiology but as the practical work of building. By shaping answers in the constant activity of our dialogue with the world, we enact the architectonics of our own responsibility. (Clark & Holquist, 1984, p. 10)[15]

For Bakhtin, authoring is not a single author expressing himself as an individual, but the act of utterance always involves the other. It is a dialogic process of expressing one's own values to another, or turning to another. Within the utterance, the dialogical principle of the contradiction between the forces of language that unify and the forces of language that stratify and diversify all is manifest through the *social* aspect of speaking to another. When one speaks, one speaks through language that is both new and creative, but also bound in tradition and culture appropriating the words and phrases of others. Todorov (1984) explained this contradiction of the utterance as follows:

---

[15]"Architectonics" or structure or construction is a term Medvedev/Bakhtin appropriated from the Western "formalists" because of their insistence on preserving the unity of form and context (Todorov, 1984, p. 38).

> The most important feature of the utterance ... is its dialogism, that is its intertextual dimension. After Adam, there are no nameless objects or any unused words. Intentionally or not, all discourse is in dialogue with prior discourses on the same subject, as well as with discourses yet to come, whose reactions it foresees and anticipates. A single voice can make itself heard only by blending into the complex choir of other voices already in place. (p. x)

Features of Dialogic Pedagogy

Because dialogic pedagogy is the newest methodology represented in this book, the remaining chapters describe it in detail; however, it is summarized here. The aim of dialogic pedagogy is to support the inclusion of voices of those who have traditionally been excluded from academic discourse, reflecting new answers to Prator's old question, "What is the nature of the learner/student?"[16]

BRANCH 1-4: USING TRADITIONAL METHODS WITHIN THE CONTEXT OF DIALOGIC PEDAGOGY

Although the audiolingual method was discredited due to the cognitive revolution, leading to today's more communicative approaches, there is much from the audiolingual method (not behaviorist psychology, but structural linguistics) that should be retained, especially in the foreign language context. For example, the situational practice dialogues can be effectively incorporated in lessons for beginners. The difference is that a more dialogic approach will encourage students not only to memorize dialogues but also to create their own. Another difference is that although the audiolingual approach viewed mistakes in pronunciation as bad habits that should be corrected, dialogic teachers would correct only those errors that actually interfere with communication. A third difference is that our attitude toward memorization of scripts would be more functional rather than focused only on the structures of the language. That is, teachers encourage the students to think more about the transactions they need to perform in the foreign language rather than sheer memorization, and teachers anticipate and present the kinds of variations that a student may encounter.

[16] Although Prator saw the discipline of psychology as the one that most closely dealt with the question "What is the nature of the student?" with respect to learning, today we would add anthropology, sociology, and ethnic and women's studies as the knowledge base to address the nature of students who have traditionally been excluded from education.

For example, if a student wants to get more information, information-gap exercises in which students are paired to ask and answer questions about a train schedule or what time a movie begins help students move from scripts to actual communication. The Rassias method, created by John Rassias (sometimes called the Dartmouth approach), moves very effectively from the audiolingual approach to use of drama. Role playing, under the guidance of a language teacher who is trained to attend to the linguistic (and sociolinguistic) use of structures students produced in the play acting, draws on students' creative, pragmatic, and playful resources of language use even as language learning beginners in the first 21 hours of instruction in the language (Rassias, 1983).

There is nothing wrong with using prepared dialogues in learning a foreign language. Questions that ESOL teachers might consider are: Are the lessons from the textbook appropriate for the aims of instruction for my students? Are the dialogues "stilted" or "natural" to speakers of the language? Are the drills and exercises well organized and easy to follow? Are they isolated sentences or longer stretches of discourse? Are there various genres in the material? Do they give students opportunities to practice—for example, through role playing or problem solving or information-gap activities that encourage students to use their emergent L2 language and to extend the range of what they can do in the second language?

Beyond the "permissibility" of using audiolingual materials in a dialogic classroom, even though the history of TESOL methods reveals the fact that audiolingualism has been supplanted by the cognitive revolution, there is a larger point to be made: The point of dialogic pedagogy is not to limit teachers to a single approach or method. Rather, it is to help teachers make thoughtful choices about how they implement the teaching and learning of a language in their classroom. No single method is appropriate for all learners or all contexts. Good teachers have access to multiple ways of choosing and working with learning materials. Dialogic inquiry helps teachers recognize the complexities of their undertaking and to ask questions that get at the many social and cultural factors that can affect (and effect) student learning (Wells, 1999).

There are four features to dialogic pedagogy:

1. *Learning in community:* Structural approaches to TESOL ignore the communal context of learning. Functional approaches begin to address the fact that learning a language takes place within and across communities. Dialogic pedagogy engages community as a site and a motivation for learning. Both Socratic and Confucian dialogues (discussed in the next chapter) posed learning as an unending dialogue in which teacher and students approach the quest for knowledge with hu-

mility. The dialogic imagination of Bakhtin emphasized the languages of social groups and communities of interaction with multiple voices and perspectives, which are historically constituted, or what he called "heteroglossic." For Bakhtin, *heteroglossic* refers to a dialectical process in which centralizing, unifying, and centripetal forces of solidarity in language simultaneously compete with those centrifugal forces that signal language diversification, and discourse in flux.

2. *Problem posing:* Learning a language is not simply a matter of following a preestablished syllabus. If we "teach to the students and not the text," as Prator admonished, then we might see language as a series of problems that students face. Dialogic pedagogy emphasizes a process of inquiry and exploration rather than "reifying any canon or particular set of materials to be learned" (Wong, 1990); this inquiry and the process of problem solving reflect Vygotsky's psychological theories of learning including the idea of the "zone of proximal development" (see branch and chap. 3). Problem posing contrasts with what Paolo Freire called a "banking pedagogy," in which knowledge is "deposited" into students. This second feature is compatible with Vygotsky's theories concerning the *social* nature of learning:

> Every function in the child's cultural development appears twice: first, on the social level, and later, on the individual level; first *between* people (*interpsychological)* and then inside the child (intrapsychological). This applies equally to voluntary attention, to logical memory and to the formation of concepts. All the higher functions originate as actual relations between human individuals. (Vygotsky, 1978, p. 57)

Students reflect on their learning strategies and draw from their own linguistic and cultural awareness as resources.

3. *Learning by doing:* Students learn language through actual communication. They experience activities, assignments, and evaluation that emphasize the dialectic of practice, dialogue and theoretical reflection, and further transformed social practice. Speaking and writing are conducted with real audiences. As Mao Zedong (1967, p. 300) said, "If you want to know the taste of a pear, you must change the pear by eating it yourself." Forms are taught with respect to their function in actual communication. The emphasis is on real life rather than on exercises. When exercises are used, they are selected carefully with respect to facilitating understanding and producing meaningful texts.

4. *Knowledge for whom:* The fourth feature is the question, "Knowledge for whom?" or "Whom does knowledge serve?" and relates to Prator's questions about the nature of students and the aims of instruction. Feminists and critical theorists such as Maxine Greene challenge us to interrogate educational participation with respect to multi-

ple dimensions of language, culture, and power (i.e., race, gender, class, ethnicity, etc.). Sociologists of education such as Pierre Bourdieu ask: Who goes to the university? How do educational practices systematically track privileged children into programs for the gifted and talented and groom them for the university and graduate programs, and how are other peoples children—the children of the working poor and racial minorities—labeled, tracked, expelled from school, placed in prisons? How can we transform the reproduction of savage inequities (Kozol, 1991) in education?

APPROACHES, METHODS, AND TECHNIQUES

Methodology is the study of pedagogical practice in the broadest, most comprehensive sense, including approaches, methods, and techniques. TESOL pioneer Edward Anthony (1963) defined methodology as consisting of *approaches*, *methods*, and *techniques*, which he conceptualized as falling within three concentric circles (Fig. 1.2).

Approaches comprises the largest circle and includes the philosophy of teaching including understandings of language and psychology and one's assumptions about language teaching (Stevick, 1988). Approaches are axiomatic, including the principles or theories of language teaching and learning. *Methods* are overall plans for implementing or putting the theories into practice. *Techniques,* still a smaller circle, are specific procedures or steps used to accomplish particular objectives.

The most often used contemporary modes in TESOL—the grammar translation approach, the audiolingual method, the communicative approach, and dialogic pedagogy—can be characterized as "approaches" using Anthony's definition. Each of these approaches includes a philosophy of teaching and theoretical perspectives on aspects of teacher/student relationships: psychology, power structures, and the nature of language. In

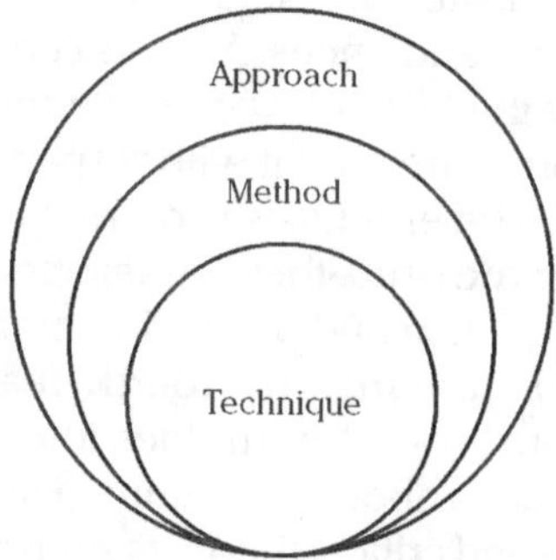

FIG. 1.2. Anthony's three concentric circles: approach, method, and technique.

the grammar translation approach, the role of the teacher is to transmit the philosophy and wisdom of ancient scholars and the culture of the academy. It predated the establishment of "psychology" as a scientific discipline in the modern university. Wherever it was practiced (whether in the United States, Turkey, or Venezuela), the grammar translation approach was modeled after the education for the upper classes using texts from classical philosophy and literature. Although the founders of this method would not consider politics to be a concern, as a traditional methodology to educate the aristocracy, it idealized the past to legitimate the claims of the ruling class (of whatever age) to have authority. Although politics may have a significant effect on students, as when disenfranchised groups gain access to classrooms, politics remain invisible within the purview of the method itself. The grammar translation method has an underlying philosophy that could be described as its approach, even if that philosophy is not explicitly delineated by its proponents.

The audiolingual method—which under Anthony's concentric circles definition is also an "approach," not a "method"—has a well-developed philosophy of teaching including a theory of psychology (behaviorism) and theory of language (structural linguistics). Likewise, communicative models are based on philosophy, psychology, and linguistic theories. In fact, the shift between the audiolingual method and the communicative methods occurred not at the level of classroom implementation (methods or techniques) but at the level of theoretical background through Chomsky's cognitive revolution advancing a new theory of psychology (cognitive) and a new theory of language (transformational, generative, or universal grammar).[17]

Theory is also central to dialogic approaches. As we discussed earlier, the theory of language includes Halliday and Hasan's functional systemic grammar or language as a social semiotic, Bakhtin's dialogics, and Vološinov's *Marxism and the Philosophy of Language* (1973).[18] The theory of psychology or the field of study that addresses Prator's question, "What is the nature of the student or learner?" is Vygotskian or sociocultural or sociohistorical psychology. Within dialogic pedagogy, philosophers include Socrates and Confucius (see chap. 2) and liberation theorists such as Freire and Mao (chap. 4). Methods, the second concentric circle, reflect general teaching processes. An example of a dialogic method would be

---

[17]See Vivian Cook's "Universal Grammar and the Learning and Teaching of Second Languages" and Philip L. Hubbard's "Non-transformational Theories of Grammar: Implications for Language Teaching" in Odlin (1994).

[18]Some attribute authorship of *Marxism and the Philosophy of Language* to Bakhtin. Whether or not Bakhtin was the main author, it is clear that he was a close associate and part of a study circle with Vološinov and Medvedev that contributed to the theoretical framework.

the use of dialogue journals, or organizing curriculum through thematic units such as "Pilgrimage, " "Bugs," or "Difference." Techniques are still a smaller circle, nestled within.[19] An example of a dialogic technique would be to ask students to brainstorm questions that they would be interested in investigating. Another example of a technique from elementary school classrooms would be "Think, pair, share."[20] First students think and write down their thoughts. Then they read their list to a partner and hear their partner's list to generate more ideas. Finally they share their ideas with the whole class.

Grammar translation, audiolingual, and some communicative approaches do not include an explicit or deliberate consideration of power structures or other political concerns in relation to teaching. In contrast, dialogic pedagogy has a central concern with power structures and their influence over the conditions of language learning. The power differences between teachers from the First World and students from the Third World are just one political aspect that influences classroom interactions. Within the dialogic pedagogy paradigm, it is important to understand how these power structures enter the classroom. The political context is part of the answer to Prator's question about the nature of the student (the student's placement or position in relation to various levels of power) as well as the aims of instruction (what help does the student need and how will we as teachers provide that).

[19]Earl Stevick coined "techneme" to speak of even smaller concentric circle within which a teacher may employ, such as minimal pair drills /b/ /v/. Another example of a techneme would be "wait time"—the amount of time a teacher pauses after asking a question. A very small technique (pausing for a few more seconds) may alter classroom interaction and expand student opportunities for participation significantly.

[20]Les Greenblatt, unpublished talk to TESOL Elementary Methods Class, University of Maryland, 1995.

2

Under the Ginkgo Tree: Learning in Community

To sit under the ginkgo tree's shade, to engage in scholarly inquiry and to ponder the human condition have historically been the privilege of the leisure classes rather than the laboring masses. Participation in academic discourse has remained almost exclusively the domain of men. At the dawn of human history, knowledge and culture were passed down through the chiefs, and the shamans or holy men.[1] Imagine Confucius and his disciples sitting under the ancient ginkgo. The cultured gentlemen (wen ren 文人 "great men") sip their tea and talk, subtly indexing the work of great poets and philosophers by reciting poetry and making clever puns. Their talk ranges from bawdy jokes to questions about the nature of justice, or what constitutes an ethical life.

Chinese women have also enjoyed the shade of the ginkgo tree, doing women's work—perhaps gathering tasty ginkgo nuts to prepare a special New Year's dish. These women might have taken a break from their labor to sit under the tree, to rest, and to reflect. However, as women, their talk—"gossip" and "old wives' tales"—however wise, was not recognized as philosophy or learning. In ancient China, women did not have a legitimate place under the ginkgo tree in the company of learned scholars.

The image of Confucius and his disciples learning in community under the ginkgo tree relates to two persistent problems in TESOL pedagogy. One question around the world is that of class size (Lo Castro, 2001; Sarwar, 2001). Dialogic pedagogy works well in small classes of 8 to 20+

[1]Socialist feminists and anthropologists tell us that before the division of labor into classes, there were matriarchal and patriarchal tribes (Morgan, 1877). With the division of society into classes, knowledge was tied to control and maintaining order. Through priests and monks, rulers kept knowledge from slaves and common people.

students—the size of ESOL classes in some elementary schools in the United States and many intensive English programs in elite universities. But it is not as easy to use dialogic approaches in classes of 35 to 45 students. In some countries foreign language classes may be as large as 50 or 60. Is it possible to have dialogic interaction in a class of 70 or 100?

Second, only men participated in the Socratic and Confucian dialogues. Exclusive access to education for upper-class males has continued. For example, the apprenticeship model, codified under feudalism in Europe into master craftsman, journeyman, and apprentice, is a highly disciplined, hierarchical transmission of cultural practices from old to young, and in most trades and crafts, is passed from fathers and uncles to sons or nephews, rather than daughters or nieces (Dobb, 1968). Is it possible to have meaningful dialogic conversations in a more diverse, inclusive community? How is it possible to develop learning in community across diverse communities?

This chapter begins with two classical examples of learning in community, the Socratic method in the West and the Eastern dialogues between Confucius and his disciples. Examples of learning through the community in TESOL classrooms follow.

EARLY DIALOGIC APPROACHES: THE SOCRATIC METHOD

Socrates called his method of inquiry *maieutic*, from the art of midwifery, *maieutike* (Bowen, 1972, p. 89). He was probably drawn to this analogy because of his mother, a midwife. The student, pregnant with thoughts, was in labor. Socrates served as the midwife, aiding the student by skillfully asking questions. Through questioning, the student gave birth to concepts and understandings that were already in his mind.[2]

According to Greek custom, a woman could not become a midwife until she was past child-bearing age. Socrates referred to this in the Theaetetus dialogue, drawing the comparison, “Like the midwives, I too am sterile with respect to wisdom” (Socrates, *Theaetetus*, 150 B.C., quoted in Bowen, 1972, p. 89). Rather than viewing the teacher as the source of knowledge, Socrates recognized that reason existed in the mind of the student. In the *Menos* dialogue, Socrates demonstrated that through proper questioning, an uneducated slave boy could reason through difficult mathematical problems and arrive at the Pythagorean theorem (Boyd & King, 1973).

---

[2]Use of the male pronoun reflects actual practice, not merely “male as norm” sexist language (in which a male pronoun refers to both females and males). All of Socrates' and Confucius's students were male.

The starting point of ignorance was important to the *maieutic* method of inquiry. A humble awareness of one's own ignorance was considered wisdom. The task of the educator/philosopher was to develop the potentialities of students by challenging students to think for themselves. The quest for knowledge was not merely a pedagogical technique, but a virtue in itself, and the quest was never completed.

Socrates employed a dialogic process, typically beginning by posing a question such as, "What is justice?" The youth would answer by giving a definition, a generalization based on experience. When Socrates questioned the youth with an exception to the definition, the youth would modify the definition. Moving from a generalization drawn from experience, through the dialogic exchange, the definition would be refined until the youth became confused and moved from "unconscious ignorance" to "conscious ignorance" (Butts, 1955, p. 55). Continuing to challenge the youth by asking more questions, Socrates helped the youth to recognize new insights.

Although Socrates had a following among his students, his method of questioning was seen as subversive to those in power in Athens. His probing, critical questions led to his eventual arrest and execution at the age of 70 for "refusing to recognize the gods acknowledged by the state and importing strange divinities of his own; he was further guilty of corrupting the young" (*The History of Xenophon*, translated by Dakyus, 1909, as quoted in Power, 1962, p. 86). Socrates' death is significant to the cause of freedom of thought and inquiry. His refusal to bow to the powers of Athens in quest of the truth made him one of the first martyrs for academic freedom in Western tradition.

TRADITIONAL EASTERN PHILOSOPHICAL ROOTS OF DIALOGIC PEDAGOGY

One of the most influential figures in eastern philosophical thought was China's "first teacher" *Kong Zi* (known in English as Confucius) (Wu, 1986), who lived during the Warring States period (ca. 500 B.C.) when China was divided into several kingdoms. Raised by a poor widow, Confucius became a public servant and sought to restore to public life the golden age of the *Zhou*[3] (Chou) dynasty. He traveled from court to court with his disciples in search of the ethical, attempting to influence public morality:

> The Analects does give us a glimpse of a credible personality, a man who was brought up in humble circumstances and was prepared to accept pov-

[3]Throughout the book I use *pinyin*, the system of romanization from the People's Republic of China, which is *Zhou*. In parentheses (Chou) is Wade Giles romanization, the system used by Dawson in the quote that follows.

erty rather than compromise his beliefs, a man who never tired of learning and who stuck doggedly to his task ("He's the one who knows it's no good but goes on trying," A 14.41), a man with a strong sense that he had a divinely appointed mission to restore the Way of the revered founders of the Chou Dynasty. (Dawson, 1981, pp. 6–7)

Above all, Confucius considered himself a scholar and a teacher (Chen, 1990). His love of learning formed the basis of his life's work:

["]At fifteen I set my heart on learning["] (A 2.4) ... for when he made no progress in public affairs or in gaining public recognition for his doctrines, he devoted himself solely to the role of private teacher, in order to distribute the fruit of his learning to others who might prove more successful in giving effect to it. (Dawson, 1981, p. 9)

D. C. Lau pointed out the importance of the distinction or opposition of *learning* (xue 學) and *thinking* (si 思) in the Confucian dialogues:

Confucius is constantly giving the advice that one should choose from what one has learned only what is good and leave out what is doubtful. The only way to do so is through thinking. There is a well-known saying in the Analects, "If one learns from others but does not think, one will be bewildered. If, on the other hand, one thinks but does not learn from others, one will be in peril" (II.15). One must learn from wise men of the past and the present, but at the same time, one must try to improve on what one has learned. Although both learning and thinking are indispensable, Confucius seems to consider learning to be, in some sense, more basic. (Lau, 1979, pp. xii–xiii)

Through teaching, Confucius sought to influence society and to bring about social reforms. Confucius did not teach a retreat from society, to be a hermit and commune with nature, but to affect social reforms in society:

Society must adjust itself to the individual in order to escape stagnation and the individual must also adjust oneself[4] to society in order to become human, and cannot live or develop oneself as a human without the help of society. So Confucius did not teach people, as the pessimists of his time did, to flee from the world and to become irresponsible hermits or political nihilists. (Chen, 1990, p. 175)

---

[4]Chen Jingpan originally wrote "himself." This book published by the Foreign Languages Press in 1990, was originally written as a PhD thesis at the University of Toronto in 1940 when male pronouns as universal were standard. I have changed the language in the quote to "oneself" to reflect contemporary language.

A central concern was attainment of *ren*,[5] to learn to be an ethical person, or as neo-Confucian philosopher Tu Wei-Ming interpreted, "to learn to be human" (Tu, 1985, p. 51). There is no easy translation of *ren*. It has been translated as benevolence, love, altruism, kindness, charity, compassion, magnanimity, perfect virtue, goodness, human-heartedness, humaneness, humanity, and man-to-man-ness (Dawson, 1981). "Goodness" and "perfect virtue" convey the centrality of virtue to *jen* but fail to show the *human* root of the word. Lawrence C. Wu therefore translated it as "*human*-heartedness," Raymond Dawson as "humane" and Peter Boodberg as "co-humanity" (Wu, 1986, p. 16). Tu Wei-Ming explained the etymology: "*jen* [*ren*] consists of two parts, one a simple ideogram of a human figure (with two legs), meaning the self, and the other ideogram two horizontal strokes, suggesting human relations" (Tu, 1985, p. 84).

The disciples quested for *ren*, typically posing the question, "Is so-and-so *ren*?" Unlike filial piety, *ren* could not be spelled out through a number of duties:

> References to *jen* (or *ren*) in the *Analects* are somewhat paradoxical. Confucius is depicted as extremely reluctant to ascribe this quality to any given individual. Indeed he expresses doubt that anyone is capable of concentrating his whole effort on humaneness for a single day (A 4.6). This reluctance to admit that anyone attains to *jen* is due to the fact that it is the quality of ideal human nature. On the other hand, since *jen* is an essential ingredient of the human being, not something which depends on anything outside himself, it should in theory be easily attainable, if men were true to their natures. "Is humaneness really so far away?" he asks. "If we really wished for it, it would come" (A 7.29). (Dawson, 1981, pp. 39–40)

According to Tu Wei-Ming, *learning to be human* is an endeavor found in Taoist and Buddhist traditions as well:

> The primary focus of the "Three Teachings" under study is self-knowledge. Since the conception of a Creator as the ultimate source of morality or spirituality is not even a rejected possibility, there is no appeal to the "wholly other" as the real basis of human perfectibility. Rather, the emphasis is on

FIG. 2.1. The Chinese character for *ren*. On the left is the character for human, and on the right, the two strokes are for "2."

[5]*Ren* is pinyin as used in the People's Republic of China. Tu Wei-Ming uses the Wade Giles romanization *jen*.

> learning to be human, a learning that is characterized by a ceaseless process of inner illumination and self-transformation. The Confucian ideal of sage-hood, the Taoist quest for becoming a "true person," and the Buddhist concern for returning to one's "original mind," are all indications that to follow the path of knowledge backward, as it were to the starting point of the true self is the aim of East Asian thought. (Tu, 1985, p. 15)

This quest for selfhood is not a heroic act of individualism or a private matter. It is a *social* rather than an *individual* pursuit:

> Ultimate self-transformation, rather than being a "lonely quest for one's inner spirituality," is a communal act. Human-relatedness is thus an integral part of one's quest for spiritual fulfillment. To take one's situated-ness[6] in a particular network of dyadic relationships as the given is not total submission to the prescribed social roles, but a recognition of the most immediate and fruitful way of initiating and completing one's task of learning to be human. (Tu, 1985, p. 19)

In ancient China and Greece, philosophy was born in communal dialogue. Suzanne Wong Scollon (1997), however, pointed out that the view of self and community in China is different from that in the United States:

> While Americans conceive of the person as colonized by biological and social constraints from which one tries to liberate oneself, the Chinese conception of the person is more that of a biological colony or community of interdependent individuals. Liberation consists in strengthening communal ties in order to resist colonization by western powers which are unified or at least homogenized not only by military and economic strength but by an ideology of individual human rights. (Wong Scollon, 1997, p. 25)

In a study contrasting English and Cantonese metaphors of self and communication, Wong Scollon found that English speakers overwhelmingly used a conduit metaphor, whereas Cantonese metaphors were somatic: Communication was conceptualized as movement of the body in the presence of other bodies. Americans communicate "in order to assert independence, in the Chinese view one communicates in order to harmonize, silence often being a salient part of the process" (p. 26).

As an exemplary teacher, Confucius instructed, disciplined, or enlightened students, but in the end, he encouraged their self-effort. The source of selfhood is inner strength. Inner strength develops not in isolation, but in *dialogic* relationship with others:

---

[6]We return to the concept of social "situatedness" through sociocultural approaches to learning such as Vygotsky and Lave and Wenger (1991) in chapter 3.

> It is only through the continuous opening up of the self to others that the self can maintain a wholesome personal identity. The person who is not sensitive or responsive to the others around him is self-centered; self-centeredness easily leads to a closed world, or in Sung-Ming terminology, to a state of paralysis. (Tu, 1985, p. 114)

As a teacher, Confucius struggled alongside his students in quest of becoming fully human. Their inquiry into the nature of *ren* (*jen*) was collaborative, an exchange in which teaching (*jiao*) and learning (*xue*) were inseparable and interchangeable. Confucius spoke candidly as a self-reflective human being, but he did not believe that he had achieved sagehood. Nor did he believe that he had been able to live out ideal relationships. Characteristically humble, his self-assessment was:

> There are four things in the Way of the profound person, none of which I have been able to do. To serve my father as I would expect my son to serve me: that I have not been able to do. To serve my ruler as I would expect my ministers to serve me: that I have not been able to do. To serve my elder brother as I would expect my younger brother to serve me: that I have not been able to do. To be the first to treat friends as I would expect them to treat me: that I have not been able to do. (Tu, 1985, p. 27)

Finally, the context of learning to be human was not only set in the midst of human relationships, but also set in the context of the universe as a reflection of Chinese cosmology. To Tu Wei-Ming in Chinese cosmological thinking:

> The familiar dichotomies such as self/society, body/mind, sacred/profane, culture/nature, and creator/creature, in light of the "continuity of being," are relegated to the background. A different mode of thinking, which emphasizes part/whole, inner/outer, surface/depth, root/branches, substance/function and Heaven/man [*humankind*], becomes prominent. (Tu, 1985, pp. 8–9)

In fact, the cosmos itself involves "dialogical interplay":

> The central question does not involve static mechanistic analytical distinctions, but subtle relationships, internal resonance, dialogical interplay and mutual influence. As a result, the "spontaneously self-generating life process." (Tu, 1985, pp. 8–9)

Central to the Chinese cosmos are the forces of *yin* and *yang*, a Taoist concept that all things and events are the product of two forces: "The *yin* is negative, passive, weak and destructive. The *yang* is positive, active, strong and constructive" (Nauman, 1978, p. 354). These oppositions do not carry connotations of good and bad; rather, they are value free like the positive and negative poles of electricity. The *yin yang* relationship is complementary, not an antagonistic relationship like good and evil (Wu, 1986) (Fig. 2.2).

The *yin* and *yang* relationship provides the Chinese cosmological basis for ethical and social teachings that all things are related and that reality is in a process of constant transformation: "Yin Yang provides the idea of harmony within creative tension" (Wu, 1986, p. 157). The sense of cosmic togetherness is evoked in a famous essay by the neo-Confucian Chang Tsai (1020–1077 A.D.):

> Heaven is my father and earth is my mother, and even such a small being as I finds an intimate place in their midst. Therefore that which fills the universe I regard as my body and that which directs the universe I regard as my nature. All people are my brothers and sisters and all things are my companions. (Chang Tsai, *Western Inscription*, as quoted in Tu, 1985, pp. 42–43)

The human being is connected to the universe, as Tu Wei-Ming put it, as the "respectful son or daughter to the cosmic process" (Tu, 1985, p. 43). There is no sense of human mastery over nature, but rather the human being is organically connected to rocks, trees and animals. This is reflected in Chinese literature such as *Dream of the Red Chamber*, in which the human hero Pao-yu was created from a piece of jade, as well as in Chinese art, where mountains flow like rivers and rocks have energy. Tu Wei-Ming (1985, pp. 43–44) explains that "all things are my companions" is reflected in talk about the different degrees of spirituality of rocks. All of this is part of cosmic transformation.

WHAT IS DIALOGIC LEARNING IN COMMUNITY?

"Community" implies a gathering of people who have long-term commitment to being together. "Learning" entails cognitive changes or the development of thought. "Learning in community" means that the cognitive changes come about because of relationships between people. "Dialogic" suggests communication–the reciprocal use of language. "Dialogic learn-

FIG. 2.2. Yin and yang.

ing in community," then, implies that through talking and listening within the context of enduring relationships, cognitive changes take place. This kind of learning has its roots in the ancient dialogues between Socrates and his students and those between Confucius and his disciples. Socrates figured out how to bring out specific knowledge in his students through strategic questioning. Confucius defined the need for both teacher and student to be humble seekers for answers to open-ended questions, and focused on essential humanity.

In the centuries since Confucius and Socrates, others have described the social nature of human learning, particularly when it comes to thought and language. For example, Vygotsky (1978) described the zone of proximal development in which a child is able to complete a task with the assistance of an adult or a more capable peer. Development of thought and language occurs on the social plane or in community before it occurs independently or individually. Jerome Bruner and associates (1983) and Courtney Cazden (1988) and others described the social nature of learning through the metaphor of "scaffolding." Barbara Rogoff (1990) used the metaphor of apprenticeship to describe children's cognitive development through guided participation in social activity. The social nature of learning means that within a community, each individual has a range of peers and therefore a range of competencies on which to draw. Further, the desire to communicate successfully within the community helps to motivate language learning (see Branch 1-2, Structural and Functional Approaches, and Branch 1-3, Contrasting Krashen's i + 1 and Vygotsky's ZPD).

Dialogic learning in community is the model for how children learn their first language (through successful and unsuccessful dialogues with one's first community, the family) (Bruner, 1983; Halliday, 1975; Ochs, 1988). It expands when children go to school through strategic questioning, mutual seeking, and opportunities for learners to develop greater competencies through examples and help provided by more capable peers and teachers as part of a wider community of learners—communities of practice at home and in the neighborhood, at school, and in the larger communities of which students become a part as they mature.

BRANCH 2-1: FUNDS OF KNOWLEDGE: EXTENDING THE ZONE OF PROXIMAL DEVELOPMENT INTO THE COMMUNITY

Learning in community refers to developing a community of learners in a class or school or learning from communities outside of the classroom walls. The Moll and Greenberg study (1990) is significant for English language teaching because teachers in Moll and Greenberg's study took the zone of proximal development out of the classroom into the Mexican American community in Tucson, Arizona. Moll and Greenberg conducted an ethnographic research project to investigate Mexican American family in Tucson. The results from the research project that they termed "funds of knowledge" would be used with teachers to develop curricular innovation in after-school labs.

Moll and Greenberg were interested in how Mexican American families helped each other through *confianza* (mutual trust) (Moll & Greenberg, 1990, p. 321), a "thick network of cooperation for daily household activities from child care to fixing cars to helping with household repairs." The Mexican American community in Tucson is connected through "kin, friends, neighbors, co-workers and acquaintances." Because Tucson is a stratified economy with 75% of the Mexican Americans in the lower paid working class jobs, Mexican wages are 80% of Anglo (or White American) wages, and Mexicans are twice as likely as Anglos to be below the federal poverty line. *Confianza* enables families to survive economic uncertainties (plant closings, layoffs, illness); to avoid expenses for auto repair, plumbers, and so on; to get jobs; and to care for and raise children to become competent, resourceful, and productive members of the community.

Moll and Greenberg understood that one of Vygotsky's theoretical contributions was to suggest that psychology should link the development of consciousness, thought, and learning to *productive* activity. This cultural, social, and historical approach to the study of human consciousness is rooted in day-to-day activities of families in working-class communities.

After studying the funds of knowledge in the communities, teachers developed modules to support student bilingual literacy development. They wanted their students to write more. Each case study of a module involved university and teacher researchers in a study group of literacy articles, demonstration lessons to generate student topics for writing and develop lessons to address student interests, and the development of a videotape as a student activity to promote literacy in the community. Learning in community involved communication with a school in Ponce, Puerto Rico, and the development of a video about Tucson to send to students in Puerto Rico.

A second case study involved the development of a construction module. Students developed models of buildings or houses with wood, paper, and other materials. The students went to the library to investigate the topic. One group wrote a detailed report of their activities. The other group developed a fictional character, Maria, who had a father who was a construction worker. The teacher invited parents to come into the class and contribute to the development of lessons and to talk about construction. This was an "*intellectual* contribution to the content and process of classroom learning. The parents came to share their knowledge, expertise, or experiences with the students" (Moll & Greenberg, 1990, p. 339). This knowledge became a part of student work as illustrated in a writing sample from a student:

> There are many people that work in construction. First there is the designer. She designs the way the inside of he building will look like. She finds the best quality furniture to match the color of the room, she also gets the rugs, curtains, etc. to match the color. The architecture designs the building. He must figure out the length, width and how many rooms there will be.
>
> The estimators figures out how much everything will cost. He tries to find the best, least expensive tools for the job. He also has to estimate how long will it take to finish, because every day they must pay money. The carpenter does all the wood work. He designs all the wood work. He designs the frame to start the building. He also does sticks so when they pour the concrete it is straight. The electrician puts the wires inside the walls for electricity. He also does the outlets for connecting things. To have lights and other needs.
>
> The plumber is someone who does drains. He does bathroom wires and he puts a hose like, so that water can come out of a fountain. (Moll & Greenberg, 1990, pp. 341–342)

This is a different approach to the typical academic knowledge that is valued in schools. Often if parents don't know English, have limited formal education, or speak a nonstandard dialect, teachers think the parents can't help their children succeed in school. When the knowledge that is valued in schools is different from that in the community, there is a cultural mismatch between what is valued in schools and what is valued in the community (Au, 1980; Ramirez & Castaneda, 1974), which can result in minority students feeling that they must "become White" or turn their backs on their families if they want to succeed in school.

With cultural and linguistic deficit models on the part of school personnel, teachers and other school staff label students as "dirty," "lazy," or "not college material" and separate working-class and racial and ethnic minority students from their more affluent, college-bound classmates. When the home language or dialect is viewed negatively, denigrated or belittled in the schools, assimilation takes place at the cost of children's identification with their home language. Through studying the funds of knowledge that exist in the community, we can anchor our curriculum in knowledge that is valued in the community (see chap. 4, Learning by Doing) (Grant & Wong, 2004).

Jim Cummins (1986) developed a framework for empowerment of language minority students that included four features:

1. Additive, not subtractive view toward the home language and culture.
2. Collaborative, not exclusionary approach to community participation.

3. Reciprocal, interaction-oriented, not transmission-oriented model of pedagogy.
4. Assessment is advocacy oriented rather than legitimization oriented.

Integrating funds of knowledge from the community into the school curriculum addresses all four features of Cummins's framework, especially the first two features: an additive approach to the home culture, and community incorporation. Funds of knowledge link knowledge of labor and productive activity and honor working-class knowledge and wisdom. We in TESOL, whether it is in EFL or ESL contexts, have a responsibility to enable all of our students to become productive, contributing citizens. Funds of knowledge can challenge us to develop curriculum that links productive activity to bilingualism or multilingualism and technologies for the future (New London Group, 1996).

The theme of "learning in community" in the English language classroom can be examined from at least two perspectives. One is to view the English language class as a discourse community itself. As teachers we seek ways in which we can increase the participation of students from diverse backgrounds and different proficiencies. Challenges within classroom discourse include how to make sure that certain students don't monopolize, or how to encourage those who are shy. Another challenge is to transform sorting and tracking patterns in classroom discourse in which college-bound students are intellectually challenged while others are provided skills and drills (Mehan, 1979). These patterns begin as early as the primary grades. Some classroom patterns and practices support learning in community and others serve to divide students and contribute to stratification. In a first-grade classroom in Canada (Toohey, 1998, 2000), ESL students were told to:

1. Sit at your own desk (instead of getting up and working with other children in pairs or groups).
2. Use your own materials (instead of sharing scissors, erasers, and crayons).
3. Do your own work and use your own words (instead of working together with other children).

Kelleen Toohey observed that these three practices set into motion "a process of community stratification that increasingly leads to the exclusion of some students from certain activities, practices, identities and affiliations." Teachers "break them apart, take them away" (Toohey, 1998, p. 80)—rather than fostering and supporting learning in community. In contrast, teachers employing dialogic approaches to TESOL support the learner as a whole person (Igoa, 1995). They look for ways to include all students, particularly those who have been traditionally marginalized by their race, gender, ethnic, social, and economic class backgrounds.

A second way to view the theme of "learning in community" is to develop opportunities for students to engage in learning from communities outside the classroom. A dialogic curriculum draws from both kinds of communities to expose students to diverse experiences, perspectives, and voices. In the first example that follows, an orientation to the United States led by the Rev. Dr. Franklin Woo, three Chinese theological students, Franklin, and I (their English language tutor) make up a discourse community. In 1986, Gao Ying, Li Yading, and Zhang Xianyong were the first Chinese students sent from the churches in China to study in the United States since the establishment of the Peoples Republic of China in 1949.[7] The second excerpt, with Father Paul Woodrum, is an example of the students having an exchange with someone from another community.

COMMUNITY BETWEEN TEACHER AND STUDENTS: SHARED UNDERSTANDINGS IN AN EXERCISE IN TRANSLATION

> A classroom performance represents a moment in which, by speaking or writing, a student must enter a closed community, with its secrets, codes and rituals. And this is, we argue, an historical as well as a conceptual drama. The student has to appropriate or be appropriated by a specialized discourse, and s/he has to do this as though s/he were easily and comfortably one with his or her audience, as though s/he were a member of the academy. (Bartholomae & Petrosky, 1986, p. 8)

The transcript that follows was taken from a class session with Chinese theological students (see appendix on the Pilgrimage Curriculum) at the home of the Rev. Dr. Franklin and Jean Woo. Franklin, a Chinese American from San Francisco, was the director of the China Program for the National Council of the Churches of Christ in the United States. He promoted dialogue and developed programs between Protestant churches in the Peoples' Republic of China and the United States. Born in China, Jean Woo worked for the Presbyterian Church and was the editor of a Chinese newsletter about Christians and churches in China. She was in charge of the students' schedules and arranged for their visits to churches in the New York

[7]See Appendix for a description of the students and the dialogic Pilgrimage Curriculum I developed to introduce them to the academic communities of Union Theological Seminary and Columbia University and the multicultural communities of New York City.

City area. The Woos had worked in Asia and the United States; they were bilingual, bicultural professional role models for the students and me in their ability to walk in many worlds.

I first met the Woos in the early 1970s when the Rev. Woo was chaplain at the Chinese University of Hong Kong. The Woos were dormitory supervisors for two of my friends who were exchange students from the University of California. Franklin and Jean took us under their wings, as we Chinese American students struggled to learn Cantonese and come to terms with our identity and cultural heritage. Many years after we met in Hong Kong, Franklin and I renewed our acquaintance in New York. He invited me to join in a similar journey of linguistic and cultural exploration, but through a different lens. This time I was an experienced English teacher and I was the local guide and cultural insider to introduce Chinese students to American culture and society, rather than the "jook sing"[8] student of Cantonese and apprentice of Chinese culture and society.

As Chinese Americans, Franklin and I have wrestled with two questions ever since we met in Hong Kong: First, what is Chinese and what is American? And second, what can we as Americans learn from China, her history and her people, and what is of value from our culture and our experiences that we can share with people in China? Sometimes the most fundamental questions are at once very simple and very complex.[9] At the core of the dialogic curriculum I developed for these students were those fundamental questions involving identity, culture, growth, and transformation.

The three Chinese students were to spend the weekend with the Woos. After the theological session, Mrs. Woo planned to take them to a yard sale and later to Columbia University to hear a lecture by a Chinese writer. The session was a follow-up to an introductory lecture by the Rev. Dr. Franklin Woo on a textbook he had selected for the students, *Constructing Local Theologies* by Robert Schreiter (1986), a Catholic theologian.

---

[8]*Jook sing* ("hollow bamboo") is the Cantonese term that describes American-born Chinese. We have no roots in China and don't know the language and culture of our ancestors. It is often accompanied by the adjective "mouh yuhng" ("usless") because, to borrow Tannen's term, we "just don't understand." We lack the memories and traditions of those who went before us.

[9]In *Write to Learn*, Donald Murray (1984) said that the subjects that haunted him before he graduated from college were the ones he was still working on. We return to good topics over and over again. I think it has something to do with commitment. When we care about a question, it involves defining and redefining ourselves in relationship to that question. If we truly invest ourselves in a subject, we become transformed in the process of learning.

Theoretical Framework for the Lesson: Theologies of Context

Historically the work of Christian missionaries has been connected to colonial conquest. The sword and the cross figure prominently as symbols of the European conquistadors and priests as they conquered the indigenous Native American people in the New World on their way to find a trade route to India and China. The Protestant missionary enterprise was closely connected to settling and occupying the land, bringing European and U.S. civilization to indigenous people and colonized people throughout the world. For example, missionaries in Hawaii made the Native Hawaiian women wear "muumuus"[10] because they considered it sinful for them not to wear clothes.

Whatever the missionaries brought from Europe or the United States was considered "good" because they equated their own culture with being God-like. The project of Christianizing was tied to educating people in European and American ways of life. The missionaries never considered that local forms of culture could be used to pray or to praise God. This would be considered "syncretism"; local gods were idols and the local culture was seen as evil. For a native person to become Christian under colonialism meant to choose not only a new religion but a new culture and new political allegiances.

Contemporary theologies of context and liberation have questioned whether European cultural forms of music, art, or dress were more "God-like" than those of the "savages." There was no reason why local music, art, or dress could not be used to praise God. The point of developing a Chinese or African or Native Hawaiian theology is to be true to the local traditions and to use the local themes and resources to understand and theorize the meaning of God.

When I arrived early Saturday morning, the students had had their breakfast and were sitting on the Woos' enclosed back porch. I set up my tape recorder in time to record Franklin asking the students to translate the second stanza of a hymn from Mandarin Chinese to English.[11] The hymn was an example of local Chinese theology because the writer drew on Chinese cultural themes to praise God.

Franklin:[12] Translate the second stanza. Look at it in Chinese and tell Shelley what it means in English. This hymn [is] by Zhao Zichen.

Gao Ying: Do you want to translate, Zhang?

---

[10] Colorful, loose-fitting cotton print dresses.

[11] Tape of session with Franklin Woo, September 12, 1987, Englewood, N.J. All of the quotations in the following translation exercise were recorded from the same session.

[12] My use of first names for the Americans and surnames for the Chinese may seem peculiar; however, it emphasizes the nationality of the interlocutor. *(continued)*

Zhang:	We ask for ... we beg our holy Father to take good care of me, so that I can do good deeds and there will issue kindness from my face or something like that ...
Franklin:	My countenance will be peaceful, gentle *yan se hui he wen*. Yeah, and then what else?
Zhang:	and then I will be ... humble.
Franklin:	yes ... humble. In humility
Zhang:	yeah, humble to teach the younger—
Franklin:	teach the young humility
Zhang:	the young generation
Franklin:	younger generation
Zhang:	yes and self control to serve the old ones
Franklin:	Yes, in discipline I serve the elders. That's very Confucian.

Zhang approached the task with humility; he expressed his doubt about the adequacy of his translation by tagging it with "or something like that," which can be seen as the proper stance of the student in both Socratic and Confucian terms.

In this and the following dialogues, Woo takes the role of Socratic midwife, helping the students to "give birth" to a translation of the Chinese hymn. In the case of Zhang, Woo affirms the student's efforts and extends them with slight corrections and clarifications. Teacher and student worked together in dialogue to achieve the task.

Following the exchange with Zhang just quoted, Franklin presented the students with a "translation" of the hymn by D. T. Niles, a Sri Lankan whose work on this text reflected his adoption of Eurocentric understandings of Christianity:

Niles	**Zhang**
Father, God in Heaven Hallowed be thy name Rule to thee be given Power and all acclaim Thee may we obey As hosts above Bread for us each day Broken by thy love	[I] beg our Holy Father to take good care of me so that I can do good deeds and my countenance will be peaceful, gentle. And then I will humbly teach the younger generation and in discipline I serve the elders.

Pointing out the essential Confucianism of the Chinese version of the hymn, Franklin declared: "He has missed the whole point of this *xu xin jiao xiao bei*!" [虛心教小輩 humbly teach the younger generation heoi1 sam1e gaau1 siu2].

---

[12] (*continued*) Use of first names in the United States conveys a sense of informality, but does not carry the connotations of speaking to a child, one's subordinate, or overfamiliarity that it could in Chinese contexts. The asymmetrical solution to the use of names in the text is only one example of the complexity of recording cross-cultural communication.

Franklin amplified his Socratic and Confucian roles with the next student, who was less skilled in English. He turned to Li Yading and asked him to translate the third stanza. When Li responded, "No, I can't," Franklin urged him three times, "Try! Try! Try!" There was a 20-second pause from the time Franklin called on Li and he answered, which to an American ear was a long time. Perhaps Li was embarrassed and feared his translation would not be as good as Zhang's. Perhaps he wanted to defer, but didn't know how to refuse politely. Li's protestation, "No, I can't," may have indicated modesty. He also may have had trouble understanding the request.

In a booming voice, Franklin repeated "Try" three times. Perhaps his repetition could be interpreted through Chinese eyes as signaling encouragement (the way a host will offer refreshments to a guest at least three times before the guest will accept). However, afterward as I transcribed the tape of the session, I detected an undercurrent of impatience in Franklin's voice when I listened to the tape repeatedly. I timed a 20-second pause between Franklin's question and Li's response. Li finally began to translate when Franklin repeated the instruction, "Try the third stanza." Despite his initial hesitancy, Li was able, nonetheless, to make a translation that was more faithful to the original than that of Niles:

Niles	**Li Yading**
Pardon as we share in thy pardoning power Keep from Satan's snare in temptation's hour In temptation's hour so from sin set us free Lord we see thy face, sons of Liberty Heirs of saving grace	I hope I have a good time today. Every moment [I] depend on Jesus. Surely as heaven is above my head, there [es] evil in my heart. I was glad to get simple clothing. As long as it keeps me warm, I don't mind it. I don't mind it if the rice is coarse. I don't mind that as long as I get the Lord's help. In 10,000—myriad—things I need the Lord's help.

Strategic Competence

The third student, Gao Ying, was the least experienced in using English. Yet despite her lack of English vocabulary, she had excellent ancillary language skills. She knew how to manage the give and take of turn-taking in English, and she parlayed her small vocabulary into larger understandings through her adroit use of interpersonal linguistic skills. In the first transcript just shown, she relegated the task of translation to a more competent student by asking Zhang (who had taught English at the university level in China) if he wanted to translate—before the teacher could choose a student to call on. In the transcript that follows, she indicates her understanding of the proceedings by laughing at the appropriate time and she makes a point that becomes central to the understanding of translation that Franklin Woo was trying to develop among the students:

Franklin: Okay, listen to D. T. Niles, our friend D. T. Niles, how he translated this Chinese hymn for the world:
"Pardon as we share in thy pardoning power"—do you find that in there? It's not in there! [Gao Ying laughs].
"Kept from Satan's snare in temptation's hour"—where did Zhao Zichen talk about Satan? *Mo gui* [devil] *mei you* [none there] [Gao Ying laughs].
"In temptations hour so from sin set us free
Lord we see thy face, sons of liberty
Heirs of saving grace."
This is garbage! He took this Chinese hymn which is very Chinese and very Confucian and made it more to his own theology. And then the fourth verse and there is not fourth verse in Chinese, he felt that the hymn did not mention the Trinity—Father, Son and Holy Ghost so he made it.
Gao: They didn't understand about Chinese culture.
Franklin: No. He doesn't. He didn't.

Not only did Gao Ying make a comment with which Franklin agreed, but she contributed to the discussion by echoing Franklin's point about the *Confucian* character of the hymn:

Gao: He didn't. I think Consu-sher ... he didn't catch Confu-sher.
Shelley: Confucius.
Franklin: He de-Confucianized the hymn.
Li: Confucius is essential.
Franklin: And he trinitarianized the hymn.
Gao: Uh. Huh.

Although Gao's linguistic resources were more limited than Li's, her participation in the discourse structure was nevertheless effective. She never attempted the translation task. Yet by laughing at the appropriate places, nodding, and commenting "uh huh," Gao was able to show understanding and agreement with Franklin's argument. Although she couldn't pronounce "Confucius" the first time, she said something close enough that I understood what she wanted to say and could provide a scaffold for her by saying the word, providing the stress on the second syllable. Because Gao initiated the comment on Confucius, Franklin commented that Niles "de-Confucianized the hymn."

The conversation between Gao Ying and Franklin continued as Franklin presented the fourth verse of Niles's "translation."

Franklin: Look at the fourth stanza:
"Grace to all men shown
All that Grace must know
God their father own.
To their father go.
Christ will come at last
Even now so near
Night will soon be past
And the dawn appear."
See this is not in there. It is not in Zhao Zichen's content. It's not in there. So the point is that D. T. Niles, in trying to introduce a Chinese hymn to the world, put in his own understanding to Christianity. He was not faithful to the beginning of local Chinese theology as expressed by Zhao Zichen. Zhao Zichen always has a *xu xin jiao xiao bei* (humbly teach the younger generation).

Gao: Uh. Huh. Very, very Confucian.

Franklin: Very Confucian. And also it reflects the poorness of Chinese society. This is a good example of how insensitive an outsider can be to the local situation. This was the trouble with the early '30s. It was very difficult. People like D. T. Niles, he is a big hero in the eyes of many of the missionaries. Oh this Sri Lankan,[13] he's such a good thinker! You know why he was such a good thinker? Because he thought like us in the West. His ideas were so similar to ours in the West that he was the best thinker in the West. People didn't know what Chinese theological thinking was like!

This time, Franklin repeats "very Confucian" after Gao Ying. Repeating what another has said (backchanneling) is similar to the counseling technique of paraphrasing to indicate understanding. Signaling agreement is what Deborah Tannen calls an "involvement" strategy, which together with its opposite, "independence," are two dimensions of *face* or politeness strategies in conversations (Scollon & Scollon, 1995, pp. 38–39). Another way of interpreting the discourse between the interlocutors in the passage just quoted is to look at the establishment of "intersubjectivity" or the way through the dialogue they coconstruct meaning. Speakers connect to each other. They are able to read and interpret each other's intentions and to "finish" each other's thoughts. We learn to be part of a discourse community through dialogic interaction.

[13]The translation of Chinese culture (China was semicolonial) by a colonized Sri Lankan or "divide and rule" is one of the key features of colonialism. Pitting different colonized ethnic groups against each other and using one group to do the policing of another (i.e., Indian and Black plantation workers in Guyana or South Africa or successive waves of Asian immigrant plantation workers in Hawaii) is a historical feature of colonialism and imperialism. Historic discursive patterns of divide and rule contribute to racism and divisions between former slaves and colonized subjects to this day. See Rodney (1982) and Takaki (1990).

BRANCH 2-2: ROGERIAN COMMUNICATION

The psychologist Carl Rogers (1902–1987) created the "person-centered approach" to therapy amidst a climate of directive therapeutic approaches (e.g., Freud and other psychoanalysts as well as behaviorist-influenced psychologists). Rogers believed that the answers to a person's psychological struggles lay within him- or herself, because people tend to move toward growth, given growth-inducing conditions. The conditions Rogers sought to have present in counseling sessions included:

- Unconditional positive regard (the counselor accepts the client).
- Congruence (the counselor must be honest rather than defensive).
- Empathy (the therapist must be able to "walk in the other person's shoes").
- Reflection (the therapist does more listening than talking and indicates understanding through reflecting both emotional and linguistic content of the client's talk).

Like Confucius, Rogers (1961) thought that the primary task of people was, as the title of one of his books reflects, "becoming human," which relates to the Chinese concept of *ren (jen)*. For Confucius, people can become *ren* within a complex relationship of social relations, involving altruistic, harmonious, and human-hearted duties and responsibilities to others (son to father—or from a less male-dominated perspective, children to parents). Rogers's system is centered on a Western conception of self. People can become fully human if they are accepted for who they are and can explore their thoughts and feelings in an accepting environment. Benjamin Whorf and John Sapir suggest that culture and language shape each other. The quest for personhood or selfhood is culturally, socially, and historically situated. One cannot learn another language without also learning other cultural perspectives, including various approaches to personhood or the self.

Similar to Socrates' approach, in which knowledge comes from within the student, Rogers believed that internal psychological conflicts could be resolved through the process of reflective listening in a supportive environment because of the essential positive nature of human beings. A main difference between Socrates and Rogers lay in their technique: Socrates often asked leading questions wherein he was directing students down certain logical paths (e.g., as he helped a slave boy reason out the Pythagorean theorem), whereas Rogers's interactions with his clients were nondirective—they were focused on the "here and now" of the patient's reality. Of course, this difference was based on the goals of the interactions: Socrates was seeking to support the development of certain kinds of knowledge, whereas Rogers was seeking to assist people in a process of self-actualization, which could come about through nondefensive reflection on events and feelings. Yet for both, the answers lay within the person with whom they were working, and both were "midwives" in helping the student/client give birth to greater understandings, whether these were philosophical or psychological insights. Teachers can use the questioning techniques of Socrates and the listening techniques of Rogers to facilitate a positive classroom environment that allows students to find and add to their linguistic and personal resources and strategies (Snow, Hyland, Kamhi-Stein, & Yu, 1996).

We size up other people in conversations. As Scollon and Scollon state:

> Language is always, inherently, and necessarily ambiguous. That leads to the second point we want to make about communication. It means that in order to communicate we must always jump to conclusions about what other people mean. There is no way around this. A crossword puzzle is much like the way language works.... When someone says something, we must jump to some conclusion about what he or she means. We draw inferences based on two main sources: (1) the language they have used, and (2) our knowledge about the world. That knowledge includes expectations about what people would normally say in such circumstances. (p. 10)

Scollon and Scollon point out that our inferences tend to be "fixed, not tentative" and that they are drawn very quickly.

What Does It Mean to Learn Another Language?

Canale and Swain (1980) pointed out that to communicate, language learners must have more than linguistic competence. They need sociolinguistic competence, grammatical competence, discourse competence, and what they call "strategic" competence. Strategic competence involves utilizing strategies to compensate for weaknesses in linguistic or grammatical competence. Deferring or fielding questions, asking for clarification, and other ways of negotiating turn taking in conversations are all part of strategic competence. From the beginning, Gao Ying parlayed these nonlinguistic competencies into effective communication.

Exercise in Translation

Franklin's exercise in translation was a metaphor for the task of the students in the United States. In a sense their experience of studying abroad would be an unending exercise in translation: to translate Chinese experiences and sensibilities to American audiences and to translate American experiences particularly in the church and the academy for the church in China. The dialogic approach enabled them to sift critically and to serve as better interpreters to foster greater communication between people of different cultural and social systems. As anthropologist Clifford Geertz (1983) wrote:

> "Translation," here is not a simple recasting of others' ways of putting things in terms of our own ways of putting them (that is the kind in which things get lost), but displaying the logic of their ways of putting them in the locutions of ours; a conception which again brings it rather closer to what a critic does to illumine a poem than what an astronomer does to account for a star. (p. 10)

Franklin positioned himself as being outraged about Niles's translation of the hymn that removed the Chinese aspects of the song. Through his outrage, he set up a context for the students of a shared community of people who were interested in a more accurate representation of Chinese Christianity. This community he set up ensured that the task he asked them to do was relevant and that he was on their side because he knew they could do a better job than the other translator. Franklin became not just a teacher (potentially a judge of students who hands out grades) but an advocate (someone who shares the concerns of students and attempts to advance students in their own goals).

All students participated despite their differing English language competencies. Two students translated; the third student did not translate but contributed to the conversation. A dialogue among students of differing abilities, particularly in the context of solving real linguistic problems (see chap. 3 on problem posing), offers students of all levels opportunities to contribute. The teacher's role is not only to facilitate the dialogue but also to assess students' contributions—perhaps through taping and analyzing student speech or conducting informal assessments. Finally, although Franklin's teaching with respect to the linguistic task of translation from Chinese to English can also be characterized as "scaffolding" (through assisting students in achieving a task by extending their capabilities) in the sense of Vygotsky, the roots of his interactions with students lie in the pedagogical techniques and philosophical questioning of both Socrates and Confucius.

The people who "sat under the ginkgo tree" in this interaction shared Chinese heritage, although they differed in language, not only because of differences in English speaking ability but also because there were differences between Chinese dialects among participants. I speak Cantonese, and the students were translating into English a hymn from Putonghua, the national language (Mandarin), which I did not understand. Franklin Woo, who spoke English, Cantonese, and Mandarin, facilitated a conversation in which all could participate across these differences by establishing shared goals, in the same way that the quest for *ren* was a shared goal between Confucius and his disciples. In the case of Woo, the goal was for students to learn English in the context of being able to "translate" Chinese Christianity in a way that valued its Chinese roots and qualities.

Yet although Woo's class focused on and affirmed Chinese cultural perspectives within the Western academy, this strategy may not always be the best approach for all student learning. The point of dialogic pedagogy is not that cultural identities must be the center of all transactions; rather, it is to have meaningful conversations that support the learning of all students. Sometimes culture will be the source and subject of those conversations; sometimes other topics will be the center. It is up to the teacher to discern the needs of the students (Prator, 1979).

It is important for us to realize that the role of the teacher of Chinese children or adolescents in the United States may be very different, as the following example shows. Donald Duk is a Chinese American 12-year-old character from a novel by Frank Chin. Donald lives in San Francisco and attends a mostly White school that is not in Chinatown.

> All his teachers are making a big deal about Chinese stuff in their classes because of Chinese New Year coming on soon. The teacher of California History is so happy to be reading about the Chinese. "The man I studied history under at Berkeley authored this book. He was a spellbinding lecturer," the teacher throbs. Then he reads, "The Chinese in America were made passive and nonassertive by centuries of Confucian thought and Zen mysticism. They were totally unprepared for the violently individualistic and democratic Americans. From their first step on American soil to the middle of the twentieth century, the timid, introverted Chinese have been helpless against the relentless victimization by aggressive, highly competitive Americans."
>
> "One of the Confucian concepts that lends the Chinese vulnerable to the assertive ways of the West is 'the mandate of heaven.' As the European kings of old ruled by divine right, so the emperors of China ruled by the mandate of heaven." The teacher takes a breath and looks over his spellbound class. Donald wants to barf[14] pink and green stuff all over the teacher's book.
>
> "What's he saying?" Donald Duk's pal Arnold Azalea asks in a whisper.
>
> "Same thing as everybody—Chinese are artsy, cutesy and chickendick." Donald whispers back.
>
> Oh no! Here comes Chinese New Year again! It is Donald Duk's worst time of year. Here come the stupid questions about the funny things Chinese believe

[14]Slang for "vomit."

in. The funny things Chinese do. The funny things Chinese eat. And "Where can I buy some Chinese firecrackers?" (Chin, 1991, pp. 2–3)

It was appropriate to appeal to nationalist and also universalizing identities and discourses in framing the tasks for the Chinese students who as adults were fully socialized to their own identities. Nothing Franklin said was "new" to them. As future leaders for Chinese churches, Gao, Zhang, and Li knew that many people had sacrificed for them to be able to study abroad. They were in the United States not for their own betterment but to serve the Chinese churches. They were selected because they were articulate spokespersons and promising leaders. Although all three had their struggles in English, particularly Gao, who had had little English preparation before coming to the United States, their own identity was never at stake.

The case is very different for young children. The children of immigrants, whether born in the United States or what the Korean Americans call "generation and a half"[15] are developing. They are in danger of losing or never fully developing their heritage language—of being "jook sing," empty bamboo who do not know their roots. It is important to not assume that any child is an expert on the culture or history of her/his parents. Somali students who grew up in refugee camps in Kenya may have no firsthand knowledge of Somalia. For English language learners who do have firsthand knowledge and memories of the home country, we must look at the social group that they belong to and the social groups in their school. If they are a minority or a member of a colonized group, they may feel uncomfortable if the teacher assumes they are different from the majority or mainstream students.

Adopted children from Korea and China may feel put on the spot if a teacher assumes from their appearance that they are knowledgeable about the countries in which they were born (particularly if assumptions are made that these students can serve as translators for ESL children). Dialogic pedagogy looks at the insider/outsider question in terms of community, recognizing that membership in a community is both forged and fluid (Leung, Harris, & Rampton, 1997). It has more to do with lived experiences, commitment, and involvement than racial appearance. All students should have options to learn about different cultures. Children from all ethnic backgrounds should study about the ways in which racial, ethnic, and religious minority groups have been oppressed and have strug-

[15]First generation immigrated to the United States (as adults having already been educated or socialized in the home country). Generation and a half came from the home country with their parents as children, having no choice in the matter. Second generation were born in the United States.

gled for their humanity, for example, the Holocaust in Nazi Germany, the internment of Japanese Americans in the United States during World War II, and the heroic struggle of the school children in Soweto, South Africa, against apartheid (Banks, 1994). Dialogic pedagogy enables students to learn more about other communities and possibly, through doing so, develop their own identification with that community. And that is important for students who can trace their roots to that community and have an inside connection as well as those who are outsiders and want to learn how to become allies.

At the same time, as James A. Banks (1996) pointed out, we need enclaves for students to explore their racial or ethnic identities (such as Black student alliances and gay and lesbian student groups). Some Native American and other minority students who have grown up outside of the reservation, barrio, or Chinatown may first recognize their ethnic identity as young adults in college, having never met students of the same background before. We also need forms for students' work on multiracial unity and justice, coalition forms which are inclusive and strive for unity and community. We need discursive spaces for both.

Who speaks for a community? As teachers we can work with our students to develop a sense of shared culture and shared community within our classrooms, our schools, our neighborhoods. The knowledge for whom question (chap. 5) asks us to look at political, economic, and social justice when we discuss community so that "community" doesn't become a sanitized concept or an exclusive club (Kiang, 1996). As teachers, we should be careful if we are not members of a community to facilitate the voices of the actual members. These are not simple issues. For adolescents, this includes the questions of what it means to belong to group, navigating changing social identities and not being accused of being "wannabes" as Laurie Olsen (1997) describes in her book *Made in America*:

> There are many paths to and aspects of becoming "American" though they all involve becoming English-speaking. And to listen even briefly to conversations among newcomers about becoming American immediately illustrates the tight connection in their minds among race, religion and language as inextricable and often interchangeable identifiers that mark one as American or not American. For newcomers, the persistent question is whether or not the path to being American is one that is really open to them. (p. 43)

Dialogic Support of Classroom Community

The chief support teachers can provide in terms of creating a dialogic community within the classroom is not subject related (e.g., making culture a center of discussion) as much as it is process related. Teaching involves knowing what to do related to the daily search for the learner's point of view (Freeman, 1996). This process includes recognizing how and why people identify with their communities/cultures and when or whether bringing those experiences into the classroom will support student learning. On the one hand, language is fundamentally communicative and people who are learning language tend to want to talk about the things that are important to them, which are often related to culture and experiences. Teachers need to be prepared to assist students in developing the skills to speak and write about the things they care about and, at the same time, to help other students in the class to become respectful listeners/readers of what people have to say (Goldstein, 2004).

On the other hand, culture and membership in communities are complex. Students may have hidden or invisible identities, including gay and lesbian students, many ethnic and religious minorities (such as Native American or Jewish), and victims of rape or other abuse (Vandrick, 1997). People's emerging and competing identities may not be easily understood, and their privacy or sense of personhood may be violated. The teacher's job is to listen and find out what students need in terms of how classroom community becomes enacted. This is not easy in a world in which there are systematic racial and class stratification, segregation and inequality, and divisions and conflicts between cultures. Imagine an ESL classroom with children whose parents are from opposite sides of a war and the potentials for misunderstandings, not just between the children but also between their families. These conflicts will not go away easily, and the classroom teacher may have a difficult time simply making sure all communications between students are respectful.

BRANCH 2-3: ON BULLYING AND HATE CRIMES

Fostering a community of learners includes a responsibility to address bullying and hate crimes. From students who have emigrated from Mainland China to Hong Kong and who are teased on the playground by the more affluent Cantonese-speaking students, to middle school Somali girls in Columbus, Ohio, who are targeted because of their wearing of the Islamic clothing, the *hijab*,[16] bullying and hate crimes affect EFL and ESL students. Although bullying often takes

[16]Bashir-Ali, K. Experiences and issues of Somali women in Columbus, Ohio. At a panel discussion at the Mershon Center, Ohio State University, Nov. 12, 2002, ESL teacher and teacher trainer talked about the game "Get Bin Laden" in which Somali students, especially girls wearing Islamic clothes, were chased on the playground.

place outside the classroom, it nevertheless affects the quality of learning within the classroom, as well as the safety of all students and their teachers. Bias, hatred, and prejudice resulting in threats, assault and battery, vandalism, and murder may be based on real or *perceived* differences in race, religion, ancestry, national origin, disability, gender, or sexual orientation.

Since the September 11, 2001 attacks, the Los Angeles County Commission on Human Relations (2001) reported "an 11% increase [in hate crimes] over the previous year, and the largest number [of victims] ever reported in Los Angeles County" (p. 3). Included in the 188 victims of anti-Middle Eastern/Muslim hate crimes were South Asians, Latinos, and Armenians (Los Angeles County Commission on Human Relations, 2001) who were attacked because they "looked like the enemy."

Critical and dialogic teachers can address bullying by uncovering assumptions and attitudes towards those who come from different communities. Sarah Benesch (1999) introduced her ESL students to the case of Mathew Shepard, a gay college student who was beaten to death in Laramie, Wyoming. Benesch, who teaches at the College of Staten Island, the City University of New York, felt a responsibility to address issues involved in hate crimes due to race, gender, and homophobia. Benesch reported:

> The unexamined assumption by many is that "heterosexual men are justified in responding to the presence of homosexual men with anger or violence to assert a traditional notion of masculinity." (Benesch, 1999, p. 577)

This assumption was initially unstated but was gradually articulated as the discussion progressed, beginning with one of the students' (whose pseudonym is Joon) dismissal of the topic as she distributed the newspaper clipping about the murder:

> "That homo guy!" As students read it silently he continued muttering, "I hate that ... Gay people. I'm gonna kill myself." After discussing the disputed facts of the Shepard murder, including whether Shepard had approached his attackers at the bar or whether they had initiated conversation with him, Roger told of once being approached by a gay coworker: "I wanted to punch him, but I had to keep my job." Then Eva told of being approached by a gay woman at a dance club, allowing the students to consider why Roger had felt threatened whereas Eva had not. Why had he wanted to beat the guy up whereas she had laughed it off and even felt flattered? Joon declared that if he were approached by a man, he would beat him up. When asked why, he said that being admired by a man would embarrass him, an important admission that led Roger to offer, "You worry that it's something about you. What do they see in me?"

Sarah Benesch characterized her role as teacher as a "conversational facilitator" and an "intervener." As a facilitator she listened, took notes, and asked questions to encourage learning in community. As an "intervener" or teacher, she probed a hidden assumption that

> homosexuals are primarily interested in making sexual overtures to and converting heterosexuals. Could this notion be based on fears some students had already raised rather than on a real threat? I asked. My other challenge was to ask the students to consider the social origins of their fears as well as alternatives to killing or beating up someone as a way of dealing with those fears. (p. 578)

For ESL students, coming from one community (a country in which they were members of the majority culture) to another may entail becoming a "visible" minority. If our students are seen as threatening, foreign, or "bad immigrants" by the new society, for us as teachers the dialogic feature of learning in community involves becoming aware of and critiquing common assumptions of "us" and "them," probing stereotypes and critically analyzing discourses that dehumanize, such as playground taunts. In dialogic classrooms, "taken-for-granted assumptions and presuppositions that lie behind argumentation are uncovered, examined and debated" (Gieve, 1998). This may involve taking up "tough topics" beyond the normal "comfort zone" for us as teachers.

Lesbian and gay students may be silent in discussions that privilege heterosexuality. Kate Evans (2002) told of her partner Annie, an art teacher at a middle school, who answered a student's question "Are you a lesbian?" by posing the following question: "Do you think this school is a place in which someone could answer 'yes' to that question and feel safe?"[17]

It is not enough to "teach tolerance," but we must also create discursive spaces where all students can grow and feel safe and respected. It is not easy to create classroom cultures that are counter to the deep-seated dominant ideologies of schools. Reflecting on Annie's question for any student who is bullied or the brunt of cruel jokes is an important step in forging classrooms and schools in which students from many walks of life can say, "This place nurtures my spirit."[18]

Dialogic Interactions in Large Classes

The question of how to forge the interactive face-to-face meaningful dialogues that are possible in a small class in a large community of 40, 50, or

[17]Reflecting on Annie's question in our schools is a very good starting point to address bullying and hate crimes.

[18]See Cummins (2000).

60 language learners is a challenge faced by many teachers all over the world (Shamim, 1996). If we teach in institutions for the elite, in intensive English programs in universities, we tend to have smaller classes as well as an institutional culture (within our ESOL centers—not university-wide) that values collaboration between teachers and collective discussion of students' progress (although as TESOL university educators, our job titles are usually "lecturer" or "instructor" rather than "professor," our salaries are low, and we are often in part-time, temporary, or adjunct positions without health insurance or benefits within the larger universities in which we teach).

Teaching in larger classrooms can be an emancipatory undertaking, in part because the students are of populations that have traditionally had less access to education than their counterparts from First-World and/or middle- to upper-class backgrounds. That said, it is important to recognize how power works in the institution and to consider what is emancipatory within the context. In the Personal Prologue, I described teaching in the British colony of Hong Kong. At one level, emancipation for the students there lay in their ability to pass tests because only then could they have access to educational and career opportunities. At another level, emancipation might have meant critiquing a system that required high-stakes testing as well as creating more post-high-school educational opportunities. In this situation, emancipatory work entails working for two seemingly opposite goals: success on the tests, and the reduction of high-stakes testing. One is a short-term survival goal for students and the other is a long-term systemic goal.

To the extent that education can be individualized in large classrooms, it should be, at least to the point that the teacher is aware of students' individual perspectives, backgrounds, and needs. Even if assignments and assessments must be standardized, there may be instances in which topics of discussion can be adapted for the interests of individuals or small groups. The literature on teaching reading and writing workshops (e.g., Atwell, 1987; Calkins, 1983) may be helpful, although it is important to recognize influence of middle-class American culture on these methods and, as Lisa Delpit (1988) pointed out, to make expectations explicit when using these strategies. Students in workshops are responsible for keeping the class running smoothly (e.g., being able to work independently, helping peers appropriately, learning to set one's own goals and tasks). This responsibility also gives students greater choices, and it creates a community that focuses on learning (Peyton, Jones, Vincent, & Greenblatt, 1994).

BRANCH 2-4: ON READING/WRITING WORKSHOP

Large-scale teaching strategies appear efficient. Each session can be planned in advance and grading is easy—using an answer key or machine scoring multiple-choice tests. The teacher can ensure that an appropriate amount of material is covered in a term. Yet when behavior problems and student failure are factored in, these strategies may not work as well as individualization—particularly when "effectiveness" is as valuable as "efficiency." Finally, large-scale strategies require the teacher to be the sole manager of the class; the students' only role is to memorize the material presented.

Reading and writing workshops allow students to work at their own pace on materials that hold their interest. The teacher facilitates students' learning, through establishing and maintaining workshop procedures, helping students make choices about their work, and keeping track of student progress. Students assist with maintaining classroom procedures and serve as resources for each other. Finally, students take an active role in their own assessment by setting goals, and keeping track of their progress.

In contrast to the way writing has traditionally been taught, real authors write for a range of audiences in a range of genres. Their process includes brainstorming, rough drafting, editing, sharing drafts with friends for feedback, rewriting, and, finally, sending the piece out for publication. The developers of the writing workshop (Bay Area Writing Project and others) thought that it would be good to bring professional writers' process in school-based writing because that might help students to want to write (the same way professional authors choose to write). See Peregoy and Boyle (1997), and Bellino (2005).

The reading workshop was developed along similar lines as the writing workshop. In Nancie Atwell's middle school, students read on average over 20 books a year according to their interests, in a variety of genres. Although Atwell's students were native speakers of English, the principle of reading books, rather than brief passages and exercises, has been used with ESL students (Rigg & Enright, 1986; Urzua, 1986) and with bilingual students to promote biliteracy (Perez & Torres-Guzmán, 1992). Those who studied emergent reading and writing practices with ESL children found that students could begin to read and write in English before they had full control over all the linguistic systems. In reading and writing workshop with ESL students, literacy is introduced immediately and students are encouraged to use their native language as well as the new language (Hudelson, 1984, 1986).

Reading and writing workshop share several features (Wulf-McGraff, 2000):

- Time. Students have time in class to read (reading workshop) and to write (writing workshop). As students work, their questions can be answered by peers, by the written material available in the classroom (such as word walls for spelling, reminders of grammatical points), and by teachers. The most effective time to intervene in a students' reading or writing is while they are doing it, and if students are only doing it at home, the teacher is missing significant educational opportunities.

- Choice. Students can choose books in the classroom or from the school and/or public library. The teacher also makes students aware of genres to write in and audiences to write for—fellow students, the wider community, and larger audiences through writing on the Internet or seeking publication.
- Feedback and dialogue. Reading conversations include connections between books by the same author and suggestions for other books to read. Feedback allows writers to figure out where their messages are effective and where they are misunderstood. Teachers can help students to give positive, thoughtful, and honest feedback.
- Community. Students work together at their reading and writing; all children can offer support, feedback, ideas, strategies, and information. While the teacher works with one group of students, others can quietly answer each other's questions.
- Structure. The workshops are highly structured so that students receive regular opportunities for reading and writing and so that students are aware that when it is time to write, that is their main task.

Reading and writing workshops consist of several types of activities:

- Activity period. Students read or write during a period of time (e.g., 25 minutes). During this time, the teacher moves around the classroom conferring with individuals. The teacher keeps track to ensure that across a week he or she has checked in with all students about what they are doing, their plans, and where they need help.
- Mini-lessons. Mini-lessons (10 minutes or so) can be presented to a whole class immediately prior to the activity period, or they may be offered to a small group of students who need help with a particular skill or concept. Courtney Cazden (1992) called mini-lessons "instructional detours." In any instructional journey, the detours, if based on students' needs, may be much more important that the original syllabus.
- Sharing. Students share in small groups or with the whole class what they have been reading or writing. This allows dialogue to take place and students receive feedback.
- Assessment. The teacher keeps track of students' work—writing, books they are reading, and contact with students. Using their knowledge of

child development and language development, the teacher chooses interventions to make with individuals and groups of students. Students also assess their own work and set goals for themselves (see chap. 4, Learning by Doing, Branch on Authentic Assessment).

Adapting Reading/Writing Workshops to Large TESOL Classes

Full-blown reading and writing workshops may not be do-able in a class of 50 students. Further, for the teacher who is making a transition to dialogic pedagogy, it may not be wise to throw out all previously used methods. Rather, the teacher may need to add new activities or procedures a few at a time across a period of several years. Here are some possible reading/writing workshop activities in a dialogic TESOL classroom:

- Texts might include "survival reading," such as manuals for a driving test or appliances, information from banks, newspapers, contracts for buying items, or recipes. Students in ESL classrooms might read for their other classes during reading workshop, which would give the teacher a chance to help and to be aware of the work other teachers are assigning.
- Writing might include writing to manage one's life: writing letters to complain or compliment service, filling out job applications, creating resumés, and writing letters of inquiry. ESL/EFL students can also use writing to advocate for their rights to an education, safe and healthy communities, and to express their political concerns.
- A textbook that has been the center of the curriculum might become a reference book for students. Or, if it needs to remain in the center, students could work through it at their own pace. More advanced students might help less advanced students.
- The sharing that is part of reading and writing workshop could be considered the place to practice speaking and listening skills.
- Students can read and write in their own language as well as in English. Teachers Rachna Rikhye and Dana Frye encourage native language use in their elementary and middle school classrooms. They have volunteer adults and other students help with translations and with the reading of the work during sharing.
- Mini-lessons can include technical aspects of language: grammar, pronunciation, and so on.
- Several things can happen at once: Most students can work independently while the teacher confers with a second group and a third group shares their work with each other. Be sure every student has access to work time as well as other activities.

- There are many forms of assessment. Your program may require testing. But you can add your own systematic, recorded observations of students, their language use, their work habits, their writing and reading, their interactions. Through observation you might learn about why and when struggle happens–so you can address it.
- Give peers specific ways they can help each other. You may have to model peer assistance to ensure that more competent peers don't simply give out answers.

Many teachers go into the field because they want to open doors for students; they want their students to succeed. They find joy when students' faces light up with new insight. These teachers find not only moments of success, but also moments of disappointment, when one realizes, for example, that only a minuscule number of students will gain access to higher education, when so many would benefit from it.

It is important not to burn out. Therefore, the project of emancipation must be seen as long term—instead of something that can be solved overnight. Sometimes progress is hard to identify and sometimes conditions degenerate. The key is to remember the importance of establishing relationships with individual students, of communicating respect for each person as a learner and human being. This may not seem like much in the face of serious systemic woes, but it is one area over which most teachers have control and it can make a long-lasting difference in the lives of individual students.

The forging of community within the classroom as a technique for giving students opportunities that extend beyond those allotted to them in oppressive systems is a complex task because it involves helping students build bridges across conflict-ridden cultural and social differences. A topic or classroom strategy in one context can be helpful to students; in another context, it can cause students to disengage from the learning process altogether. The struggles that many students face can be overwhelming to the teacher and, unfortunately, it is in these situations where teachers may face large classrooms full of students whose intellectual potential may be cut off prematurely.

When teachers find out their students' needs and interests, when teachers take steps toward incorporating these needs in the classroom, when teachers take care of themselves so they remain able to be a resource for their students, then classrooms become places of support and growth for everyone. The scholars under the ginkgo tree were historically a homogeneous group; today's classes are much more heterogeneous and the challenge for teachers, those who facilitate scholarship, is to help the scholars express their concerns and their joys and to listen to the concerns and joys of others.

IN SEARCH OF AMERICAN CULTURE: VISITS AND VISITORS

Another aspect of community consists of the visitors or guest speakers who come into the classroom to share their lives. Visitors can support students learning. For instance, a visit with a Chinese student with more experience in the United States supported the position of Zhang, Gao, and Li, and the visit of a gay Episcopal priest challenged them (as they challenged him) to think about their own cultural assumptions. As with the conversation described earlier, students participated in these events at their own level of language proficiency. Their participation included preparing and delivering an introduction to the visitor and preparing and delivering a talk for the visitor about an aspect of their own work in China and the United States.

During the first semester of the Pilgrimage Curriculum we had two visitors. The first was Hu Yang, my classmate at Columbia Teachers College, who was a doctoral student in the English Education Program. I thought that the students would enjoy hearing about the experiences of another student from China, particularly because Hu Yang had such a beautiful command of English. Hu Yang, while not a model for the students' content area, theology, was a model as an English language learner from their context, the People's Republic of China. She spoke about her impressions of graduate school in the United States, how she had adjusted to graduate studies, and about her strategies in improving her English.

The second visitor was Father Paul Woodrum, an Episcopal priest who came to talk about gay liberation and the church. Before each session, a student was asked in advance to introduce the visitor and lead the discussion. This assignment gave students a chance to do some research and to prepare a statement in English. I had checked out books on gay liberation from the library, including theological works on homosexuality from a variety of perspectives, and had given them to Zhang Xianyong to select a few articles for the class to read before the discussion. Zhang prepared an introduction of the Rev. Woodrum using Paul's resume. Looking straight into the camera as he made the initial introductions, Zhang's moderating was skillful, despite self-consciousness induced by the presence of the video camera and the hand-held microphone. His speech was clear and deliberate as he read the introduction he had prepared. He also made an extemporaneous reference to the photos that Paul had shared with us of handcrafted church vestments.

Although Zhang's introduction made numerous references to Father Woodrum's involvement in gay rights, I learned after the priest had left that Zhang, Li, and Gao had not inferred that Father Woodrum was gay. Paul did not fit their image of a gay person. He had a moustache, wore glasses, a conservative dark suit, and a clerical collar. He was a distinguished-looking, middle-aged, White male. Gao Ying blurted out, "But he was a *nice* man and a scholar!" At first I thought that students did not infer that Father Woodrum was gay because they had had no previous exposure to openly gay people. Later, after listening to the video tape, I noticed that there were linguistic and pragmatic reasons why the students would not infer that Paul was gay. Paul used the third person "he, she, or they" to speak authoritatively about gay and lesbian people (as opposed to using the first person "I" or "we"). The students may have interpreted his use of the third person as indicating that he did not belong to group about which he was talking; they saw him as an Episcopal priest with an active ministry to gays and lesbians.

Zhang described Paul's involvement with gay rights in his introduction. He then asked the students to say a few words of introduction. He started to call on Li Yading and then turned jokingly to Gao Ying, when Li deferred to her:

Zhang:	And now we three students from China will say a few words about ourselves, our purpose in coming to the United States and something about our daily lives and study in this semester in New York City. And now, Li Yading will be the first.
Li:	Oh lady first!
Zhang:	Lady first! [Laughter as Zhang hands the microphone to Gao Ying]

Gao Ying introduced herself after responding to the joke. Then Li Yading began the dialogue on the gay question. Zhang framed the dialogue by identifying our topic of discussion to be the issue of gay civil rights. He provided background information to Paul about the students' previous exposure to the question by seconding Li's point about the students' surprise to encounter active gay and lesbian organizations on the various campuses.

Zhang asked me to say a few words. I responded by introducing the students as the first to be sent from the churches in China to study in seminaries in the United States since 1949. I stated that we hoped that this was only the beginning of more exchanges between Christians in China and in the United States. I hoped that Paul would share from the American cultural context some of the key controversies in the church over gay rights, such as ordination of gays and lesbians and ministry to the gay and lesbian community.

Zhang called on Paul to speak to us. Paul began with the development of the gay rights movement as part of a larger, civil rights movement beginning with the Black civil rights movement. He described the Stonewall riots in New York City, which for many marked the birth of the gay and lesbian movement in the United States.

As Paul described gay and lesbian caucuses in the churches and the various positions taken by the churches, I interjected to repeat a point to Gao Ying, who nodded her head as if to indicate she understood Paul's point (which was about gay Roman Catholics who had to meet in a Unitarian church). When Zhang asked if they were excommunicated, Paul replied that they were not and clarified that as individuals they could receive mass, but as a gay group they could not go to church. I asked whether the gay synagogue was Reform, Conservative, or Orthodox. Paul wasn't sure, but indicated that while there were some each, the majority of gay practicing Jews were Conservative.

Before Paul went into a discussion of ethics and sexuality and the Biblical questions, he paused for questions and Zhang Xianyong asked about terminology:

> I notice in your talking you does not like to use *homosexuality*, this word. You used *gay*. Or perhaps, in my understanding, you don't want to connect the gay community with homosexuality.

Paul responded that "language was often used to oppress people" and compared the terms "Black," "Nigger," and "Negro."[19] He explained:

> *Homosexual* is a strange word, it is a psychological term that was coined in Germany at the end of the 19th century. It combines a little Greek and a little Latin. It is a clinical term and it places the emphasis on sex. And people who are homosexual by that category prefer the term *gay* or *lesbian*. That's *their* choice. The other term puts people in a psychological category and suggests illness or something wrong. I mean most people don't go around saying, "You know, I'm heterosexual."

Paul later talked about the relationship between power and those who controlled the food supply and sex. When Gao Ying looked puzzled, I repeated key phrases of what Paul said, and Gao Ying nodded to indicate understanding. Paul talked about how different cultures controlled sexuality and gave the example of the conflict in the New Testament of the Jews practicing polygamy and the Gentiles practicing monogamy. He raised the contemporary controversy in Africa within the Anglican church over polygamy.

Paul discussed the few Biblical references to homosexuality. For example, Paul felt that *eunuch* was a code word for homosexual when Jesus

[19]"Nigger" is extremely derogatory, signifying White racial superiority. After the Black Power and Black liberation movement, "Negro" was replaced by Black, Afro-American, and African American.

said, "There are those that are born eunuchs, those who are made eunuchs, and those who become eunuchs." Throughout this discussion, Gao Ying was given the words in Chinese for "Gentile" and "eunuch" by Zhang Xianyong.

When Paul asserted that the Bible didn't really deal with homosexuality, Zhang challenged this by raising a number of Biblical passages. The first was a passage from Romans in which Saint Paul admonished against engaging in unnatural sex. Father Paul Woodrum responded by asking, "What does Paul mean by nature?" Zhang answered, "What is normal, acceptable." Paul then argued:

> Yes, nature is custom, it is normal. It's very cultural. St. Augustine said what is "nature" is the Platonic ideal, the image we should aspire to.... And this is true for Plato, Augustine, Aquinas. Modern times when we talk about nature, it's about what is observable scientifically. If Paul says it's not natural for men to have sex with men and women to have sex with women, he is saying that it is not custom. If Augustine says it, it does not live up to our ideal. If a scientist says he hasn't observed it, he is probably not a good scientist.

When Zhang challenged Paul to discuss Sodom, Paul answered that the issue in the story of Sodom was not homosexuality, but the question of hospitality, how to treat a guest.

Finally the discussion turned to homosexuality in China. Zhang responded:

Zhang:	It [homosexuality] is not cultural acceptable.
Paul:	But it exists, doesn't it?
Zhang:	Yes, in our literature. In some novels and short stories we may come across such sexual behavior among the same sex.
Paul:	What about in real life or is it all hidden?
Zhang:	In my opinion these literature writing is just something reflected from real life so I'm sure homosexuality also exists.
Paul:	Probably what happens is that it is hidden. Nobody thought there were that many in our society. The estimate is in every culture, genetically they are approximately 10% of the population.
Zhang:	I think in this society the environment and situation is more suitable for it to develop. According to our culture, according to our traditional ethics, one will not or dare not develop such a tendency.

Li then asked, "I want to know the attitude towards homosexuality of most churches in the United States." Paul cited the differences in treatment between the more open denominations and the more repressive ones. He raised an example of a Methodist bishop in Texas who had died of AIDS and had led a dual life. Paul was critical of the church for forcing a hypocritical life on its gay and lesbian clergy. He drew the parallel in treatment of gays to ordination of women. Zhang mentioned that the first female to be ordained in the Anglican church was a Chinese woman who now lives in Canada.

The session closed with a presentation for Paul by Gao Ying on the Chinese Christian Church. She showed us photographs: an ordination, students at Nanjing Seminary, and Chinese paper cuts of Biblical scenes. The paper cuts evoked immediate response from Paul, who tried to identify the various scenes. She also showed a journal from the seminary, which Zhang explained was an English translation of their original theological review that had been supported by friends abroad. I noticed that they had one of Gao Ying's sermons in the journal. By showing the photos, paper cuts, and journal from China, Gao Ying was able to convey experiences of Chinese Christians. When she asked Paul if he had any questions, he commented that he was honored to be with the students and returned to one of the themes that we discussed throughout the year: the challenge of interpreting what the students would learn in Western seminaries for Chinese Christians. When he commented that what they learned in the Western seminaries might not fit local Chinese conditions, the students agreed. This was their challenge: to sift though what they learned and critically appropriate what was suitable for their own context.

The dialogic method, which employed oral dialogue and student writing, created a vital relationship between reading, writing, and experience. Because of differences in English language ability, the students' interactions were uneven. Zhang was a full participant, posing questions concerning terminology and challenging Paul's Biblical interpretations. Li was not as active as Zhang, but asked questions. Gao Ying listened and struggled to understand, but did not ask questions. She participated by making her presentation on the churches in China. However, Li and Gao had further opportunities to struggle with Paul's message in their journals, class discussions, and a visit to a gay and lesbian meeting at Union Theological Seminary the following semester.

The gay/lesbian question proved to be challenging for the students from the standpoint of coming to terms with their own cultural biases. They had had exposure to Black theology in China and were familiar with Mao Zedong's essay about the Afro-American people's struggle. Curricula about hunger, war, immigration, and racism were familiar themes.[20] During-

[20] Gao Ying's comment "but he seemed like such a nice man" may seem naive. But her actual level of heteronormality were not any more deep-seated than those of many of us in the United States who do not want to be oppressive or hateful, but may marginalize gay and lesbian students. What is particularly "sinful" from a Christian perspective or "left dogmatism" and "sectarianism" from a Marxist perspective is to utilize religious or political ideals to oppress, repress, and dehumanize others. In the United States some "Third World" people of color activists, myself included, have been guilty of imposing heteronormality in the interest of antiracist, working-class, or national liberation struggles. See Zia (2000).

ing the second semester, Gao, Li, Union student Ken Guest (who had lived in China), and I went to the McDonald's on 125th Street [21] and had a discussion about gays and lesbians. Ken told us that he had heard it estimated that over 50% of the students at Union were gay or lesbian; Union is one of the few seminaries that accepts gays and lesbians. There are some professors who write about gay theology and ethics as well as support groups for students. We talked about gay and lesbian families and I told them about my brother's friend from high school, a gay man who donated to a sperm bank and found out to his delight that he had a 9-year-old daughter who was being raised by a lesbian couple.

Philosophically, as we discussed the question of universal standards, Li struggled with the notion of what was Chinese and what was Western. Although he wanted to learn and be accepting of differences cross-culturally, he had trouble dealing with homosexuality in the Chinese context. He felt that it was abnormal. Ken and I pushed Li, who was at a clear disadvantage in English, to explain his position. When he said he was open-minded, I retorted that this was a relative question.[22] Gao Ying laughed and pointed to Ken and me and nodded and repeated, "Relative, relative!"

I agreed with Li that each society has its own problems. It would be incorrect to impose Western gay/lesbian liberation or feminism on China from the outside. But just as there are indigenous efforts on the part of women in China, there are gays and lesbians in China.[23] Gao Ying was surprised to hear from Ken Guest that a particular street in Shanghai was a gay hangout and that a number of gay people had talked to him when he was in China. She had lived in Shanghai and never knew such a street existed. When Li and Gao returned to China, would they hear their voices?

Having visitors to a classroom can challenge students to use language for real purposes through their preparations for the visit. It can challenge students' cultural understandings as well, helping them to find ways of dealing with aspects of their new culture that may be opposed to their prior understandings. This learning is not easy, nor is it always comfortable. There may be no conclusions drawn; an event of this sort may not lead to neat resolutions in the minds and hearts of students or visitors.

---

[21]The McDonald's on 125th Street in Harlem has pictures of famous African Americans on the wall. The students asked if the restaurant was owned by Blacks. No, was my guess.

[22]In one of her classes, Professor Maxine Greene commented in self-conscious irony that although she wanted her students to be independent critical thinkers, she wanted them to think like her. I understand completely.

[23]The Chinese Psychological Association no longer views homosexuality as deviant.

BRANCH 2-5: BRINGING DIVERSE COMMUNITIES, PERSPECTIVES, AND VOICES INTO THE CLASSROOM

Teachers of English as a foreign language may challenge, "Of course in New York City, the opportunities for learning from diverse communities are tremendous—going to Harlem, Chinatown, and getting a gay speaker are worlds away from my class of Midwestern middle school students!"

Developing opportunities for students means "thinking outside the box." An EFL middle school teacher in Japan who wanted to find opportunities for her students to speak English reasoned that a temple would be a good place for her students to find English-speaking tourists. She arranged for a field trip, preparing her students with a brief set of questions to use in interviewing English-speaking tourists.

Begin with your own community. Remember, your guests do not need to be native speakers of English. Be sure to think about ways to incorporate a variety of regional and cultural dialects to your curriculum and do not limit yourself in terms of economic standing. For example, in the United States, there may be Appalachian, Creole, or Native American speakers.

If there is a neighborhood that represents a culture you want to learn more about, look for small businesses there and visit them in order to make contact. If there is a college or university, make contact with faculty and students. Most universities have offices that assist international students and faculty, which might be a good starting point.

Other sources of diverse voices in English might include documentaries and movies, newspapers and magazines, television (e.g., recordings of news programs), short-wave radio broadcasts, and the Internet.

Although giving students access to a range of voices in English is important, it is also a good idea to give students a chance to get to know people in their own community, some of whom may not speak English. The parents of your students are a good starting point. Perhaps one of them knows how to do certain kinds of folk art and could share that art form even using English. As the teacher, you can provide your students with English vocabulary to discuss what has been shared.

Finally, consider sharing your guests with the larger school community and look there for possible guests. Think across the district as well as within your school.

Bringing new voices into the classroom is often a matter of finding one person and then asking that person for other contacts. It is a matter of building from year to year and keeping your eyes and ears open as you go about your life outside of school. You might run into someone at the grocery store or at a temple, mosque, or church function or at a party or anywhere who could come to your classroom and talk with your students.

As with the caveat about using culture as a point of conversation within the classroom, teachers must be aware of the developmental needs of their students. It was appropriate to have the theological students engage with gays and lesbians because they were likely to come across this issue in their schooling and professional work. Teachers need to choose who might be invited. Certainly students who are learning English need to be exposed to the varieties of English they will face, including regional and cultural dialects (Wolfram, Adger, & Christian, 1999). They may also benefit from talking with parents of children in their own class as a way of demonstrating that the school values its students' cultures. Without adults in their lives showing what they value, children may think that their parents' languages "don't count" in an English-speaking society. An Asian American teacher in Arlington, Virginia, invited her own parents to come into her classroom to speak Tagalog to her fourth-grade students; this encouraged English language learners in her class to bring their parents to share other languages and also encouraged children to continue to learn their own native languages.

Yet many students are part of marginalized groups, wherein the dominant culture views the home culture as "the enemy." These children may renounce their culture and language to demonstrate their patriotism or allegiance to their new country. In this instance, bringing home languages and cultures to school may be challenging and painful; many teachers may wish to spare children this pain. Still, children are exposed to pain all the time, as in the bullying that has contributed to school shootings in the United States (in Columbine, Colorado, for example).[24] Ignoring that pain can have tragic consequences.

Dialogic pedagogy, with its focus on community building within the classroom and between the classroom and the larger community, offers the possibility of confronting some of the painful issues such that people on all sides can hear each other and perhaps begin to relinquish the idea of taking sides. Human history is filled with examples of individuals who have faced conflict between groups—whether it is the story of Romeo and Juliet from conflicting families, the White and Black abolitionists in the United States who joined forces and risked their lives to assist African Americans fleeing slavery, the people of Europe who hid Jews or helped them to escape during Hitler's reign, or teachers who reach out to students

[24]Twelve students and a teacher were killed and 23 others were wounded before their teenage assailants took their own lives at Columbine High School in Littleton, Colorado on April 20, 1999. The shootings not only aroused concerns about school safety, gun control, and violence, but also caused educators and policymakers to focus on issues of the bullying, intolerance, and alienation that is often a significant part of school culture. See: http://www.rethinkingschools.org/archive/13_04/edit.shtml

different from themselves—and have learned about these people's lives, struggles, and dreams, thereby leaving behind their own prior ideas.

The shade of the ginkgo tree is cool even on a hot day—or at least cooler than the surrounding areas in the sun. Historically the tree has been a source of comfort for those who share its shade because whether they were a group of male scholars or a group of women doing "women's work," they were alike enough that they shared basic assumptions. Now the tree shades people from all walks of life. Like Confucius and Socrates, the teacher asks wise questions to help scholars from around the world and all life conditions work from the stance of the humble seeking of knowledge. It is never easy, and all teachers struggle with individual situations that are new and even heartbreaking. But the establishment of relationships across the cultural boundaries is the best we can do to help people express themselves successfully, listen to each other with respect, and ultimately make choices about how to engage with the polyglot, multicultural world we inhabit.

3

Taste of the Ginkgo Nut: Problem Posing

With the exception of a few saplings that came directly from Japan, it appears that most of the oldest Ginkgos growing in North America were imported from England as seedlings, which most likely had been raised from imported Japanese seed. By the late 1800s and early 1900s, after the original American introductions started producing seed in abundance, Ginkgo became popular as a street tree on the east coast, primarily in urban areas from Boston to Washington, D.C. ... The horticulturist's love affair with the Ginkgo began to fade in the 1920s and 1930s when many of the widely planted seedling street trees began reaching sexual maturity. At this point, ovulate trees started producing large quantities of seeds, which, when crushed by passing foot traffic, resulted in a foul-smelling mess, reminiscent of the odor of vomit. In the horticultural literature, this scent is variously referred to as "disagreeable," "evil," "offensive," "disgusting," "repulsive," "nauseating," and "abominable."

—Del Tredici, 1991, p. 6

The fruit of the ginkgo tree is "smelly" and its nut is an "acquired" taste. It is used in the Buddhist "Tsai" 齋 or vegetarian Chinese New Year's dish. For a member of the Chinese community, the smell and the taste of the ginkgo nut may symbolize good fortune and the new year, and evoke warm memories of loved ones, "comfort food," grandma's home cooking. Other ingredients for this dish include "faat tsai" 髮菜/發菜, a black hairy-looking moss, whose name is a homonym for "prosperity"; "won yee" 雲耳, cloud ears, a black fungus; mung bean thread (also used prominently in Korean, Thai, and other Asian cuisines); dried pressed bean curd; and the *very* strong-smelling preserved bean curd. To someone outside the community, who has never tasted "Tsai," whose first association with "fungus" is athlete's foot, and whose first encounter with the ginkgo fruit was to step on it, creating "a foul-smelling mess, reminiscent of the odor of vomit"—the smells and tastes of this dish may seem unappetizing or even repugnant.

Teaching a foreign or second language can be as strange and exotic as introducing a foreign smell or taste. The sounds and tones, the placement of the tongue, the ways of expressing oneself in a foreign language can be to a beginning language learner very uncomfortable, as unappetizing or repugnant as the smell of the ginkgo fruit. Important questions for TESOL professionals include: How do we enable the foreign language and culture, the foreign smells and tastes to become familiar? How do we expose our students to multiple experiences, perspectives and discourses? How do we develop in our students the appreciation for different ways with words, different metaphors, different literatures, registers and genres? How do we enable our students to be full participants in more than one speech community and to walk in multiple worlds (Valdés, 2004)?

BRANCH 3-1: FREIRE AND PROBLEM POSING

Freire called for a "problem-posing" concept of education as an instrument for liberation:

> Problem-posing education, responding to the essence of consciousness—*intentionality*—rejects communiques and embodies communication. It epitomizes the special characteristic of consciousness: being *conscious of* not only as intent on objects but as turned in upon itself in a Jasperian "split"—consciousness as consciousness *of* consciousness. (Freire, 1970, pp. 66–67)

A communiqué is an official bulletin that announces something and is given to the press or the public. It is a one-way transmission of meaning by an authority. In contrast, "communication" implies a two-way dialogue (notice the "di-" prefix, which also implies "two") and does not invoke authority within that transmission of meaning. When teachers use communication instead of communiqués, they help students take charge of their own learning. When students do this, they are likely to be motivated to succeed.

Karl Jaspers (1883–1969) of the "Jasperian 'split'" was a German psychologist who pointed out that people are nonrational. What is significant is not simply knowledge but also the emotional "take" people have on those facts. Teaching is not simply a delivery of a set of facts to a group of people, but it entails engaging with how students will relate to those facts as whole, emotional people. For example, American students studying Middle Eastern politics or religion after September 11, 2001, may have a different emotional take on those subjects because of the events on that day. For some, the events of that day may motivate them to understand more about what happened and why. Others may be so traumatized that they will push away greater understanding because they do not have the ability to deal with it. If we view teaching as choosing facts to transmit, then we miss the affective aspects of teaching and we may fail to teach more often than we would like. As teachers, we must be conscious of our students' consciousness.

With the problem-posing method of education, student and teacher roles are transformed through a process of dialogue. All are responsible and education becomes a mutual process, which is world mediated:

> Education is thus constantly remade in the praxis. In order to *be*, it must *become*. Its "duration" (in the Bergsonian meaning of the word) is found in the interplay of the opposites *permanence* and *change* ... problem-posing education—which accepts neither a "well-behaved" present nor a predetermined future—roots itself in the dynamic present and becomes revolutionary. (Freire, 1970, p. 72)

Henri Bergson was a French philosopher who considered two opposing inclinations: life, which is ever-changing, and matter, which is static, what Freire refers to as "permanence" and "change." Bergson pointed out that our perception of time is not by the clock but rather by what he called "durée," duration. When we dread something, time seems to pass slowly; when we are absorbed in something, we do not sense the passage of time.

As teachers we can be seduced by the promises of the permanent. If I use the same syllabus as last year or the same text, then I can predict what will happen. At the same time, I might not reach all students with this. In fact, I might only reach the docile students, the ones who are already privileged within the system. If I can use a problem-posing approach, in which I as a teacher do not know the answers but am willing to work with my students to find them out, then I am working within a "dynamic present." I may not be able to predict the future—what and how students will learn, but they will be learning. I may experience the time of my teaching not as a series of minutes to be counted but as an excitement of the moment of discovery, which erases that clock sense of time. When I teach like this, I am working with change rather than static things and this teaching becomes revolutionary; it supports the kinds of change that end oppression.

This chapter presents problem posing, the second feature of dialogic approaches to TESOL, which is contrasted to what Freire calls "banking education." The metaphor of developing a taste for the ginkgo nut is related to dialogic approaches to second-language learning through the work of Vygotsky. Acquiring a taste—a sense of the aesthetic—for anything from food to music to literature can be understood through Vygotsky's theories. His concepts of tool, symbol, and mediation provide a theoretical framework for a problem posing approach to learning. Examples in this chapter focus on student teachers working with secondary students from a variety of educational backgrounds, including those who, due to war and economic hardship, have had little or no previous schooling.

WHAT IS PROBLEM POSING?

Learning another language, like learning any complex skill—such as installing an air conditioning unit, playing the violin, caring for animals, doing T'ai Chi Chuan, or making pottery—can be daunting. Whether the aim of instruction is to learn English for academic, professional, or vocational purposes, the task can be overwhelming for teacher and student alike because there is so much to learn. The tendency for the ESOL teacher, then, may be to cram as much into the curriculum as possible. For example, when I was teaching the Pilgrimage Curriculum (see Appendix), the more I learned about what would be required of students in graduate school seminary programs, the more there seemed to be to learn: how to use a word processor, write academic papers, listen to lectures, use a research library, speak at conferences, and "do theology" in English.[1]

Because of the sheer volume of material to be learned, it is easy to slip into a transmission model of teaching, in which the teacher "transmits" knowledge to students. Although this might seem to be an efficient way to teach, it is not, because it fails to engage with the students' purposes for learning. First-language acquisition revolves around a young child's desire to communicate; it is not undertaken systematically and yet in a matter of 3 years, with no previous language learning experience, children master grammatical and cultural aspects of language and develop a large vocabulary. Obviously, second-language learning in a classroom is different from first-language learning under the tutelage of one's family. Yet when people's needs to communicate are engaged, they learn quickly. Likewise, students who are bored or disengaged fail to learn, no matter how efficiently a curriculum is "delivered" by a teacher.

[1]In the course we audited at Union Theological Seminary, Prof. Christopher Morse assigned an "Utrum" paper in which students were required to write their understanding of a theological problem in the format of a medieval proof, alternating arguments for and against. The more I found out about English for theological purposes, the longer was my list of teaching points.

When a curriculum is preestablished as a set of materials to be learned, this requires students to use a single learning modality, memorization. Memorization is an effective learning strategy, but it is not the only learning strategy and it is not the most successful way of reaching students who have had little experience with school or who are disenfranchised from the educational system in some other way.

Another way of learning is through solving problems. Learning based on problem solving is vivid—it becomes embedded in the mind through the emotional experience of success. To learn a new mathematical concept such as multiplication, for example, one can memorize a procedure or one can have the experience of using manipulatives (small items that can be counted) to figure out what multiplying does. When children simply memorize a procedure, they often do not understand what they are doing and they are not likely to be able to apply that process outside of a narrow range of problems. They might "know" the process but they cannot apply it to a novel situation.

In contrast, when children are presented with manipulatives and a series of problems that involve grouping, they can, over time, figure out an abstract way to represent their actions. When they have figured out the process, they remember it and they can apply it to new situations because they understand what they are doing. Memorization has its place in learning math—once children understand the concept of multiplication, they need to learn their "times tables." But it is much easier to memorize when one understands the utility of what is being learned.

On the surface, problem posing appears to take more time than the transmission model of teaching. Yet because problem posing engages the students in powerful learning and it provides a context for memorization, it is a more effective way to teach. Therefore, a problem-posing approach to TESOL emphasizes the process of learning *as much as* (not more than) material or "canon" to be mastered. Students must play an active role in their education, and they will if they are a part of a community of learners involved in dialogue, questioning, debate, and analysis. As we saw from the dialogues of Confucius and Socrates, that there is not always a "correct" answer to questions. Instead, the quest for knowledge unfolds through open-ended dialogue. There are many ways to present satisfactory solutions to the problem, and the dialogue unfolds as an expression of human freedom situated within specific, material and historical circumstances (Greene, 1988).

Problem posing has roots in meaning making. First, language learning involves complex meaning making. There is nothing simple about language learning. Previous chapters have explored some of the political stakes. It is also important to be aware of the aesthetic dimensions of language learning: To learn a language is to learn a culture, including learning what counts as taste. Vygotsky's theories of art form the basic understandings we must have in order to bring the richness and complexity of language learning to the fore in our classrooms, in order to pose problems worthy of solution.

BRANCH 3-2: PROBLEM POSING AND HIGH-STAKES TESTING

What does a teacher do when high-stakes testing is central to the ESL program? Teaching to the test is another form of transmission teaching—a worse form because the curriculum does not even derive from the teacher (who could best understand students' needs by drawing from the perspectives of the students themselves) but rather from outside the classroom or even school or community. At the same time, as mentioned in chapter 2, one way to be an emancipatory teacher, to help our students gain more educational and career opportunities, is to help them succeed on tests, particularly when we have students from populations that have not traditionally succeeded in education (Valdez-Pierce, 2003).

There are three strategies to use when tests are central to the system and the teacher cannot change that fact. First, it is important for the teacher to become aware of what is on the test. Over the course of teaching in a dialogic way, test skills and materials will arise spontaneously in conversation and in students' work. The teacher can "cover" these points as they arise—pointing out that a particular concept or type of vocabulary will be on the test, keeping track of which points have been discussed, and looking for opportunities to present the remaining points. Students may not receive a review of concepts in the order in which they might be presented on the test; however, if students are actively using their new language to read, write, speak, and listen, then surely that which is being tested is present. It is a matter of identifying the test skills and helping students to understand that they are developing these skills.

Second, instead of teaching *to* the test, we need to teach *beyond* the test. We need to help students gain sense of ownership over the language they are undertaking to learn such that the test material is easy. For example, if students, through their process of problem posing and solving in English, come to use grammatically complex sentences with a wide range of vocabulary, test review becomes a matter of pointing out to them what they can already do and then helping them to learn the test jargon for what they already know. Because the learning goal is well beyond the test material, the test material is less of a stretch for students—the same way that athletes practice tasks that are beyond those which they will complete in a competition. Baseball players warm up with two bats so that a single bat will feel light when they are swinging to hit the ball. Because dialogic pedagogy embraces complex interactions, the language that students use is likely to become more complex early on. The teacher's job, near test time, is to help students remember the concepts they have learned and show students (and possibly their parents) how those concepts are related to the test.

Finally, it might be appropriate in some classrooms to pose the test itself as a problem (Shohamy, 2001a). Students can learn about the history of the test and statistics associated with it. Who tends to pass and who fails? What characteristics of the test contribute to the pass/fail rate? What are the consequences of passing or failing? What does the test purport to measure? How does it do so? Is that a reasonable procedure? What is the utility of the test in the larger social context? As students read the test critically, they may become engaged in developing strategies for succeeding on it—and this motivation might help them to undertake any memorization that might be necessary. In the case of testing in which large numbers of students are likely to fail, a critical look at the test may help students keep a sense of their own value regardless of their score.

Second, the metaphor for language learning needs to be reexamined in relation to problem posing. Acquisition leads us as teachers to focus on input and transmission. Participation, as we show later, allows us to recognize the reality of idiosyncratic forms of progress. The fruits of these understandings can then be seen in the problem-posing classrooms of student teachers (discussed later) and in other settings (in branches).

THE TASTE OF THE GINKGO NUT: WHAT DOES IT MEAN TO ACQUIRE TASTE?

In my family we value cuisine above many other semiotic systems. We pride ourselves on our cooking and we live to eat. I remember watching my American-born grandmother, Yen Yen 仁仁, cook her prized duck feet dish. She would say with a sense of insider superiority, "Chinese people really know how to eat" [tong4jan4sin1sik1sik6 唐人先識食]. Her generation of Cantonese people in America (common, working people, both China- and American-born like she was) called themselves "people of the Tang Dynasty" 唐人 tong4jan4, a period from 618 to 907 A.D. in which Chinese culture flourished.[2] My grandmother's choice of the verb *to know*

[2]In the novel *Accordian Crimes* by Annie Proulx, European immigrants within the United States referred to themselves not by village or family by country—became "Italian." Similarly, the dominant Chinese districts in the early years were from the four villages from the southern province of Kwangtung: Toishan 台山, Hoiping 開平, Sunwui 新會, Yanping 恩平—but in the United States became the "four villages" sei yahp 四邑, and the others who spoke a city dialect closer to Cantonese became identified as "three villages" sam yahp 三邑. To Americans they became "Chinese," a larger national grouping.

"sik" (from zi3 sik 1 知識) or knowledge in "Chinese people really *know* how to eat" reflected a stance of insider or local knowledge (Geertz, 1983). Our theories of knowledge, or our epistemologies are situated with respect to our histories and identities.

For my grandmother's generation, appreciation for good food was part of being Chinese. Chinese cooking is a highly developed semiotic system—an art form—a craft to which one apprentices oneself for years. It involves texture, timing, ingredients, presentation, and a whole system of balance—"hot" [jit6 熱] versus "cold" [laang5 冷], "dry" [gon1 乾] versus "wet" [sap1 濕]—a philosophy of health in which the human body and what is eaten relate harmoniously to balance of the elements in the universe.

Developing a palate is cultural. Tastes are acquired. We are not born with a taste for the ginkgo nut—just as we are not born with a taste for macaroni and cheese, candied yams, pigs' feet, Vegemite, chorizo, hot dogs, pizza, snails, frog legs, squid, fu fu, curried goat meat or black bean sauce. And yet one can acquire a taste for "sushi" or "escargot" or "pigs' feet" or "grunge music" or "Cantonese opera" or "Bach" or "Bartok" or "bluegrass" or "cake walk." One can acquire an appreciation for Shakespeare or Dostoevsky or Tang Dynasty poetry. It is possible to broaden one's tastes, to expand one's sense of the aesthetic, to have a more intercultural and international perspective.

As discussed in chapter 1, Halliday and Hasan defined language as a semiotic system. Cuisine, music, and painting are like language because they are also semiotic or meaningful systems. How we acquire tastes or how we develop the aesthetic dimension (for cuisine, music, painting or other art we appreciate) is a semiotic problem. The acquisition of taste comes about from being aware of the history and possibilities within the system. For example, at first, individual pieces of an unfamiliar form of music may seem indistinguishable. Only after one has heard a range of pieces—becoming aware of its history and how the music works (what harmonies, rhythms, timbres are "allowed" within the system)—can one distinguish between pieces and come to appreciate quality.

Appreciation for cuisine, music, or painting is like language—a cultural, historical, and *social* problem. Cuisine, like other semiotic systems, is a human product and a human process. It is a system of meaning involving our senses (our biological inheritance) and the material world. Through human labor or human activity there is the creation of both an aesthetic and cultural dimension of food preparation.[3]

---

[3]As cuisine and talk about food is local, the romanizaiton for the Chinese characters in the above section is not pinyin but Cantonese. Yen Yen [仁 仁] is Toishan (Taishan) dialect for grandmother [奶奶]. The Linguistic Society of Hong Kong Cantonese Romantization Scheme, or known as *Jyutping*, was designed and proposed by the Linguistic Society of Hong Kong in 1993. See the Hong Kong Linguistics Society at http://cpct92.cityu.edu.hk/lshk/

LEV VYGOTSKY ON ART AND LITERATURE

Vygotsky was an avid reader and was literate in eight languages: Russian, German, English, Hebrew, French, Latin, Greek, and Esperanto (Berk & Winsler, 1995). He translated into Russian and wrote introductions to major works from Europe such as Freud and Piaget. He brought to his study of aesthetics, knowledge from diverse fields including medicine, law, philosophy, literature, theater, psychology, and education.

The problem of the aesthetic was one of Vygotsky's first intellectual concerns (Wertsch, 1985). Rather than seeing psychology as a combination of stimulus and response, the way many of his contemporaries did, Vygotsky was concerned with higher order mental or thinking processes, such as voluntary attention and memory. His doctoral dissertation explored the aesthetic dimension of Shakespeare's play *Hamlet*. Vygotsky was interested in accounting for the development of consciousness, aesthetic appreciation, and creation of culture, including language and literature.

One of Vygotsky's lifelong preoccupations was to deal with the paradox of the aesthetic dimension being both social and individual, both inherited and unique. Taste is also individual and unique. No one person's tastes are identical to another's, yet our tastes are not our own—they are influenced by our family, culture, and history. Stamped with our class and educational background, our aesthetic sense is deeply ideological.[4]

Tools, Symbols, and Mediation

What makes humans different from other animals? At the heart of the answer is language and culture. Marxists answer that tools are what make humans different from other animals because humans are able to not only live within the environment, but to transform their own habitat. For Vygotsky, tools and symbols are what separate humans from other animals. Animals, including humans, have senses, and emotions, but humans alone have language, consciousness and a sense of *beauty*.

One of the major influences on Vygotsky was Karl Marx, who discussed the tools and labor in setting humans apart from other animals in his essay "Alienated Labor":

> The practical creation of an objective world, the working-over of inorganic nature, is the confirmation of humankind as a conscious species—being, that is, as a being that relates to the species as to her/himself and to her/himself as to the species. It is true that the animal, too, produces. It builds itself a

[4]Mao's article "Yenan Forum on Art and Literature" in *Selected Works of Moa Tse-tung* poses the challenge to artists and intellectual workers that their art take a stand with the oppressed, that it be used in the service of liberation. This article is related to the fourth feature of dialogic pedagogy that we discuss in chapter 5, which poses the question, "Knowledge for whom?" or who does knowledge serve?

> nest, a dwelling like the bee, the beaver, the ant, etc. But it only produces what it needs immediately for itself or its offspring: it produces one-sidedly whereas humankind produces universally; it produces only under the pressure of immediate physical need, whereas humans produce freely from physical need and only truly produce when they are thus free; it produces only itself whereas humans reproduce the whole of nature. Its product belongs immediately to its physical body whereas humans can freely separate themselves from their products. The animal only fashions things according to the standards and needs of the species it belongs to, whereas humankind knows how to produce according to measure of every species and knows everywhere how to apply its inherent standard to the object: thus humankind also fashions things according to the laws of beauty. (Marx, in McLellan, 1977, p. 82)

The human taste for beauty, the aesthetic, is not peripheral to human production; it is central—or it would be in a world in which production was not alienated from the producer. This understanding is the basis for the entire Marxist project: how to overcome alienation and exploitation, which prevents people from being able to "reproduce the whole of nature" and to "[fashion] things according to the laws of beauty." In Marx's ideal society, where labor is not alienated, men and women can engage in fishing in the morning, hunting in the afternoon, and being artisans at night.

Like Marx, Vygotsky recognized the centrality of tools and human activity with respect to creativity and aesthetics. In Marx's example of architecture, creating the human habitat is different from the honeycomb or ant farm. Human labor led not only to the production of material goods to satisfy human need, but the creation of things of beauty. Vygotsky elaborated on Marx and Engels's concept of tool by delineating between physical or material tools and sign or symbolic tools, including language (John-Steiner & Souberman, 1978). Of particular importance for Vygotsky is the role of language as a symbolic tool in the development of consciousness and higher order thinking:

> Vygotsky brilliantly extended this concept of mediation in human—environment interaction to the use of signs as well as tools. Like tool systems, sign systems (language, writing, number systems) are created by societies over the course of human histories and change with the form of society and the level of its cultural development. Vygotsky believed that the internalization of culturally produced sign systems brings about behavioral transformations and forms the bridge between early and later forms of individual development. (Cole & Scribner, 1978, p. 7)

Vygotsky observed that the development of thinking occurred largely through the mediation of language. Children develop human reason and other complex mental operations such as memory through social interaction; they are not born with it. They develop these abilities through a process of dialogic interaction with the significant people in their lives who care for them—their parents, other family members, caregivers, teachers, and other children. Adult speech regulates a child's behavior and enables him or her to solve problems, and ultimately to become independent and self-regulating.

Developing a sense of the aesthetic or what constitutes "good taste" (in cuisine, a "palate") reflects cultural knowledge, which, in Vygotskian psychological theory, like all higher mental functions, is *social* before it is *individual*:

> Every function in a child's cultural development appears twice, first on the social level and later, on the individual level; first *between* people (*interpsychological)* and then, *inside* the child (*intrapsychological*). This applies equally to voluntary attention, to logical memory, and to the formation of concepts. All the higher functions originate as actual relations between human individuals. (Vygotsky, 1978, p. 115)

Like other forms of cultural development, acquiring a sense of appreciation for any aspect of culture, including the taste for the ginkgo nut, is a complex matter.

The development from social/external to individual/internal is not mechanistic:

> Although Vygotsky regarded mental functions as internalized social processes, he was careful to note that they were not the result of children simply mimicking features of social interaction. His vision is very different from traditional behaviorist and social learning views which regard development as a consequence of modeling and reinforcement and as directly shaped by or copied from external sources. Instead Vygotsky regarded children as active agents in development, contributing to the creation of internal mental processes by collaborating with others in meaningful cultural activities. (Berk & Winsler, 1995, p. 23)

Problem posing emphasizes the fact that we can't "cram" language, concepts, facts, or impose a sense of the aesthetic. Instead, through problem posing, and learning in community, students learn the new language through dialogue and meaningful activity.

For Vygotsky, mediation was vital to the development of language and thought: "An activity that is generative of higher mental processes is a socially meaningful mediated activity. The source of mediation is either in a material tool, in a system of symbols, or in the behavior of another human being" (Kozulin, 1990, p. 114). Tools and mediation help a child in a task. For example, in Reading Recovery, an early literacy program for first graders, children are encouraged to use a finger to point to the words as they read a text. As children develop more familiarity with the text and fluency in reading, they are told to use "only their eyes" (Clay & Cazden, 1990).

Tools, Symbols, Aesthetics, and Second-Language Learning

All along in this book, it has become clear that learning a language is much more than memorization of vocabulary and grammatical structures. The context of language learning is influenced by social and political structures, including the relative position of the first language to a language of world conquest, such as English (Pennycook, 1994b).

We can contrast the power of English with the language of former colonized countries. "Intellectualization" of Filipino, or developing the resources of the language in the Philippines for scholarly discourse (as the medium of instruction in secondary and tertiary education) cannot be taken for granted:

> The aspiration for Filipino is that it will be intellectualized to the extent that scholars can use it to discuss their field of study, be this in the humanities, social sciences, national sciences, technology, or business; in short, that Filipino can be used the way English has been used for many years in the Philippines, as a code for academic discussion, research, and publications. (Bautista, 1994, p. 115)

Further, language consists not simply of structures but is itself affected by social contexts, including a concept of the aesthetic. To learn a new language is to engage with a foreign sense of beauty; part of meaning making, including comprehension within a second language, involves understanding the aesthetics embedded within that language. Finally, language learning, whether the mother tongue one learns first or a subsequent language learned at a later time, can be best accomplished with symbolic and material tools that help new speakers succeed at the tasks they have set for themselves. Tools assist students in solving the problems they encounter in the process of learning a language.

BRANCH 3-3: LEARNING FROM READING RECOVERY IN ELEMENTARY ESOL CLASSROOMS

A problem-posing approach to literacy focuses on the process as well as the product. Problem posing asks students to reflect on their own learning, including the metacognitive question, "What makes a good language learner?" ESOL and bilingual students of all ages can benefit from strategy instruction in learning how to read. Here's an example from elementary schools in a National Reading Research Center—University of Maryland—Arlington Virginia School District Project research project (1992—1997).

There were three goals in the project, which used Reading Recovery principles (Wong, Groth, & O'Flahavan, 1994) to teach reading to ESOL elementary school students:

1. To get the students to read progressively difficult books at the pre-primer level at school, at home and at school again. Fluency and confidence came through getting the students to read repeatedly and extensively.
2. To develop independent reading strategies so that they could figure out new words themselves.
3. To have students learn how to work together in groups.

A problem-posing approach involves organizing the class so that the teacher can lead small groups instead of working with a large class all the time. This includes getting students used to a variety of grouping strategies. Elementary ESOL and classroom teachers organized centers so that students could engage in various activities in different parts of the room. They had students work in groups and pairs to enable the teacher to work with individuals or a group of two to five students for 15 to 20 minutes.

During small group time, the teacher developed two charts with the students. One was titled "What Good Readers Do" to summarize strategies that students used to try to figure out a word they didn't know. These also included "clues" that one student would give to another. The students were allowed to help the reader—only after the reader asked for help—not saying the word, but by giving a clue. Here are some strategies that teachers wrote on the charts through discussion with the students:

Look at the picture.
Start over again.
Skip the word and then come back.
Look at the first letter.

Strategies were added to the charts each time a group met, and each group had its own chart. This process helped students use multiple cues: meaning cues, (what "makes sense"), syntactic clues (what "sounds right"—drawing on students' grammatical competency)[5] and phonemic clues ("what does it *look* like"—visual clues).

---

[5]This strategy for beginning second-language learners will not be as useful as it is for native speakers, because beginning learners do not yet have competency in the L2 to be able to judge what "sounds right."

Each group also developed a chart based on "How to Work Together in a Group." Here are some examples that first and second grade students came up with:

Give the reader time to think.
Don't take someone's turn.

A problem-posing approach involves assessing individual progress as well as developing clear directions, routines, and schedules for classroom management so that students can work independently individually, in pairs, and in small groups. Effective development of cooperative learning and strategies for group work takes time. If you have never worked with groups before, don't be discouraged if your first attempt is chaotic. Read up on group work and cooperative learning techniques (McGroarty & Holt, 1993). Observe other teachers (including videos). Start small. As the Zambian proverb says, "Start where you are, but don't stay there."

CLASSROOM DISCOURSE AND THE METAPHOR OF PARTICIPATION

A number of second language researchers are moving away from the metaphor of "acquisition" to the metaphor of "participation" (Lantolf & Pavlenko, 2000). The problem with "acquisition" is that it is atomistic and regards language learning in terms of lexical items or linguistic structures, rather than discourse in use. Chomsky's cognitive model of acquisition posited a biological endowment that enabled humans to acquire language the way that birds can fly. He called this innate capacity for language the mysterious "black box" or language acquisition device (LAD). Krashen's concept, i + 1, developed the acquisition metaphor for second-language acquisition. The + 1 refers to the structure of acquisition to be acquired next, assuming that all second-language learners progress in roughly the same sequence of acquisition. It tended to assume that you have either "acquired" a structure (i.e., "s" for a plural marker in English) or not.

The Vygotskian perspective views learning as a dynamic zig-zagging process:

> As cognitive tools are used, the people who use them change. Also, significantly, the tools themselves transform and are adapted to meet new requirements of new and unpredictable activities. (Kinginger, 2001, p. 421)

Students progress, but they can forget or go backward. Some elements of language learning develop rapidly, others at a slower rate. Performance in a task is determined by the social and historical context of the speech (or writing) situation. This includes the political power between the participants (including class, race, gender, ethnicity, and other dimensions of stigmatized group relations). Participation rather than acquisition as a metaphor highlights power relations, enabling the contradiction to be resolved through a dynamic group process. Learning is achieved through collaborative problem solving.

"Vygotsky's major insight regarding the ZPD [zone of proximal development] was that instruction and learning do not ride on the tail of development, but instead blaze the trail for development to follow" (Dunn & Lantolf, 1998, p. 419). This is important for us as teachers because the responsibility for the ways in which we organize our classrooms can be decisive in learning. If we are working with nonmainstream students, what Lisa Delpit (1988) called "Other People's Children," Vygotskian sociocultural concepts enable us to develop a dialogic I–thou (Buber) relationship rather than a deficit, deficient orientation. This is critical in TESOL/BE (Bilingual Education) when many of our students have had interrupted schooling, have been in refugee camps, have been the victims of war and violence, or have personally witnessed the injury or death of family members, neighbors, and friends due to war. Vygotsky and his colleagues were engaged in extending education to those who had been historically excluded—retarded and disabled children, rural peasants, ethnic minorities, and indigenous tribe people. Their work has direct relevance in educating nontraditional students in TESOL today.

A key theoretical point is the notion of "ripening." This means being able to recognize the "teachable moment," when a student is ready for an epiphany. The teacher (or a peer) can bring the student to new understandings at these moments through providing social support. For a teacher, that means the difficult work of assessing the relevance of particular "errors" or "mistakes" in problem solving. For example, in ESL for math, if a student makes a mistake in a mathematical problem, what is the source of difficulty? Is it a math fact (i.e., $8 \times 7 = 56$), or is it a mathematical concept? Or is it a second-language issue? Sometimes for ESOL students, the problem is that procedures for "showing" work (or notation) vary from one educational system to another (Wong & Teuben-Rowe, 1997).

A student's participation may be to present a partial solution for a problem. The teacher can use a variety of assessment techniques as well as questioning techniques to help students work within their "zone of proximal development," and thus to change the nature and quality of their participation within the classroom. Mistakes and partial solutions, then, do not represent failure as much as they represent opportunities for learning. Teachers can recognize these opportunities and help students gain new understandings through the process of discussing problems and their solutions.

COLLABORATIVE RESEARCH WITH STUDENT TEACHERS: TOOL AND MEDIATION IN CLASSROOM INTERACTION

Shelley Wong and Suhanthie Motha with Dana Frye, Will Roberts, and Charles Wang

This section focuses on problem posing using Vygotsky's concepts of tools, symbols and mediation in teacher education, by providing some examples from a collaborative research project at the University of Maryland. The project occurred during the final semester of a master's of education (MEd) TESOL program with certification for kindergarten through Grade 12 (K–12). Dana Frye, Will Roberts, and Charles Wang were full-time student teachers for 8 weeks in an elementary school setting and then 8 weeks in a secondary school setting. Suhanthie (Su) Motha, a doctoral student in TESOL, was their supervisor, and I was the professor of the course. We used a sociocultural theoretical perspective to analyze how Dana, Will, and Charlie developed a repertoire of curricular and instructional strategies to address equity in classroom interaction.

BRANCH 3-4: HOW DIALOGIC INQUIRY SUPPORTS AGENCY IN NOVICE TEACHERS

> "You lose opportunities if you aren't willing to go off track to take advantage of the structuring in possible open time—-a conceptual space that you are trying to create. That's what I've seen time and time again: giving the answer if there isn't an answer. [We should] let them think about it! Students will start to think about it.... If you fill the silence, then you aren't giving people a chance to think." (Dana Frye)

A theory of teacher education must expand the subjective factor or consciousness of the teacher to support agency. You can't become a reflective practitioner (Valli, 1992, 1998) without practice or without reading theory such as Vygotsky and TESOL methodology. There must be an experiential component that involves actual teaching or support of teaching, such as being an aide, a volunteer, or participant observer. Consciousness emerges through a dialectical and recursive process of teaching, identifying problems for analysis, studying theory and research, narrowing the divide between theoretical knowledge and practical knowledge, summing up and evaluating and analyzing ways to rethink and adjust, and revision. Reflection involves shifting through and interpreting and reinterpreting how we "read" or understand the voices and discourses of our students and ourselves.

Teacher educators should remember that development in a domain, whether mathematics or second-language teaching, is initially regulated externally and socially. Kathryn Au (1990) pointed out that speech makes a person's thoughts accessible to the processes of social influence (I would add "and vice versa"). Di Bello and Orlich (1987) suggested that the act of speaking makes one's understanding explicit. Individuals may have a sketchy comprehension of an idea but be unaware of exactly what they know or don't know. Studying Vygotskian theory and critical discourse analysis, keeping journals, engaging in seminars, and carrying out observations allow preservice teachers to remain focused on "blazing a trail of development."

As a graduate student in psycholinguistics class, Charlie made a presentation on Vygotsky. His handout, examples, and lecture were so outstanding that all his classmates clapped for him. I remember later asking him about the sociocultural theories and his hesitation in assigning Vygotskian terminology to his own teaching. He was pleased to hear from Su and me that we recognized the application of Vygotskian theories in his classroom practice, and that we saw him skillfully mediate student problem solving based on his knowledge of their skill level (math facts vs. concepts). In describing their conceptual frameworks, the student teachers developed metaphors. Charlie described working within a student's zone of proximal development as "bumping heads":

> A lot of it's new, and we need to scaffold. You know, they need to bump their heads ... well, with word problems, the goal is how the students discriminate, what they need to read and what they don't. I'm there to help them along and explain to them if they don't understand this word or what the important word is. It's more or less up to them to figure out.

Student teachers do not need years of teaching experience to theorize about their own practice. Sociocultural theory helps us to appreciate that the ontogenesis or development of teachers, just as their ESOL students, does not occur in a vacuum; it is a dialogical process of engaging in situated, social practice and reflection. Vygotsky argued that psychological theories didn't develop exclusively through controlled experiments or introspection. The same is true in developing a theory of language education. We develop theories about teaching and learning languages through doing and through being part of a community, engaged in meaningful problems that emerge from our own teaching.

Teaching is social activity, but it can also be isolating—especially if there is only one adult in the classroom. We must offer student teachers and beginning teachers opportunities to engage in meaningful discussion about their pedagogy, to gain feedback and support on their teaching, and to receive additional suggestions for analyzing the problems on which they are working (Motha, 2003). Gallimore and Tharpe (1990) drew attention to the importance of institutional contexts for assisted performance for teachers and administrators as well as students. Schools must be structured so that teachers can share insights and draw on each other's support and expertise. Gallimore and Tharpe point out the importance of principals going into classes, teaching, modeling good practices of leadership, and working with students' suggestions to transform schools. Becoming a good teacher is a lifelong endeavor, rather than something that can be "achieved" in one or even five years. Experienced teachers can help to identify critical problems in their own teaching—the big problems—for example, how to develop assessment that will support instruction, how to organize one's classroom for maximum interaction and independent work for students in a variety of grouping strategies, which can help novice teachers, but you will notice that the best teachers continue to work on the same problems all of their lives.

Su and I used a variant of Fanselow's (1987) technique "Focus" to observe the three student teachers. As we observed each student teacher in her/his secondary school placement, Su and I tallied the number of utterances addressed to and from each student in a class we observed. We then met with the three student teachers in a biweekly seminar to examine the counts, revise their accuracy, and discuss the changes student teachers planned in order to transform the patterns of classroom interaction. (For example, "Encourage more participation from student A.") The student teachers experimented with strategies to facilitate student participation, recorded their reflections in journals, and collaboratively analyzed the evolution of their strategies in the seminars. In the final week of student teaching, Su and I returned to the classrooms and again recorded the counts of student–teacher interaction, then met with each of the student teachers to present them with the final counts and discuss the changes that had taken place.

Mediation Through Material Tools

The student teachers used physical tools as well as sign systems or speech as a "tool of the mind" to facilitate second language learning. Charlie Wang used tools to teach the concept of "standard unit of measurement" for an ESL math class for middle school students. There were only five students in the class—they were part of a special program for students who had had interrupted or no previous schooling. Physical tools figured prominently in Charlie's lesson:

> "Everyone take some of these paper clips and lay them side by side across your desk in a line. How many paper clips are there? What if we measure the desk with these rulers? Are the rulers bigger or smaller than paper clips? So will there be more rulers? What if we use our hands?"

Using the language of discovery (Bruner, 1985), leading the students through the lesson using demonstrations, problem solving, and dialogic questioning, Charlie introduced the concept of standard measurement. He wanted the students to discover for themselves the utility of having a common standard unit of measurement as opposed to the imprecision of measuring "with one's feet." He also wanted to teach estimation. He asked the students to use their feet, their hands, paper clips, and rulers to measure their desks, the floor, and lines drawn on the chalkboard and paper.

Charlie asked various students to measure the length of the classroom with their feet. First he asked one of the boys, Nestor,[6] to measure the classroom, and wrote the number of Nestor's feet on the board. Then he asked Ms. Fuentes, the cooperating teacher, to measure the room with her feet. Charlie observed, "Ms. Fuentes has little feet. Do you think that she will need more or fewer feet than Nestor?" One of the students (perhaps associating "small" with "fewer") answered "fewer." Charlie responded, "Let's see." Charlie posed a constant stream of questions to the students so that they would themselves be able to actively participate in solving the problems, moving from what Vygotsky called "everyday concepts" to "scientific concepts." As Gallimore and Tharp explained:

> All concepts develop through language use accompanying joint activity. Everyday concepts are closely tied to the specific objects and conditions that their names represent. The word for an object is a part of the object, an attribute of the object as integral as its color, smell, or size. Words in the everyday realm, cannot be detached and manipulated in the young child's mind separately from the image of the phenomenon represented.
>
> In schooled concepts, words are wrested from their designata and manipulated in the mind independently of their images. Many of these new schooled words are themselves imageless and serve to link and manipulate other words. The student's attention shifts from sign–object relationships to sign–sign relationships (Wertsch, 1985). A system of words develops, with units of decontextualized words, rules of use, rules of transformation, and an emphasis on these internal relationships.

[6]Pseudonyms for the ESOL students and cooperating teacher.

> Vygotsky argues that the unique route to higher-order verbal thinking is the experience of schooling. Schooling detaches the word from its designation and attaches it to a generalization. This shift is of profound importance because only if the word is freed of its sensory impedimenta can it be manipulated voluntarily and with conscious awareness. Written speech must have more words, be more precise, and be more expanded than verbal speech, because it cannot rely on paralinguistic elements such as tone and gestures. This enforces an experience of language as system. This systematicity—self-contained and self-sufficient—is what allows language to be unhooked from the sensory world, to be taken in hand by the thinker, to be used as a tool for thought. (Gallimore & Tharp, 1990, pp. 193–194)

In a following student teacher seminar, after looking at the counts of participation that Su and I shared with Charlie, he identified a boy and a girl as students with whom he wanted to increase interaction. At the next seminar, we brainstormed, and Charlie developed the following possible strategies:

1. Giving instructions verbally and reinforcing them by writing on the board or overhead projector in order to reduce confusion and increase comprehension.
2. Tapping into students' prior knowledge.
3. Maintaining written records of students' recurring problems and progress.
4. Eliciting answers from students with more developed skills and asking for confirmation from those less likely to have correct responses.
5. Relying on visual cues.
6. Peer correction, for instance, asking: "Is that what everyone got?"
7. Asking open-ended, discovery-oriented questions so that students could participate without fear of giving an incorrect response.
8. Rather than correcting an incorrect response, asking the student to describe the process and providing scaffolding so that he or she could discover the correct response somewhat independently.

To Charlie, scaffolding and participation were tightly connected, and in the context of scaffolding, he was mindful of students' affective needs. For instance, while describing his progress with a student who was struggling with a word problem, he noted that his encouragement and investment in the student helped the student to learn:

> It's that first step, he can't take it on his own. If it looks way too confusing, he needs me to say: 'I know you can do it.' Because what he sees is the 100 words, and that is overwhelming. It's only three sentences. He doesn't have

> the confidence to take risks, but when he has guidance, he does quite well. (Seminar, 04-08)

and:

> With word problems ... it's more or less for them to figure out. I'm there to help them along and to explain to them if they don't understand this word, or what the important word is. (Seminar, 04-08)

Charlie, too, noticed a relationship between encouragement and participation:

> Carlos isn't lazy, he's just scared. He seems to have anxiety, and having him read to me and acknowledging that he is doing it correctly encourages him to make an effort. (Seminar, 04-28)

Charlie believed that his determination to address not only academic needs, but the whole person, and attention to the affective needs of the student, supported the student's active participation in the class.

Charlie expressed admiration for the determination of a Somali girl who the previous year had started school for the first time at age 13:

> She will raise her hand to ask for clarification and will ask again and again. She has no problem announcing that she got the wrong answer so that she can find out where she made her mistake. Her goal is to understand it all as opposed to getting by with 50%. She announced to everyone that she had the wrong answer because she wanted to figure out what was wrong ... she has no problem asking you to repeat it two or three times because her goal is to understand, so she will seek the clarification. I feel that if she does get the wrong answer, I need to go over the problem step by step so that she can master it. (Seminar, 04-28)

Another student's participation appeared to have increased, and Charlie suggested that drawing pictures to explain word problems had helped her because she had more confidence when she understood the problems and got the answers.

> She said, 'I'm finished' when everyone was still working. It gave her a sense of pride. Out of the five she finished first. She's worked very hard to get where she is. (Seminar, 04-28)

Mediation Through Symbolic or Sign Systems

Vygotsky pointed out that sign (language as a means of social intercourse) and tool (as a means of labor of mastering nature) were mutually linked and yet separate in the child's cultural development. Vygotsky (1978) placed both sign and tool under the more general concept of "indirect (mediated) activity" (p. 54). He linked the concept of mediated activity which he "invested with the broadest possible meaning," to Hegel's characteristic feature of human reason:

> Reason is just as cunning as she is powerful. Her cunning consists principally in her mediating activity which, by causing objects to act and react on each other in accordance with their own nature, in this way, without any direct interference in the process, carries out reasons' intentions. Marx cites that definition when speaking of working tools, to show that man "uses the mechanical, physical, and chemical properties of objects so as to make them act as forces that affect other objects in order to fulfill his personal goals." (Vygotsky, 1978, p. 54)[7]

Dana Frye developed a unit on diversity. She was concerned about the racial hierarchies and the social pecking orders she saw in the high school. She had heard students make derogatory racial comments. Her lesson contrasting the words "same" and "different" provided the language for conceptual, higher order, critical thinking for students of various levels of English language proficiency. She provided students who had limited lexical resources with questions on flashcards that they could use as prompts when engaging in discussions with peers about the peers' home and communities.

BRANCH 3-5: ZPD AND QUESTIONING TECHNIQUES

> Krashen saw movement from one state of interlanguage competence to the next as ultimately a fixed and predictable process, independent of cultural and historical influence. Thus for Krashen, an individual's linguistic future is certain; for Vygotsky, the future is open, uncertain and depends on the material and interactional (i.e. cultural and historical circumstances in which the individual is situated. (Dunn & Lantolf, 1998, p. 422)

Novice teachers often want to know how to ask "higher order" questions. Sadker and Sadker (1994) pointed out that teachers tend to give differential feedback to girls and boys. Girls tend to be told "Good," and are not forced to defend or elaborate their positions. But boys are challenged by teacher ques-

[7]Vygotsky explained that tools and signs could neither be considered isomorphic with respect to the functions they perform, nor an exhaustive list of mediated activities: cognitive activity is not limited to the use of tools or signs.

tioning and are encouraged to provide more detail, or to extend their answers. How does a teacher become aware of these interaction patterns and how can a teacher develop a repertoire of dialogic questioning strategies? Studies such as Hugh Mehan's recitation script (Mehan, 1979), Sarah Michaels' sharing time (Michaels, 1981), Courtney Cazden's classroom discourse (1991), and Au and Kawakami's talk story (Au & Kawakami, 1985) disclose discursive patterns that segregate, separate, or differentiate students (Toohey, 2000). Another way is to videotape or audiotape one's teaching and to conduct critical discourse analysis to uncover patterns in interaction. There is no substitute for "learning by doing."

By working collaboratively with teachers who have diverse experiences and strengths, we can work within our various zones of proximal development and provide social and pedagogical support for each other. It is very difficult to see patterns in one's own teaching. Teachers need support and a team to give them the encouragement and perspective to *be able to identify potential* both in our students and ourselves. Because the mediating role of teacher–student interaction and discourse is so complex, it is easy to become bogged down in the technical aspects of counting. One can count the number of turns and never analyze the significance of the counts or generate pedagogically sound alternatives. By becoming part of a collaborative team that counts and codes utterances or turns, a teacher can be enabled to see patterns that she or he would never be able to see individually. Finally, to be observed, supported, and affirmed as a teacher by other teachers is very important. The feminist pedagogy of the support group is a good model for going into each other's classes to coach, support, observe, and *listen and learn* rather than tell and teach. In the end, teacher change is self-generated. Each teacher will herself or himself generate changes. So although it is helpful to watch other teachers and see the way that they interact, one cannot blindly copy someone else. In the end each teacher must begin from where she or he is and find ways to come into her or his own.

In a study by Katherine Au (1990) on sociocultural perspectives on teacher education, an experienced home economics teacher who was learning the KEEP literacy system to work with Native Hawaiian students[7] pointed out the complexity and difficulty of acquiring practical knowledge of teaching:

> I don't know if some [other teachers] would admit that maybe things didn't go too well. You're real prideful of your teaching and what you do. And the only think you hear from other teachers [is] "oh, I did this and it was great." You know, all you hear are the good things.... But you don't want to go and say, "you know, I really bombed," ... because then you think they're going to think, "well she's not good teacher." When it's really just, you know, teaching's a hard thing. (Au, 1990, p. 286)

Yes, teaching is a *hard* thing. It is extremely situated. And to get to know every new context or group of students is challenging. And yet this is our job and our vocation. It takes a long time to develop as a teacher. The first years of teaching can be a nightmare, as evidenced in the high turnover rate.[8] Vygotsky's revolutionary perspectives for language minority students provide a challenge to teachers that cannot be solved by individual teachers, overnight. Novice teachers need allies; they need mentors. A transformative agenda in teacher education must have both the visions of Vygotskian revolutionary theory, but also the pragmatic issues of survival, of getting to know the students and the school culture and of finding allies and neutralizing hostile elements.

Will focused on instructional conversation, on questions he could use to develop higher-order thinking skills. His cooperating teacher had given him a list of questions designed to challenge students, and he posted this by his desk. Questioning figured prominently in the reflections of all student teachers. The ways in which student teachers approached problem posing was to focus on what the student already knew, and to accept what was partially correct. Will, for example, found that accepting the partial answer provided a point of departure for scaffolding his instruction:

> When I plan lessons, I try to think about questions, the specific questions to those who don't participate as much. I really try to *bring* them to a reasonable answer.... I think that one thing is that I try to accept whatever answer they give, and go from there ... from whatever starting point that is. (Will Roberts)

Problem Posing Works for Students and Student Teachers

Problem-posing-centered teaching occurred in these examples on two levels. On one level, the student teachers created problem-centered classrooms. In Charlie's class, the students learned about standard measurement, for example, through engaging with the problem of communicating about length. Charlie allowed his students to use physical tools to make measurements and symbolic tools to discuss those measurements. Dana's students learned about diversity through considering the problem

[8] About 42% of all U.S. public schools have no minority teachers. Minority students make up 33% of enrollment in U.S. public schools, while minority teachers make up 13.5%. Early in the 21st century, the percentage of minority teachers is expected to shrink to an all-time low of 5%, whereas 41% of American students will be minorities (National Center for Education Statistics Digest of Education Statistics). National Center for Education Statistics data show that 20% of teachers will abandon their profession within the first 3 years, while 9% will leave within their first year. Others estimate that as many as 50% of new teachers leave within the first 5 years.

of how students get along in the high school. Will's concern was to engage students in high-level thinking.

At a second level, the student teachers were involved in a problem-posing student teaching seminar. Using the tool of systematic observation of classroom interactions, the students considered how they encouraged student interactions. They reflected on their knowledge of power in the classroom and made decisions about how they would help every student participate—because they recognized that participation is key to learning another language.

FEMINIST PROBLEM POSING

Feminist ways of knowing or methods of inquiry open up alternative ways of *posing* or *constructing* the problems of investigation or identifying the challenges or dilemmas of a particular field (Pavlenko, 2004). Second, they explore alternative explanations and analysis that provides spaces for voices that have been absent from the academy in the past (hooks, 1981; Belenky, 1986). Finally, they scrutinize the role of the researcher, social scientist, or evaluator (Harding, 1987, 2000).

In probing the role of the researcher, it is important to ask who conducts the research, their stance vis-à-vis the subjects of their research, and their positioning within unequal hierarchical relationships (Wong & Teuben-Rowe, 1997). This is important for us in TESOL when our students come from working-class and poor communities or come from countries or racial, ethnic, or religious groups that are seen a threat by the mainstream. Critical race theorists and critical multiculturalists have suggested that marginality can be utilized as a resource (Kubota, 2002). It is important to note the multiplicity of perspectives that are presented by critical feminism, which sees women's experiences in the plural. African American feminists (Collins, 1990) and other feminists of color (Anzaldùa,1987; Matsuda, 1996; Moraga & Anzaldùa, 1981) are critical of representations of "women" that are racist or have taken Whiteness as the norm. In contexts in which the majority of students are non-White, and the majority of teachers are White, it is important to interrogate racism.

I first became introduced to feminist theories of knowledge as I prepared to teach the Chinese Theological students.[9] The problem of feminist or "womanist" (Williams, 1996) readings or interpretations of text can be found in the following example: "How could a slave owner, a White man,

[9]The "learning by doing" aspect of exposure to feminist theology for me as the ESOL teacher and the Chinese theological students involved attending lectures, reading books and articles, and participating in women's conferences, as discussed in the following section.

and his slave, an African American woman, both consider the Bible to be a sacred text and the word of God?"

Feminist Christian liberation theologians look at the ways that religion has been used to both "foster liberation" and "maintain oppression" (Welch, 1985, p. 15) They are critical of the ways in which women emulate Jesus' suffering and passively accept their own victimization:

> The qualities that Christianity *idealizes*, especially for women, are also those of a victim: sacrificial love, passive acceptance of suffering, humility, meekness, etc. Since these are qualities idealized in Jesus "who died for our sins," his functioning as a model reinforces the scapegoat syndrome for women. Given the victimized situation of the female in sexist society, these "virtues" are hardly the qualities that women should be encouraged to have. (Daly, 1973, as quoted in Welch, 1985, p. 15)

The patriarchal "virtues" of women Mary Daly discusses in Christianity have a parallel in traditional China. Confucian "virtues" of women were passed on through the three Obeys and four Virtues: Obey your father as a child, your husband as a married woman and then your son as a widow (Levy, 1968). Here Confucian refers to the ideology criticized by Chinese intellectuals in the May 4th movement (see Branch 4-4: John Dewey in China) that ruled China for thousands of years, rather than the Confucian dialogues of the man Kungze or the original teachings of Confucius. Although the Confucian hierarchy respected the elderly, its patriarchal nature restricted respect and deference to men. The elderly woman was subservient even to her son, who was the "head" of the household. Women were a commodity. Child marriage developed as poor families received dowries for their daughters, who worked as child servants in wealthier families. Wealthy men had concubines, whereas poor male landless peasants who could not afford the dowry for a wife had no families. In times of floods, famines, or drought, poor peasants would sell their daughters or abandon girl babies. Preference was given to sons, who were valued because they would continue the family line rather than daughters, who "belonged" to their husband's family after marriage[10] (Snow, 1983).

---

[10]Sadly, many of the problems that the Chinese women's associations battled in the 1950s with the establishment of new marriage laws to fight against women's oppression are back in China today with the opening of capitalist forces. Freedom of movement to economic zones has led to prostitution of rural girls. With China's "one child" policy and medical technology that enables one to know the sex of any embryo, once again there is tremendous imbalance of girls and boys per 100 children.

BRANCH 3-6: WOMEN'S WAYS OF KNOWING

Feminist and womanist intellectual work in the academy has opened up new epistemological perspectives in history, politics, economics, and how we view science and inquiry (Harding, 1987; Weedon, 1987; Weiler, 1988, 2001). An example of "women's ways of knowing" is given in the work of Carol Gilligan, a development psychologist.[11] In her book *In a Different Voice*, Gilligan poses questions of about voice and relationship:

> My questions are about psychological processes and theory, particularly theories in which men's experience stands for all of human experience—theories which eclipse the lives of women and shut out women's voices. I saw that by maintaining these ways of seeing and speaking about human lives, men were leaving out women, but women were leaving out themselves. In terms of psychological processes, what for men was a process of separation, for women was a process of dissociation that required the creation of an inner division or psychic split. (Gilligan, 1993, p. xiii)

Gilligan wrote about a study on moral development in which two 11-year-old children, Amy and Jake, were given a moral problem to solve:

> A man named Heinz considers whether or not to steal a drug which he cannot afford to buy in order to save the life of his wife. In the standard format of Kohlberg's interviewing procedure, the description of the dilemma itself—Heinz's predicament, the wife's disease, the druggist's refusal to lower his price—is followed by the question, "Should Heinz steal the drug?" (Gilligan, 1993, pp. 25–26)

Jake's response, that Heinz *should* steal the drug, was based on the following reasoning:

> For one, thing, a human life is worth more than money, and if the druggist only makes $1,000, he is still going to live, but if Heinz doesn't steal the drug, his wife is going to die. (Why is life worth more than money?) Because the druggist can get a thousand dollars later from rich people with cancer, but Heinz can't get his wife again. (Why not?) Because people are all different and so you couldn't get Heinz's wife again. (Gilligan, 1993, p. 26)

Jake scored well on Kohlberg's six-stage theory of moral development. Because Jake incorporated logic and was able to differentiate morality from law (Jake had

[11]It is important to recognize the pioneering work of Gilligan and others in opening fields that have previously held a male-as-norm standard. The grass-roots student movements for ethnic and women's studies and often unrecognized work of institutionalizing women's studies, sometimes one course at a time, have begun to make an impact, little by little.

said, "the judge would probably think it was the right thing to do," "the laws have mistakes, and you can't go writing up a law for everything that you can imagine," and "the judge should give Heinz the lightest possible sentence"), he was seen as having a principled conception of justice, which Kohlberg equated with maturity in moral development.

In contrast to Jake, Amy's response to Heinz's dilemma was rated as "evasive and unsure," "stunted in logical development," and "reflecting an inability to think for herself." She replied that Heinz *should not* steal, but did not seem to have resolved the ethical dilemma posed by the problem:

> Well, I don't think so. I think there might be other ways besides stealing it, like he could go borrow the money or make a loan or something, but he really shouldn't steal the drug—but his wife shouldn't die either.

Asked why Heinz should not steal the drug, she considers neither property nor law but rather the effect that theft could have on the relationship between Heinz and his wife:

> If he stole the drug, he might save his wife then, but if he did, he might have to go to jail and then his wife might get sicker again, and he couldn't get more of the drug, and it might not be good. So they should really just talk it out and find some other way to make the money. (Gilligan, 1993, p. 28)

Amy sees the dilemma as a problem of relationships. Because of the wife's illness, Amy sees the wife's need for her husband to continue over a period of time. Just as she ties the wife's survival to the preservation of relationships, she considers the value of the wife's life in a context of relationships. She sees the problem in the druggist not responding to human need, "if somebody has something that would keep somebody alive, then it's not right not to give it to them," and she considers the problem in the dilemma to arise not from the druggist's assertion of rights but from his failure of response.

On the six-stage scale of moral development, Amy's score was a full stage lower than Josh's. She lacked Josh's rational approach to the law, and as the interviewer conveyed throughout, that Amy and Josh were constructing the problem in different ways: the repetition of questions, "Why Heinz should not steal the drug, she simply repeats, 'Because it's not right.'" Sensing that she was not providing the correct answer, Amy's confidence began to diminish and her ability to communicate her answer gave her a lower score for cognitive reasoning—her answer was seen as lacking in systematic thinking, showing a reluctance to challenge authority, naive and immature.

Gilligan pointed out:

> Just as Jake is confident "the judge would agree that stealing is the right thing" for Heinz to do, so Amy is confident that, "if Heinz and the druggist had talked it out long enough, they could reach something besides stealing." (Gilligan, 1993, p. 29)

The interviewer's problem in failing to understand Amy's response took for granted that the two children were answering the same questions. But the children were really solving two very different moral dilemmas:

> Amy is considering not whether Heinz should act in this situation ("*should* Heinz steal the drug?") but rather *how* Heinz should act in response to his awareness of his wife's need ("Should Heinz *steal* the drug?").... In the interviewer's failure to imagine a response not dreamt of in Kohlberg's moral philosophy lies the failure to hear Amy's question and to see the logic in her response, to discern that what appears, from one perspective, to be an evasion of the dilemma signifies in other terms a recognition of the problem and a search for a more adequate solution.
>
> Thus in Heinz's dilemma these two children see two very different moral problems—Jake a conflict between life and property that can be resolved by logical deduction, Amy a fracture of human relationship that must be mended with its own thread. (Gilligan, 1993, p. 31)

Gilligan's work in psychological development asks us to look critically at the role of the researcher in how the questions are posed. We cannot take for granted, even though the interviewer asked both children the same sets of questions, that the task was able to measure moral development. Universal scales of development that reflect male (or for that matter, White, Western, or upper-middle-class) norms may not adequately measure all students. Gilligan pointed out that in Kohlberg's scale, what Jake sees that Amy does not is clear, as Jake's response is rated a full stage higher than Amy's in moral reasoning. But if posed the question "What does she see that he does not?" Kohlberg's scale has nothing to say. A deeper inquiry into "what does Amy see that Jake does not" may create spaces for perceiving multiple ways of knowing and being in the world.

Not all women know in the same ways. Gender is mediated by class, race, ethnicity, sexual orientation, and many other constructions of difference with respect to hierarchies of knowledge and power in academic institutions. Testing of human development involves scales, ranking, and too often linear paths for development. Gilligan's research points out that development may not occur in a straight line and that our scales of measurement may be flawed. Dialogic inquiry into women's ways of knowing—in all their varieties—is important for all of us—female and male—in TESOL as we search for ways to affirm, challenge, and extend ways that students come to know.

Why is it that most of the great philosophers and writers from classical times until the present are men? Why is it that historically—in any field—the 10 great books have been written by men or that only 1 out of 12 writers are women (Olsen, 1978)? Feminist theories of knowledge emphasize opening the traditionally male-dominated canon. Instead of grand master narratives and unitary, universal standards for truth, they emphasize the multiplicity of perspectives. In the area of literature, just as the work of African American authors, both women and men, has completely changed the teaching of English, Greene (1988) pointed out that the discovery of women novelists has expanded the horizons of those reared in the traditions of so-called "great" literature. The "classics" have been read through new critical perspectives:

> The growing ability to look at even classical works through new critical lenses has enabled numerous readers, of both genders, to apprehend previously unknown renderings of their lived worlds. Not only have many begun coming to literature with the intent of *achieving* it as meaningful through realization by means of perspectival readings. Many have begun engaging in what Mikhail Bakhtin called "dialogism," viewing literary texts as spaces where multiple voices and multiple discourses intersect and interact (1981, pp. 259–422). Even to confront what Bakhtin calls "heteroglossia" in a novel is to enlarge one's experience with multiplicity of perspectives and, at once, with the spheres that can open in the midst of pluralities. (Greene, 1988, p. 129)

One of the contributions to problem posing of women's studies and ethnic studies is the unearthing of voices that have been excluded from the history texts. An example from the field of church history is the story of how African slaves became Christians and established churches. An example in women's studies is to look at the lived experiences of women garment workers or the struggle for women to gain the vote. Through the slave narratives and through oral history projects, we in TESOL who are ourselves the descendants of slaves or indigenous or colonized people or who teach the descendants of slaves or indigenous or colonized people can redefine, rethink, and re-vision whom knowledge serves.

A synonym for "language" is tongue; of course, the word "language" comes from "lingua," which means "tongue." When we learn a foreign language, we wrap our tongues around foreign words the same way we might open our mouths to a new food when we are in a new-to-us culture. In both cases of learning language and trying new foods, we experience a strangeness that may not be pleasant. In time and with experience, the new becomes "familiar"—like the old language we learned from our family; we *acquire* not so much a series of grammatical rules and a vocabulary, but through *participation*, we acquire taste—an aesthetic appreciation for the new language and other cultural forms of production in that new language. Feminist and womanist problem posing can open new criteria for ethics and morality and create new spaces for the creation of aesthetics and tastes.

4

Learn by Doing

If you want knowledge, you must take part in the practice of changing reality. If you want to know the taste of a pear, you must change the pear by eating it yourself.

—Mao, 1967, "On Practice," p. 71

The essence of dialogue itself is the word. And within the word are reflection and action. If there is reflection without action, you have "verbalism." And if reflection is sacrificed, you have "activism."

—Freire, 1970, p. 75

Feminist challenges reveal that the questions that are asked—and even more significantly, those that are not asked—are at least as determinative of the adequacy of our total picture as are any answers that we can discover. Defining what is in need of scientific explanation only from the perspective of bourgeois, white men's experiences leads to partial and even perverse understandings of social life.... Notice that it is "women's experiences" in the plural which provide the new resources for research. That is, women come only in different classes, races, and cultures: there is no "woman" and no "woman's experience."

—Harding, 1987, p. 7

Among my favorite teaching materials is a set of cards produced by the University of Michigan in the audiolingual days.[1] I have used the stick-figure cards of a person "reading a book," "waiting for a bus," and "going to bed" to introduce and teach verbs. In teaching a beginning language learner, a two-dimensional stick figure drawing may be more useful than an actual ginkgo tree to focus attention on the generic word "tree" along with other basic vocabulary: "house," "bus," "school," "work." Beginners may not want to invest the time to learn the details and qualities of the ginkgo tree or its fan-shaped leaves with ridges, which grow from nub-like buds.[2] They may not want to learn the specialized terms such as "buds" or "twigs," "bark" or "trunk," or to distinguish between a "maple" and a "fir" or a "ginkgo," but may be satisfied at first to learn only the generic word "tree." Although a botanist studying English may be interested in specialized terminology, other beginning ESOL students may have other priorities for language learning.

In determining the content of instruction, the needs of the students must be taken into consideration (e.g., How much vocabulary should be introduced in a lesson? What are the most important terms and expressions for students to know?) Proceeding from basic materials such as dialogues and simplified readers and moving to authentic materials provides a classroom language experience that is in meaningful chunks and not overwhelming in the amount of detail, which can be frustrating for the beginning language learner.

At the same time, we should not have a "stage approach" and say that we *first* deal with simplified and scripted materials *before* we introduce students to natural language and authentic texts. Beginning students of all ages can benefit from interaction with second-language (L2) speakers and use of television or radio shows, films, newspapers, and books with the support of the teacher. And conversely, intermediate and advanced students who read and respond to authentic L2 materials such as "real" books, magazines, and articles can also benefit from formal instruction in grammar, linguistic exercises, and mini-lessons that focus their attention on structures of the language with which they have difficulty.

---

[1]Although the University of Michigan cards are no longer available, there is a book for teachers (Wright, 1984) that shows "easy to draw" stick figures. A word of caution: Stick-figure representations are culturally very specific, and figures that may seem unambiguous in one culture may be problematic in another. Ask one of your students to serve as a cultural informant and "pilot" your stick-figure drawings. It may help you get a sense of whether your students understand the contexts you are trying to establish through your drawings.

[2]The ornamental shape of the leaves may be a reason the ginkgo was selected as a symbol of the Weimar Republic in Germany (personal contact with German teacher and OSU graduate student Cynthia "Max" Schilling).

A critical feature of dialogic approaches to TESOL is "learning by doing." Yet how do we develop a meaningful, balanced curriculum that moves from props to life, from drilling and formal instruction to actual use of the language, from scripts to spontaneous dialogue? How do we teach our students meta-cognitive strategies for language learning (Oxford, 1990)? What is the proper relationship between authentic uses of the language (writing for real audiences, real purposes, for publication, content-based ESL) as opposed to formal teaching of grammar (Cazden, 1992; Celce-Murcia, 1998; Larsen-Freeman, 2003)? There are no simple answers to these questions. Imagine the following prescriptions:

> 70% "Real" communication and 30% feedback, exercises to instruct in lexical–grammatical issues.
>
> 70% Scripted dialogues, pattern practice, and 30% use of the target language for actual interaction.

We can't have a "formula" approach to learning by doing. Depending on the context of instruction, the educational background, level of proficiency, and age of the students, there may be an argument for any number of effective combinations.

As stated in the previous chapter, Vygotsky (1978) formulated a useful principle for addressing this problem: Any function in a child's cultural development appears twice, or on two planes. First it appears on the social plane and then on the psychological plane. It moves from what Vygotsky calls "inter-psychological" (the social) to "intra-psychological," (internalized individually), from joint problem solving, to being able to solve a problem independently. An example in which teachers exploit this principle comes from emergent literacy in primary schools, where teachers organize the classroom into a number of reading events of varying levels of student independence. Social forms of reading lead to independent reading (Table 4.1).

The teacher exercises the most control and responsibility for the reading act in "read alouds," in which s/he reads large picture books to the children. In "shared reading," the teacher has the whole class read certain words or repeat certain phrases. In "guided reading," within small groups of two to four children, individual children take turns reading with teacher and peer support. In "buddy reading," two children read to each other. And in "independent reading" a child reads alone. Children take home books to read to family members that they have already practiced reading independently at school (Ruopp & Wong, 1995). Performance with assistance precedes individual competence (Clay & Cazden, 1990).

This chapter addresses principles of learning by doing so that teachers can incorporate experiential dimensions of language learning into their classrooms (Nunan, 1999). The Chinese characters for student are "learn" and "growth, alive or life."

TABLE 4.1
Roles in Emergent Literacy

Reading Event	*Teacher's Role*	*Children's Role*
Read alouds or storybook reading	Teacher models reading to children and poses questions	Students answer questions about the narrative, and conventions of text (what is the title, the author, plot, setting, characters)
Shared reading	Teacher reads most of the story	Students read certain words and phrases (usually repeated patterns in the text)
Guided reading	Teacher introduces the story, manages the turn-taking, and focuses student attention on reading strategies (What do good readers do?) and working in a group (How do we work in a group?)	Students take turns reading pages of the book.
Buddy reading	Teacher circulates to observe students or works with small groups of students or individual students	In pairs, students practice rereading to each other a book that they have already read in a group.
Independent reading	Teacher circulates to observe students or works with small groups of students or individual students	Students read books that they have already read in a group for increased fluency and confidence
Books home	Teacher monitors student progress through collecting parent signatures, or organizing students to assume record keeping, or distributes stickers to those who have read at home	Students read to a family member (or stuffed animal) books that they have already read in a group for increased fluency and confidence, and parents sign that the home reading has taken place

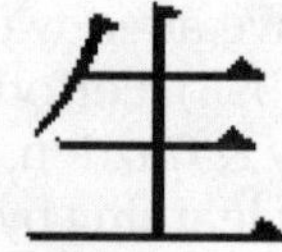

FIG. 4.1. "Student" is composed of the two characters "learn" (on the left) and "growth, alive or life" (on the right).

This chapter begins with a discussion of Marx, Mao, Freire, Dewey, Bakhtin, and feminist ways of "learning by doing," discussing its relevance for foreign and second-language teaching. In the second section of the chapter, examples come from the Pilgrimage Curriculum I developed for the Chinese theological students.

PHILOSOPHICAL ROOTS OF CRITICAL PEDAGOGY

Critical/dialogical ESOL pedagogy relies on a wide range of political and/or educational theorists, including Freire (Auerbach, 1992; Wallerstein, 1983), Bakhtin (Hall, Vitanova, & Marchenkova, 2004; Maguire, 1999), Vygotsky, (Newmann & Holzman, 1993), and Foucault (Benesch, 2001; Diaz-Rico, 1998, 2004). These thinkers have addressed disparate issues, from the essentially social nature of learning (Vygotsky) to the inclusion of oppressed voices in the classroom (Freire); from the complex, dialogical nature of language (Bakhtin) to the nature of knowledge and power (Bourdieu, 1991; Foucault, 1972). What these scholars have in common is that they were strongly influenced by the ideas of Karl Marx, or, in the case of Dewey, by Hegel, whose philosophy undergirds that of Marx. Some educational theorists sanitize Vygotsky of his political background and thought.[3] Yet to truly understand how and why these theories work, we must understand their Marxist roots. This is particularly critical as we come to consider the relationship between theory and practice, a common theme among these theorists.

Across many centuries, philosophers have attempted to address questions such as who we are in the world (which they call *metaphysics*) and how we know what we know (*epistemology*—the nature of knowledge). Although it is difficult to summarize the works of many lifetimes, there are two important, contrasting themes that emerge across the history of Western philosophy. One is sensory based. We can know what we see and we are products of the world we sense. The other could be considered idea based. It suggests that although there are things we cannot sense, such as another person's thinking or the idea of beauty, these things are nevertheless important to the human experience and they profoundly shape who we are. Although there are also many other important philosophical themes, both of these themes have been central to the history of educational ideas.

"Learning by doing" is a theory of knowledge involving *praxis*, that is, the practical application of (and reflection on) theory, through practice. Marx's philosophy was influenced by Immanuel Kant (1724–1804), who

---

[3]A notable exception is Newmann and Holzman (1993). Newmann and Holtzman do not shy away from the political dimensions of Vygotsky.

posed the major epistemological (knowledge) and metaphysical (nature of human experience) questions of the 19th century (Balmuth, 1968). Unlike Hume, a forerunner of the 20th century behaviorists who believed that human reason was merely a reflection of sense perception, Kant believed that reason was involved in all human judgment, from mere perceptions of individual objects to higher levels of experience. According to Kant, beyond perception and understanding, reason seeks to uncover the totality of conditions of all experience. But here reason is confronted with nonrational circumstances that lie behind that to which the categories apply: those "things in themselves," which are logically prior to phenomena as experienced.

The philosophical, epistemological, and metaphysical problem posed by Kant was taken up by Hegel, who saw that Kant's critical understanding of the *limits* of reason itself reflected a new and higher stage in the development of reason. Hegel took the investigation of reason into *time*—whereas previously *space* played the major role in conceptual thought elaborated in the sciences (Lefebre, 1969). In the preface to *The Phenomenology of Hegel*, translated by Walter Kaufmann, Hegel compares the history of philosophy concerning scientific knowledge to the flower and fruit of a tree:

> The bud disappears as the blossom bursts forth, and one could say that the former is refuted by the latter. In the same way, the fruit declares the blossom to be a false existence of the plant, and the fruit supplants the blossom as the truth of the plant. These forms do not only differ, they also displace each other because they are incompatible. Their fluid nature, however, makes them at the same time, elements of an organic unity in which they not only do not conflict, but in which one is as necessary as the other; and it is only this equal necessity that constitutes the life of the whole. (Hegel, 1969, p. 8)

Reason grows and changes across time through a dialectical process: Older forms of reason become negated by newer forms. For example, Hegel's addition of the concept of time contrasts with previous spatial concepts of reason. It was created in response to those older concepts and to some extent it opposes and displaces the older ideas.

Another example might be the influence of multicultural understandings on the process of teaching reading. In the 1950s in the United States, basal readers (reading textbooks for young children, which feature a controlled vocabulary) almost exclusively featured middle-class European Americans. The Civil Rights, Black Power, and Black consciousness movements eventually influenced reading practices: Multiculturalism suggests that children need to see themselves in the books they read. Modern basal readers reflect this newer form of reasoning, and the people in the books represent the many cultures that are present in the United States. Although the newer basal readers may still suffer from "tokenism" and reflect biases and stereotypes, it is no longer acceptable to ask children to read from a monocultural reading series. In many newer textbooks, the newer reasoning process has supplanted the older one.[4]

For Hegel, reason was constantly in flux and developing:

> There is an absolute movement, in consciousness and reality, of the idea of "world." Hegel calls this movement and its end the Absolute Idea, World Spirit, or "Geist." The historical movement of the Absolute Idea follows the dialectical form of a continuous triadic development of rational fulfillment. The nature of this concrete whole is understandable only by philosophic reflection. (Freedman, 1968)

In this way, Hegel provided a historical interpretation of Kant's logical analysis of the limits of reason. The historical movement of the Absolute Idea was the modern state:

> Without the state, the elements that compose social reality—the "estates," the crafts and corporations, subdivisions like municipalities and families—would fly apart. Without its rules and regulations there would be a breakdown of objective morality (manners and customs, morals) and of subjective morality (sense of duty, sense of obligation) alike. Human history attains its peak in the modern constitutional state. There is nothing further to look forward to in the womb of time or to expect from human endeavor. Marx took a diametrically opposed position. (Lefebre, 1969, p. 26)

To Marx, who followed Hegel and based his philosophy on many of Hegel's ideas, the modern state was a part of the superstructure. Like other institutions, the state, rather than being the culmination of human history, was dependent on historical conditions. That is, political structures, like philosophical ideas, shift through negation. Older political structures become displaced by newer political developments. Where a political structure is, in terms of its history, determines the nature of the governments to which it gives rise. The state, like other parts of the superstructure—all ideas, culture, thought—has a historically given material basis. As Marx and Engels wrote:

> The ideas of the ruling class are in every epoch the ruling ideas: i.e. the class, which is the ruling *material* force of society, is at the same time its ruling *in-*

[4]There is still a great deal of work to be done to challenge White Eurocentric, male-as-norm biases in textbooks, and reactionary currents to "turn back the clock" and "return to basics."

> *tellectual* force. The class which has the means of material production at its disposal has control at the same time over the means of mental production, so that thereby, generally speaking, the ideas of those who lack the means of mental production are subject to it. The ruling ideas are nothing more than the ideal expression of the dominant material relationship, the dominant material relationships grasped as ideas; hence of the relationship which make the one class the ruling one, therefore the ideas of its dominance. (Marx & Engels, 1947, p. 64)

Ideology is the set of ideas that are necessarily part of the superstructure. Different superstructures have different ideologies. The classic Marxist perspective on ideology is that it serves the ruling class. The ideology of a monarchy includes the belief that one person is born to be king and this person has absolute authority over everyone else. The ideology of capitalism is that the capitalist, the person with the money who owns the factory or the corporation, has the right to control the working conditions of the employees. Before the labor union movement in Appalachia, for example, this meant that coal mine operators owned the houses and the stores and paid the miners in scrip instead of money. Miners could only use the scrip to pay rent to the company and to buy their groceries and supplies at the overpriced company stores. Miners worked extremely dangerous jobs (the companies were not interested in mine safety practices that would cost money or time) and ended up in debt to the company rather than ahead. This sort of exploitation was acceptable to the ruling class. This type of reasoning only began to be negated by the labor union movement of the workers, which the companies fought violently. The strength of the labor movement has rested on its ability to unite workers despite management's attempts to divide workers across race, gender and immigration status[5] (K. Wong, 1995).

What is so powerful about ideology is that it validates exploitation, oppression, and inequality as morally justifiable. Italian Marxist Antonio Gramsci (1971) explained that in advanced capitalist countries the ruling class rules through ideological dominance or what is called ideological hegemony through the civil institutions of society—through consent, not primarily through coercion—although there are prisons, police, and the military. Engels called democracy the best possible shell for capitalism. Ideological hegemony is so powerful that it is "normal," even sacred or "God-given." For that reason, the Marxist critique of the distortions of ideol-

[5]Although Asian Americans have been part of the U.S. workplace for over 150 years, unions in the United States historically viewed Asian immigration as a threat that would lower wages and working conditions of native-born workers. The new labor movement combines union organizing and the struggle for the rights of all workers, including undocumented workers (Delp, Outman-Kramer, Schurman, & Wong, 2002).

ogy—for example, racism or chauvinism that divides workers and other oppressed people and prevents them from uniting—is an essential component to organize against exploitation and oppression.

Another very important component of the Marxist conception of ideology is the relationship between the superstructure and the economic base. The economic base or means of production is comprised of the forces of production (which includes the technological level of development of the society, whether plows, industrial factories, or modern-day computer technology) and the relations of production (the class relationships including the obligations of feudal lords and peasants under feudalism). There is a dialectical relationship between the economic base that engenders the superstructure and the superstructure that reflects back on the base.

Marx has been criticized for economic determinism and mechanical materialism (not seeing the independence of the superstructure, nor the role of consciousness in making history). He has also been criticized for dichotomizing "science" against ideology and for only seeing ideology as "false" and science as "real." Given the historical times in which Marx wrote and the revolutionary purpose of his writings, these criticisms seem unfair. For Marx to unlock the secret of exploitation under capitalism and to grasp the emancipatory role of the working class when the bourgeois revolutions against feudalism were underway was visionary. When others saw the relations of the market to be a "free" contract between workers and industrialists, Marx showed the hidden exploitation through disclosing the contradiction in the commodity.[6] *The German Ideology* must be understood as a polemic against idealism, which was the dominant perspective in 19th-century European philosophy, as we saw already.

The major areas from which Marx developed dialectical or historical materialism were German philosophy (i.e., Kant, Hegel, Feuerbach), English political economy (i.e., Adam Smith and Ricardo), and French socialism (i.e., Saint-Simon, Fourier, Proudhon). Others, notably Vygotsky and Bakhtin, developed Marxist theory in the areas of psychology and linguistics. We talked about Vygotsky's psychology exploring consciousness and the development of higher order thinking in previous chapters. We now turn to Bakhtin and the authors of *Marxism and the Philosophy of Language*, V. N. Vološinov and P. N. Medvedev, for their contributions on the role of "dialogic" in language and ideology.

---

[6]It is beyond the scope of this book to introduce Marx's critique of capitalism. It's difficult to present Marxist epistemology, especially dialectical materialism or practice, without utilizing the concepts. I encourage readers who are not familiar with Marx to begin with *The German Ideology* and the *Communist Manifesto*.

BAKHTIN'S "DIALOGIC" THEORY OF IDEOLOGY

How can a dialogic theory contribute to an understanding of epistemology? Ideology for the Bakhtin Circle was not necessarily used in a negative or pejorative sense (unreal or false). Vološinov and Medvedev suggested there were different domains or regions of ideological production (science, literature, everyday speech genres) and that each reflected or refracted reality (and other such ideological spheres) in particular ways (Vološinov, 1973). The various domains reflected both the semiotic material used in their production and the position and stance of the speakers in society (Hodge & Kress, 1988). The sign was a site of contestation and struggle. Ideology for the Bakhtin Circle was broadly construed as any "signifying practice or meaning endowing activity" (Gardiner, 1992, p. 71): "The ideological sign is not autonomous, but connected to wider social contradictions and the dynamics of revolutionary historical change" (Gardiner, 1992, p. 79).

BRANCH 4-1: SEMIOTIC THEORY

Semiotics is the study of "signs," or meaning-making processes. Originally, "semiotics" came from pathology, or the study of the signs of disease. With linguist-philosophers such as Charles Sanders Pierce and Ferdinand de Saussure, semiotics came to be understood as the study of any type of sign in society.

According to Saussure, a linguistic sign is composed of a concept (signified) and a sound/image (signifier).

> The linguistic sign unites not thing and name, but concept and sound/image. The latter is not a material sound, a purely physical thing, but the psychological imprint of the sound, the impression that it makes on our sense. The sound-image is sensory, and if I happen to call it "material" it is only in that sense, and by way of opposing it to the other term of the association, the concept, which is generally more abstract. (Saussure, 1966, p. 66)

Saussure's background was in historical philology, the study of changes in sounds in Indo-European languages (Hodge & Kress, 1988). Looking at how languages developed historically from Latin to French or Spanish, the very existence of different language and the variety of signifiers in different languages, Saussure concluded that "the bond between the signifier and signified is arbitrary." For example "the signified 'ox' is pronounced on one side of the border as *b-o-f* and *o-k-s* on the other" (Saussure, 1966, p. 68).

Saussure's analysis distinguished between linguistic "signs" and "symbols" because the associative bond between signified and signifier is never wholly arbitrary; it is not empty, for there is the rudiment of a natural bond between the signifier and the signified. The symbol of justice, a pair of scales, could not be replaced by just any other symbol, such as a chariot....

The word *arbitrary* also calls for comment. The term should not imply that the choice of the signifier is left entirely to the speaker (we shall see below that the individual does not have the power to change a sign in any way once it has become established in the linguistic community); I mean that it is unmotivated, i.e., arbitrary in that it actually has no natural connection with the signified. (Saussure, 1966, pp. 68–69)

Social Semiotics

Saussure and to a lesser extent Pierce could be characterized as the founders of "mainstream" semiotics (Hodge & Kress, 1988). In contrast, social semiotics focuses on language in context in the tradition of linguistic anthropologists such as Boaz, Malinowsky, and Firth, who were critical of ethnocentric perspectives and saw their task as being in part to dispel myths of "primitive" people, cultures and languages without a written form. Halliday and Hasan (1985) pointed out that B. Malinowski first developed the term "context"—context of situation and context of culture (con = with text) to accompany his descriptions of Kirwiwinian, the language of Trobriand Islanders. Their language of navigation without the context of the situation of a fishing expedition would not make sense to a European audience. Originally he developed the system of text and context of situation and context of culture for studying "primitive" people. He later realized that text and context of situation and context of culture could be applied to European languages.

In contrast to mainstream semiotics in the tradition of Saussure, which focused on linguistic forms separate from their actual use, Halliday and Hasan (1985) developed a three-part system (field, tenor, and mode) to analyze semiotics in which the *social* placed a central role. Field refers to "what is going on?" Tenor refers to the relationships between the participants. Mode refers to the type of text—oral or written.

Hodge and Kress (1988) took Halliday and Hasan's social semiotics in an explicitly political direction by inquiring about the connection between the broader society-wide dimensions of ideology or history and language. Fairclough (1989) directed our attention to the societal relationships of power in both text interpretation and text production, which are missing from Saussure, and sender A–receiver B models. Through critical discourse analysis, we as teachers can analyze which perspectives are foregrounded in the textbooks, videotapes, and images we select (or are selected for us) in our classrooms.

Dialogics plays a significant central role in understanding the sign. Rather than conceptualizing the sign as a formal symbol or an abstraction, it is placed within the context of living people through their dialogic social interaction. Ideology (and all language) is placed within social activity and given a material basis through expression of meaning. It is always "embodied in some signifying practice or semiotic material (words, gestures, etc.) if these ideas or beliefs were to have any social efficacy whatever" (Gardiner, 1992, p. 71). Ideology is not abstract but a material force for social transformation.[7]

Another significant development of the dialogic approach to ideology is the Bakhtinian treatment of subjectivity or agency. One speaks not from some self-sufficient preconstituted entity, but through "rented" words, through the struggle between contending "voices" or discourses. There is open-endedness and possibility in the multiple meanings that are presented in the practical context of social intercourse.

Dialogic interaction does not take place free of social or historical constraints. Actual discourse is organized into "speech genres." They regulate various kinds of social activity with respect to content, linguistic styles, and compositional structure. Speech genres mediate between the larger or macro forces of sociopolitical and economic life and language:

> Not unlike Foucault's "orders of discourse" (1977), genres regulate what can and cannot be said in given situations, by facilitating certain forms of communication within proscribed limits and suppressing others. A tacit understanding of these generic forms is, of course, not innate, but learned; it is acquired like any other cultural knowledge through socialization into a particular socio-cultural environment. As reflexive social actors we eventually master (with greater or lesser degrees of success) a repertoire of practical skills pertaining to the production and consumption of a vast array of signs and messages ... such a communicative competence (described variously by Bakhtin as "apperceptive background" "dialogizing background" or "social purview" enables us to tailor a given "speech plan" in response to the relevant generic constraints and varidirectional social contexts. (Gardiner, 1992, p. 82)

This has tremendous bearings for us in TESOL and sheds new perspectives on what it means to learn a language, and to acquire the discourse, the language of social groups. Genre theories have important implications

[7]Gardiner added that Bakhtin "emphasizes the importance of the body as the site for ideological inscription and *Rabelais and his world* can in fact be read as an extended treatise on the semiotics of the body—a 'somatic semiotics' (or bawdy language) which reverses the traditional hermeneutic emphasis on the interpretation of texts of a written or oral nature" (Gardiner, 1992, p. 71).

for teaching at elementary and secondary levels as well as in English for special purposes in postsecondary education (Belcher, 2004; Hyon, 1996). Utilizing Bakhtin's speech genres and the languages of social groups provides a theoretical perspective on the nature of language that enables us to support the development and appropriation of voice in academic writing, which occurs in specific speech communities or communities of discourse. Learning through doing involves learning how to speak in the language of the Western academy through participation in specific discourse communities. For example, the Chinese theological students learned English for theological purposes by doing theology, by participating in worship services and church conferences, and by writing for theological and church publications. The genres in which we work, whether a lab report or a radio talk show, are the texts or utterances produced by living speech communities.

As Vološinov put it in his brief but important essay "Discourse in Life and Discourse in Art":

> The behavioral utterance always joins the participants in the situation together as co-participants who know, understand, and evaluate the situation in like manner. The utterance, consequently depends on their real, material appurtenance to one and the same segment of being and gives this material commonness ideological expression and further ideological development. (Vološinov, 1976, as quoted in Gardiner, 1992, p. 82)

Because of Bakhtin's emphasis on the ongoing nature of dialogism, its unfinished quality—"there is no first word nor last word," open-endedness and multiple voices—dialogism (as opposed to monologism or the authoritative voice of the Church or the State) has been seen as a valuable theoretical resource for those who want to open spaces for different voices (Greene, 1988). The Bakhtinian relational, dialogic aspect of language has been taken up by feminists, both critical and poststructural, in their quest for voices from the ground up, those that have been silenced and submerged in the critique of master narratives (Luke & Gore, 1992) This has significance for us in TESOL in teaching students who are new to the discourse community of the Western academy (Starfield, 2002; Zamel & Spack, 1998).

Bakhtin's theory of language focuses on the "doing" aspect of learning by doing. Language is not just a system, like a game of chess, to which Saussure compared it; it is a vibrant, constantly changing entity. We are born into a system of signs—none of us invented the languages we speak. We sometimes struggle with the inability of our languages to express our experiences and may "break rules" or coin new expressions. Bakhtin's theory suggests that we have an active role to play in our use of language;

our "doing" language is transformative not only of ourselves but also of the language itself.

BRANCH 4-2: MAO ZEDONG

TESOL readers in many parts of the world may be surprised to see a serious treatment of Mao's contributions to epistemology. After the ultra-left excesses of the Cultural Revolution in China, in which knowledge that was anything "feudal," "foreign," or "bourgeois" was literally burned and destroyed, many may opt for pursuit of knowledge that is "objective" and "disinterested" rather than standing for the interests of oppressed peoples. With the whole-scale market reforms that have transformed China's economy propelling her, and the dissolution of the former Soviet Union, there is cynicism concerning the failures of communism. The criminal abuses that have been carried out under the name of Marxism and socialism in many parts of the world have made many question the gap between theory and practice.

In some parts of the world, even reading Mao, Freire,[8] or Marx may make one suspect. TESOL university students and professors in certain countries live in fear of discussing anything that may be perceived as "political" and being reported on by spies. In certain countries, such as Colombia, the cost of being associated with the left leaves scholars in danger of assassination by right wing terrorists.

In addition, in the United States—unlike Mexico, Canada, Europe, Japan, or Australia—there historically has never been a strong Marxist intellectual tradition in the universities. In fact, during the 1950s there was the anticommunist McCarthy period, which continued to have a chilling effect on the ability of Marxist intellectuals to teach and publish throughout the 20th century.[9]

Although Marxists such as Freire and Vygotsky have had an impact in foreign and second language teaching and more broadly in the field of education, Marx himself is rarely cited. And yet Freire's *Pedagogy of the Oppressed* and Vygotsky's *Language and Thought* and *Mind in Society* cannot be fully understood without understanding Marxist philosophy and political economy.

Many have looked to the West to locate foundations of dialogic and critical education in ancient Greek civilization. For example, James Gee (1990)

[8]One of my undergraduate students at the University of Maryland asked if the Maryland State Department of Education knew that we were reading Freire, a communist.

[9]There was also severe repression of the Black liberation movement, which emerged from the civil rights movement. The leadership of the Black Panther Party was systematically eliminated and the COINTELPRO operations led to infiltration, disinformation, and discrediting. Leaders like Fred Hampton were shot in their beds.

traced critical literacy from Plato to Freire. Claude Goldenberg (1991) attributed the origin of the "instructional conversation" to the Socratic method. In preparing the Chinese theological students for graduate study in the United States in 1987–1988, I sought foundational sources for dialogical pedagogy in the East as well as the West. So I went to Confucius as well as Socrates, Mao as well as Freire. Attempting to wrestle with Mao, the Chinese revolution, the role of the May 4th movement, and modern and traditional Chinese intellectual thought was a way to better understand the realities of the Chinese students I worked with.

Those of us in the field of teaching English to speakers of other languages, who have been trained in Western universities, have a lot to learn from the non-Western sources of knowledge and intellectual traditions of our students. English-language learners from non-Western contexts bring rich resources to the philosophy of knowledge and ways of knowing the world (Tyson, 1998). However, their epistemologies "don't count" within transmission models of education, which equate learning English with assimilation or acculturation to the Western academy. A dialogic approach to TESOL in which students learned to represent Chinese Christians and the churches in China, through dialogue with diverse voices, enabled them to develop their own voices by being true to their own cultural context and identity. This was in keeping with their charge from the Christian Council to "seek common ground." Their pilgrimage became the occasion for many individuals and institutions to contribute to international educational exchange as well as ecumenical and interfaith relations.

At the heart of dialogic pedagogy is the view that learning is reciprocal and that we as TESOL professionals have as much to learn from our students as they do from us. There are dialogic approaches to education not only in the West, but from all over the world.

Mao Zedong's Theory of Learning by Doing

I hazard a guess that in terms of the number of people reached, Mao has made a greater contribution to mass literacy than almost any other person in the 20th century.[10] Mao's revolution was built on educating illiterate workers, peasants, and soldiers. The raising of the educational standards, health, and well-being of Chinese workers, peasants, and soldiers was a remarkable achievement, given the oppressive semifeudal and semicolonial warlord systems, natural disasters, and wars.

[10]Xu De reports that of the four titles that Mao was given during the Cultural Revolution, the one that he was said to have preferred was "Great Teacher." The other three were Great Commander in Chief, Great Leader, and Great Helmsman (Xu, 1992, p. 68).

Mao had a lot to say about education and epistemology. His theory of knowledge was integrated throughout the revolutionary movement, whether it was leading an army, increasing production, or creating literacy campaigns. He believed that illiterate peasants could become good soldiers, and could beat a professional army if they were trained. In fact, the Red Army taught soldiers to read by pasting characters on the backs of the soldiers while they marched (Snow, 1968).

Mao's article "The Important Thing Is to be Good at Learning," addressed to the Red Army, pointed out the importance of learning through *doing*: "Our chief method is to learn warfare through warfare" (Mao, 1971, p. 62). Mao emphasized that even if recruits had not gone to a military academy, they could learn to fight if they were good at *learning* while they were fighting. There was "no Great Wall" between the ordinary civilian and the soldier. Mao cited the Chinese adage, "Nothing in the world is difficult for one who sets his mind to it" (Mao, 1971, p. 62). To be good at learning was a virtue. Yet one also had to have humility. Mao contrasted a humble attitude toward learning with the "know-all":

> This most ridiculous person in the world is the "know-all" who picks up a smattering of hearsay knowledge and proclaims themselves "the world's Number One authority," this merely shows that they have not taken a proper measure of themselves. Knowledge is a matter of science, and no dishonesty or conceit whatsoever is permissible. What is required is definitely the reverse—honesty and modesty. (Mao, "On Practice," 1971, p. 71)

For Mao, knowledge came from practice: "If you want knowledge, you must take part in the practice of changing reality. If you want to know the taste of a pear, you must change the pear by eating it yourself" (Mao, "On Practice," 1971, p. 71). Significant to this was the relation between theory and practice. To Mao, "The truth of any knowledge or theory is determined not by subjective feelings, but by objective results in social practice" (Mao, "On Practice," 1971, p. 68). He acknowledged the truth of Lenin's claim, "Without revolutionary theory, there can be no revolutionary movement," but explained that revolutionary theory must be a guide to action; it was not to be applied dogmatically.

Mao's thesis that practice and knowledge reinforce each other in a dialectical progression is a practical approach to solving problems. It can be applied to entering a new culture or learning a new language. For cadres who were assigned to enter a new area and work with the people there, Mao offered a Marxist approach to getting involved and learning about the terrain or the ways of doing things in the local area.[11] Mao emphasized participation and summing up one's experiences into rational knowledge:

> As to the sequence in the process of cognition, perceptual experience comes first; we stress the significance of social practice in the process of cognition precisely because social practice alone can give rise to human knowledge.... Knowledge begins with experience—this is the materialism of the theory of knowledge. (Mao, "On Practice," 1971, pp. 74–75)

Mao identified a dialectical relationship between the perceptual and rational stages of knowledge:

> To think that knowledge can stop at the lower, perceptual stage and that perceptual knowledge alone is reliable while rational knowledge is not, would be to repeat the historical error "empiricism" ... fully to reflect a thing in its totality, to reflect its essence, to reflect its inherent laws, it is necessary through the exercise of thought to reconstruct the rich data of sense perception, discarding the dross and selecting the essential, eliminating the false and retaining the true, proceeding from the one to the other and from the outside to the inside, in order to form a system of concepts and theories—it is necessary to make a leap from perceptual to rational knowledge. (Mao, "On Practice," 1971, p. 75)

Mao's understanding of the relationship between these stages of knowledge brings to language learning the importance of repeated attempts to understand and use the language to communicate. There is an understanding on the part of the learner that through the "rich data of sense perception," one will struggle to attribute meaning.

Another device characteristic of Mao is learning from models. In analyzing production, warfare, or political campaigns, Mao used positive and negative models as examples. When used with dialogical inquiry and criticism, models can be valuable pedagogical tools. If the models are used only to deposit knowledge that is a foregone conclusion, rather than as tools for discovery, they are what Freire called "banking pedagogies." Freire's notion of the teacher–student relationship emphasizes mutual discovery and exploration. In "banking pedagogies," however, the teacher discusses reality as if it is "motionless, static, compartmentalized and predictable" (Freire, 1970, p. 57). The task is to "fill" the students with the con-

---

[11]Mao's theory of knowledge is similar to the situated learning (in which anthropologists or cultural psychologists learn in situ)—with revolutionary stance, viewpoint, and method. Red Army or Eight Route Army and party cadres were instructed to stand with the people and to learn the local habits to win over local people to the Red Army. The three rules of discipline and eight points of attention included "Do not steal a needle or pin from the people," and "Replace all the doors when you go." These rules, which the new conscripts learned to read by posting the characters on their backs as they marched, enabled the idealistic ragtag Red Army to win over peasants who were tired of the piracy of warlord armies made up of conscripted soldiers.

tents of the teacher's narration: "Words are emptied of their concreteness and become a hollow, alienated, alienating verbosity. The outstanding characteristic of this narrative education then, is the sonority of words, not their transforming power" (Freire, 1970, p. 57). Students are receptacles and education is the act of depositing. The teachers are the sole source of knowledge. The authoritarian teacher–student relationship mirrors other oppressive relations in society.

If, however, models are used with genuine dialogue, teachers and students will learn from each other. Similarly in politics, the revolutionaries will not only teach, but learn from the masses or what Mao calls "mass line": from the masses to the masses. If the approach is only *to* the masses, the approach is not transforming, but is dominating. If the approach is only *from* the masses, the approach is similarly not transforming, but is backward or "tailing" of the masses, rather than providing leadership.

Finally, Mao's theory of knowledge addresses the question "knowledge for whom?" (discussed in chap. 5). There is no such thing as "knowledge for knowledge's sake"; knowledge must serve the masses, not the exploiters and oppressors:

> Our literary and art workers must accomplish this task and shift their stand; they must gradually move their feet over to the side of the workers, peasants and soldiers, to the side of the proletariat, through the process of going into their very midst and into the thick of practical struggles and through the process of studying Marxism and society. Only in this way can we have a literature and art that are truly for the workers, peasants and soldiers, a truly proletarian literature and art. This question of "for whom?" is fundamental; it is a question of principle. (Mao, "Yenan Forum on Literature and Art," 1971, p. 262)

Mao called on intellectuals to utilize their knowledge for the workers and peasants by going among them, becoming one with them and learning from them.

BRANCH 4-3: CLAIMING THE RIGHT TO SPEAK

Dialogue is the encounter between men (humans), mediated by the world, in order to name the world. Hence, dialogue cannot occur between those who want to name the world and those who do not wish this naming—between those who deny others the right to speak their word and those whose right to speak has been denied them. Those who have been denied their primordial right to speak their word must first reclaim this right and prevent the continuation of this dehumanizing aggression (Freire, 1970, pp. 76–77).

Freire talks about silencing. One of the features of oppressed people is that they can be silenced or they may not speak up for themselves.[12] Traditionally, in addressing "acculturation" and second-language acquisition, researchers have not questioned the inequitable power relations between the dominant-language group and indigenous people or immigrant groups. Perhaps as social scientists wanting to be objective, they have not chosen to question the inequalities, but only to describe them as "social factors."

An example of theorizing "social factors" without looking at the dimension of power is John Schumann's acculturation model or social distance theory (Schumann, 1976, 1986). Hermalinda Cancino, Ellen Rosensky, and John Schumann studied six Spanish speakers acquiring English without formal instruction in naturalistic settings; the two children, two adolescents, and one of the two adults all made improvement in their English. The researchers looked carefully at negation, with learners beginning with a "no" verb (reflecting the Spanish structure), which was replaced by "don't." Following a common sequence of development, learners acquired other auxiliaries, "can't" and "isn't," and finally the entire English "do-support system" including "doesn't" and "didn't" (Hakuta, 1986). Only Alberto, a Costa Rican man of 33 years old, failed to improve. For the feature that they studied, negation, Alberto's speech continued to be No + verb. His negation pattern "No go to work" was "fossilized" or didn't change.

Schumann theorized that Alberto's interlanguage did not develop further due to "social distance" between himself and the target group. Alberto was a laborer. He watched Spanish-language TV and listened to Spanish radio. He had little contact with the target language group.

Schumann developed an acculturation model based on the causal link between acculturation and second-language acquisition (SLA). SLA is just one aspect of acculturation, and the degree to which the learner acculturates to the target language group will control the degree to which a person acquires the second language. Schumann states that the model argues for acculturation and against instruction. According to Schumann, if acculturation does not take place, instruction in the target language will be of limited benefit to the language learner.

In critiquing Schumann's model, Bonny Norton (1998, p. 15) pointed out:

> The Acculturation Model does not take into account that in general, the second language (L2) group is far more vulnerable to the "attitudes" of the dominant group than the dominant group is vulnerable to them. It is the L2 group ... that (is)

[12] They are, as Jean-Paul Sartre (1966) called it in *Being and Nothingness*, "a class in itself" rather than "a class for itself."

> more invested in the relationship than the target language group. The model, in other words, does not address the fact that immigrant language learners are generally in a relatively powerless position with respect to the target language community and that their group identity, culture and values may be under siege. Specifically the model does not acknowledge that inequitable relations based on race and ethnicity may compromise attempts by the second language group to maximize their contact with target language speakers, notwithstanding the positive attitudes of the second language group.

Significant to the "target language community" is whether the language learners are perceived of as "good immigrants" (like us) or "foreigners, not to be trusted," "lazy, slow, dirty," "they breed like rats" (like them—the Other). In discussing two studies of Finnish students in Sweden (Skutnabb-Kangas & Toukomaa, 1976) and in Australia (Ilpola, 1979), Ovando and Collier (1985) attributed difference in academic achievement to differences in social status. Although Finnish and Swedish languages are more similar than Finnish and English, because Finns are discriminated against in Sweden, they did not achieve academically in schools. The processes of labeling and cultural deficit theories in the schools made them products of institutional school failure in Sweden. Conversely, they were looked on as the "good immigrants" in Australia because of the color of their skin. In comparison to the Aborigines and darker skinned immigrants to Australia, Finnish students in Australia did very well. Ovando and Collier (1985) pointed out that the critical issue in these two studies may not be "cultural-mismatch" but the differences in social status and power between Finns in Sweden and Finns in Australia.

Another example of the problem of silencing from Bonny Norton's research is Eva, an immigrant woman whose Canadian co-worker asked incredulously, "How come you don't know him. Don't you watch TV. That's Bart Simpson." Eva was silenced: "It made me feel so bad and I didn't answer her nothing. Until now I don't know why this person was important" (Pierce, 1995, p. 10).

What Norton calls the *right to speak* would be to say something like, "No I don't. Does it matter?" Or, learning that Bart Simpson is a cartoon character on a popular show, one might reasonably retort, "What difference does it make if I know or do not know who Bart Simpson is?" We all have gaps in our knowledge—even members of a culture—but the differences in power relations between the Canadian woman and Eva and the implication that "there must be something wrong with you if you don't know" were enough to silence Eva. In relating back to ESL teaching, Norton (1998, p. 16) pointed out that in English-speaking countries like Canada and the United States, as teachers,

> it is crucial that we acknowledge the inequitable relations of power between target language speakers and second language learners so that we can support learners

as they claim the right to speak. "Right to speak" refers not only to the target language, but the mother tongue.

Paolo Freire's Pedagogy of the Oppressed

Paolo Freire shared Mao's concern that knowledge be used in the service of the oppressed. In his *Pedagogy of the Oppressed*, Freire integrated Christian ("the least of my brethren") and Marxist approaches in answering the question "knowledge for whom?" In his preface, Freire stated:

> This admittedly tentative work is for radicals. I am certain that Christians and Marxists, though they may disagree with me in part or in whole, will continue reading to the end. But the reader who dogmatically assumes closed, "irrational" positions will reject the dialogue I hope this book will open. (Freire, 1970, p. 21)

Freire's work is compelling because at its core is the key to education: for humanity to become more human. Just as for Confucius selfhood is the process of becoming human, of the attainment of *ren* (*jen*), for Freire the justification for a pedagogy of the oppressed begins with the discussion of the problem of humanization. Like Mao, Freire talks about humanization for the poor and the powerless, those whose humanity is denied.

As a Marxist, for Freire the problem of dehumanization is not merely an "ontological possibility" but a "historical reality": "Within history, in concrete, objective contexts, both humanization and dehumanization are possibilities for a man (person) as an incomplete being conscious of his (one's) incompletion," (Freire, 1970, p. 28). The origin of dehumanization lies in the contradiction between the oppressors and the oppressed. It is the result of an unjust order. This contradiction can only be resolved through the efforts of the oppressed themselves:

> This, then, is the great humanistic and historical task of the oppressed: to liberate themselves and their oppressors as well. The oppressors, who oppress, exploit and rape by virtue of their power, cannot find in this power the strength to liberate either the oppressed or themselves. (Freire, 1970, p. 28)

Freire distinguishes between "true generosity" and "false charity." False charity encourages the victims to extend their hands in supplication, whereas true generosity encourages those hands to work to transform the world. The transformation must come from the oppressed and those who are in solidarity with them. Like Mao, Freire's pedagogical method is integrally bound up with the struggle for liberation:

> This pedagogy makes oppression and its causes objects of reflection by the oppressed, and from that reflection will come their necessary engagement in the struggle for their liberation. And in the struggle this pedagogy will be made and remade. (Freire, 1970, p. 33)

In the tradition of Socrates and Marx, Freire utilizes the metaphor of the midwife to describe the process of learning as an act of liberation:

> How can the oppressed, as divided, unauthentic beings, participate in developing the pedagogy of their liberation? Only as they discover themselves to be "hosts" of the oppressor can they contribute to the midwifery of their liberating pedagogy. As long as they live in the duality in which *to be* is *to be like*, and *to be like* is *to be like the oppressor*, this contribution is impossible. The pedagogy of the oppressed is an instrument for their critical discovery that both they and their oppressors are manifestations of dehumanization. (Freire, 1970, p. 33)

Like Mao, Freire appreciated the necessity of resolving contradiction not in idealistic terms, but through understanding the objective situation and working to transform it: "This solution cannot be achieved in idealistic terms ... the oppressed ... must perceive the reality of oppression not as a closed world from which there is no exit, but as a limited situation which they can transform" (Freire, 1970, p. 34). Like Mao, Freire saw that the oppressed must liberate themselves in the context of a world that is changing. Learning takes place through practice in transforming the world.

Freire on Learning by Doing

As Freire and other liberation theologians point out, *praxis* includes action and reflection: "When a word is deprived of its dimension of action, reflection automatically suffers as well; and the word is changed into idle chatter, into *verbalism*, into an alienated and alienating 'blah'" (Freire, 1970, pp. 75–76). In the dialogue that Freire would have us engage in, action and reflection are constitutive elements of *the word*, the essence of dialogue. If action is sacrificed, what results is "verbalism." If reflection is sacrificed, what results is "activism," or "action for action's sake": Either dichotomy, by creating unauthentic forms of existence, creates also unauthentic forms of thought, which reinforce the original dichotomy between theory and practice (Freire, 1970, pp. 75–76). For learning by doing to occur, there must be reflection. Reflection occurs through dialogue with other oppressed people and those who seek to end oppression. Freire considered dialogue to be the practice of freedom.

> If it is in speaking their word that humans, by naming the world, transform it, dialogue imposes itself as the way by which people achieve significance as human beings. Dialogue is thus an existential necessity. And since dialogue is the encounter in which the united reflection and action of the dialoguers are addressed to the world which is to be transformed and humanized, this dialogue cannot be reduced to the act of one person's 'depositing' ideas in another, nor can it become a simple exchange or ideas to be 'consumed' by the discussants. (Freire, 1970, p. 77)

Dialogue requires "profound love for the world and for humankind," (Freire, 1970, p. 77). It also requires humility and faith in humanity's power to "make and remake, to create and re-create, faith in one's vocation to be more fully human (which is not the privilege of an elite, but the birthright of all men and women" (Freire, 1970, p. 79). With love, humility, and faith as the foundation for dialogue, the relationship that the participants develop is incompatible with banking pedagogy.

Freire also adds that the dialogue must exist with hope:

> Hope is rooted in humanity's incompletion, from which they move out in constant search—a search that can be carried out only in communion with other human beings.... If the dialoguers expect nothing to come of their efforts, their encounter will be empty and sterile, bureaucratic and tedious. (Freire, 1970, p. 80)

Finally, for Freire, dialogue must be critical:

> Dialogue may not take place unless the dialoguers engage in critical thinking—thinking which discerns an indivisible solidarity between the world and humanity and admits of no dichotomy between them—thinking which perceives reality as process, as transformation, rather than as static entity. (Freire, 1970, pp. 80–81)

Through dialogue, the search begins for program content. Rather than the content of education being determined by the teacher, the program content is fashioned (through a dialogic process). In an interview with the French philosopher Andre Malraux, Freire explained by way of a quotation from Mao: "You know I've proclaimed for a long time: we must teach the masses clearly what we have received from them confusedly" (Freire, 1970, p. 82). Freire referred to what has been popularized in China as "mass line": from the masses to the masses. The starting point for the program content of education or political action "must be the present, existential, concrete situation, reflecting the aspirations of the people" (Freire, 1970, p. 85).

By rooting the content of education in political action of the masses, Freire places the quest for knowledge at the service of transforming the world. Theories are developed and refined through trial and error. It is not easy to acquire that knowledge. Making mistakes is inevitable. But as Mao said, "The important thing is to be good at learning."

BRANCH 4-4:
ON LEARNING LITERACY BY DOING

Dialogic approaches to TESOL stress that learning to listen, speak, read, and write is interactive and interconnected (Belcher & Hirvela, 2001). Students must develop a sense of audience and must learn to anticipate the questions of their interlocutors. Learning the conventions of academic discourse and establishing intersubjectivity between a writer or speaker and an audience have been described with the metaphor of "joining the literacy club." In gaining entrance to the club, it is important that students not be forced to leave their language behind. This is a cultural as much as a linguistic issue. For us in TESOL, developing our students' voices is as important as helping them to conform to the rules of the academy. We must work on both in a process of activity, discussion, feedback, and reflection.

Throughout this book there are examples of learning literacy by doing. In chapter 2, reading and writing workshops were discussed. This technique uses authentic texts and places students in situations in which they can talk, listen, read, and write for real purposes; they use language to learn language. Likewise, Reading Recovery techniques are discussed in chapter 3. Reading Recovery offers students multiple opportunities to read books on their own level in supported settings and independently (Lyons, Pinnell, & DeFord, 1993). It also helps students to become aware of their own strategies for approaching texts, to be conscious of their ability to learn. Mao stated that one could learn to fight while fighting if one was good at learning while fighting. Helping students engage with their own strategies is one way to teach them to become good at learning reading while they are reading (or writing, speaking, or listening).

Many other literacy strategies can be adapted to second-language learners at all educational levels, such as whole language, classroom drama, the language experience approach, journaling, classroom publication programs, and so forth. The key ideas to learning by doing are:

- Use simple and complex models. Do this in a dialogic way, rather than telling the students a conclusion about what they are seeing. Ask what they see in the model and how it relates to what they know. Simple models might be stick-figure drawings to learn vocabulary. Complex models might be collecting and discussing letters to the editor of a newspaper as a model for persuasive writing.

- Help students learn how to learn while they are doing, to become aware of their meta-cognitive strategies. When they come across a new word, what can they do to figure it out? When they are beginning a new piece of writing, how might they get started (brainstorming, freewriting, talking with a friend, looking through journal entries, etc.)?
- Knowledge comes from practice. Give students multiple opportunities to practice in real settings. If they are learning how to use the library, visit the library several times and practice looking up and finding things.
- Remember, teaching is a dialogue, not a communiqué (see Branch 3-1: Freire and Problem Posing). Any approach, method, or teaching strategy can become a communiqué or a dialogue depending on how the teacher handles it. Questioning techniques (mentioned in chaps. 1 and 3) in which the teacher asks open-ended questions and elicits from students their interests are good starting points for creating dialogue.
- Finally, as teachers, we need to be aware of who is served by knowledge (chap. 5). A literate person has opportunities to influence the world; a nonliterate person can reach fewer people and has less of an opportunity to develop a comfortable life. The purpose of teaching literacy is to give students greater choices, which leads to humanization, in the terms of Confucius and Freire.

John Dewey on Learning by Doing

Like Mao and Freire, John Dewey saw the importance of moral education. John Dewey, who was a professor at Columbia Teachers College, considered morality to be the most important part of education. To Dewey, moral education would enable the student to develop identification with society and to develop a sense of social responsibility. The ideals of Dewey's morality included democratic values such as the opportunity to develop to one's full potential, regardless of one's background and status, and "open-mindedness," which included overcoming prejudice, pride, and selfishness.

> Both Dewey's and Mao's similar notions on the social characteristics of schooling and moral education to a large degree relate to yet another similarity in their theory—their epistemology. First, both agree that knowledge consists of experience and can only be acquired through active human inquiry in experience. Human experience as a whole can be divided into different levels. It is the higher level of experience—experience by experiment according to Dewey or the conceptual state of experience according to

> Mao—that brings the real leap in learning and acquisition. Later experience also serves a check-up for true learning and leads to further experiments, learning and growth. (Xu, 1992, p. 99)

Also similar to Mao and Freire, Dewey saw the value of reflection (Dewey, 1997). Experience in itself might not lead to knowledge nor be part of a larger moral vision of social transformation. Experience could only have educational value when there were connections drawn between the experience and other experiences. The teacher was important in guiding and challenging students to make connections between daily experiences, society and moral principles:

> The teacher will find every subject, every method of instruction, every incident of school life pregnant with moral possibility. (Dewey, 1909, p. 59, as cited in Xu, 1992, p. 46)

For experience to be educative entailed a process of reflection involving both longitudinal and lateral development. It involved an experimental approach to inquiry and the development of a scientific approach. Like Freire's "activism" action without reflection, Dewey stressed that it was "reflective experience—with thinking—not merely doing" (Xu, 1992, p. 100) for there to be any educational value in "learning by doing."

Although Dewey and Mao had similar perspectives on the centrality of "learning by doing," their starting points were different. Dewey began with "a firm belief in western science and philosophy of the relational world; Mao with a mixture of Chinese tradition and Marxism" (Xu, 1992, p. 101). Dewey and Mao answered the question, "Knowledge for whom?" differently. Dewey advocated that education should be based on Western science and was to be modeled on the Western academy (i.e., American universities in China). Education should serve society, and his vision of social progress was the newly developed industrial world and bourgeois democracy. For Mao, educational ideas reflected Marxist political ideology and focused on social and political transformation through revolutionary struggle.

The origin of the centrality of experience in their theories of knowledge may be Hegelian philosophy:

> There is one common source in their philosophy, which might explain some similarity in their notions of experience regarding the wholeness and the relational property of experience. That is Hegel, whom Dewey studied intensively, and to whom Marxism is greatly indebted, for his dialectic philosophy. (Xu, 1992, p. 101)

Maxine Greene attributed significance of the Hegelian roots of Marxists and John Dewey, who "found his philosophical maturity in Hegelian philosophy" in the "crucial connection between the attainment of freedom and the consciousness of some larger, encompassing whole" (Greene, 1988, p. 40). Dewey rejected Hegel's Absolute Spirit but kept the Hegelian view of dialectical change and development. In contrast to the 19th-century social Darwinists, such as William Sumner, who saw corruption and poverty as "natural selection" in laissez-faire capitalism, Dewey saw in Darwin a different vision of social evolution:

> A view of open-ended development enhanced by a conception of dialectical interchange that would overcome old dualisms and discontinuities.... The invention of cultures was seen as a break with natural selection. Capable of thinking and choosing, capable of communicating and transmitting valued ways of life, men and women could direct the course of future evolution. No longer subject to the repetitive patterns laid down by instinct, they could be educated to pose questions, to pursue meanings, to effect changes, to extend control. Making more and more connections in their own experience, reflecting on their shared lives, taking heed of the consequences of the actions they performed, they would become aware of more and more alternatives, more and more experiential possibilities. (Greene, 1988, pp. 42–43)

Dewey's theory of experiential education, which is connected to his vision of "a great society," is relevant to us in TESOL as we search for connections between learning by doing and intentional connections between education and transformation in society.

BRANCH 4-5: JOHN DEWEY IN CHINA

Those of us educated in the United States may be more familiar with the pragmatism of John Dewey than the Marxism of Mao Zedong. Yet there is a connection at least between Dewey and China shortly before Mao came to power. Dewey lived and lectured in China from 1919 to 1921, at a time when Chinese intellectuals and the Chinese revolutionary movement were searching for direction. Dewey became one of the most influential American philosophers in China in the first half of the 20th century before the founding of the People's Republic of China. "Learning by doing"—which in China was associated with both Mao and Dewey—was in complete contrast to traditional Confucian education and the examination systems under Imperial China. Because of the severity of China's national crisis, Dewey's progressive American educational perspectives and Western science and democracy contended with Marxism and the Bolshevik Revolution as the way forward for China's political, social, and economic salvation.

When John Dewey arrived in China, the country was divided into various fiefdoms controlled by warlords and their private armies. Foreign powers controlled parts of China, and if foreigners committed crimes, they were not tried in Chinese courts. There were signs in the parks in the foreign-controlled areas in Shanghai that said, "No dogs or Chinese allowed." The 1911 Revolution had overthrown the Manchu dynasty and the imperial system that had ruled China for centuries. But Dr. Sun Yat-sen, the founder of the Chinese Republic and leader of the Kuomintang Party, did not have control over China. In 1916, Chinese intellectuals such as Hu shih, Ch'en Tu-hsiu, Dean of College of Arts and Sciences at the Peking University, and writer Lu Hsun called for a "New Culture Movement" and a "Chinese Renaissance" (Schurmann & Schell, 1967). With the end of the emperor and China being divided, the New Culture Movement proclaimed the need to end the rule of "Confucius and Sons," which led to stagnation and feudalistic family structures that oppressed women and the young. It called for the use of vernacular Chinese instead of classical Chinese so that the people could understand and learn to read. They wanted to reform education and modernize China. The women's movement called for a wide range of demands, from the end to the practice of arranged marriages, concubines, and foot-binding, to women's suffrage and education.

The New Culture movement developed rapidly into an anti-imperialist student movement in 1919, coinciding with Dewey's arrival in China on May 1, 1919. Dewey's visit to China coincided with the May 4th Movement when Chinese intellectuals debated Chinese language, culture, and politics. This provided an opportunity for Dewey to introduce American democracy, science, and progressive educational models to China.

The May 4th movement of 1919 developed in response to the news that the Paris Peace Conference—the British, Americans, and French allies of the First World War, who had defeated the Germans—would give the Japanese the concessions the Germans had controlled in China in Shantung Province (Chow, 1960). Chinese troops had dug trenches in World War I for the allies in France, and yet rather than receiving equal treatment, as had been promised by Woodrow Wilson, China was treated as a colony of Japan and as a vanquished army. The students from Peking University suspected that the Chinese government had capitulated to the agreement, rather than standing up for what had been promised by Woodrow Wilson. There was tremendous outrage in the American betrayal because many idealistic Chinese students had seen American democracy as a model for China. This created complications for Dewey and his American educational models. Many of the students who had been inspired by Dewey's progressive messages of social responsibility became disillusioned by Western democracy and inspired by the Bolshevik Revolution. Could China also have a successful revolution like the Bolsheviks?

Russia under the Czar was called a center of "Oriental despotism" and was considered, like China, to be backward. Some Chinese revolutionaries were encouraged by Lenin's teachings on bourgeois democratic revolution:

> Lenin admitted that it was unlikely a proletarian revolution could occur in colonial and semi-colonial countries in which, like China, the proletariat was weak; and he maintained that the hold of foreign imperialists must first be broken. He then advanced the argument that since the bourgeoisie was anti-imperialist, the proletariat could unite with them in the first stage of the revolution to destroy foreign domination.... Chinese intellectuals had found a Western ideology which suited China's immediate problems: China's two main enemies were the "feudal" institutions of the past and the imperialist nations, which were slowly seizing control of China's economy. (Shurmann & Schell, 1967, pp. 4–5)

Chen Tu Hsiu, Mao Zedong, and others founded the Chinese Communist Party in 1921. Chou Enlai and others in France who had also been radicalized by the Paris Peace Conference founded a branch of the Chinese Communist Party in France. Chen Tu Hsui, one of the key theoreticians of the New Culture Movement, who had been fired from his position at Peking University due to his participation in the May 4th Movement, became the first General Secretary of the Chinese Communist Party.[13]

After the establishment of the People's Republic of China in 1949, during the 1950's, the Chinese Communist Party led campaigns for land reform and collectivization; it led ideological campaigns against feudalism and imperialism. When Confucianism and Hu Shih, one of the intellectual leaders of the May 4th Movement who promoted Western science and democracy, were criticized, John Dewey's American pragmatism and liberal bourgeois perspectives were also criticized. This reached a height during the Cultural Revolution (1966–1976), when everything old or foreign was seen as reactionary.

Today in China there is a more open climate to reappraise the contributions of Confucius, Hu Shih, and Dewey. Rather than see them only as reactionary, intellectuals in China are studying them and finding that not only are Dewey and Mao different, but that they also have similarities. Tu Wei-Ming characterizes the Post-Cultural Revolution current appraisal of Dewey, Mao, and Confucius as follows:

---

[13]From 1921 to 1949, the Chinese revolution developed through the Republican China period through two united fronts of the Chinese Communist Party and the Kuomintang, including the united front to oppose Japanese occupation and finally a civil war. See Snow (1968) and Belden (1970) for American journalistic accounts of the Chinese Revolution. For an introduction to modern Chinese history through literature, read Pa Chin's *The Family* and Han Suyin's *A Many Splendoured Thing, The Mountain is Young, The Crippled Tree*, and *A Mortal Flower*.

> Prior to the Tiananmen (The Gate of Heavenly Peace) tragedy in June 1989, the fruitful interaction among three newly emergent currents of thought—democratic liberalism, Confucian humanism, and Western Marxism—had generated unprecedented vitality of the Chinese intellectual scene for almost ten years. The spirit of reform since 1979 encouraged freedom of thought and freedom of expression. An upsurge of interest in liberal democratic ideas prompted an overall reevaluation of Hu Shi. This created new possibilities for representing Dewey's pragmatic insights to a Chinese audience. Ingenious attempts to study Mao's traditional roots offered fresh perspectives on Mao's indebtedness to Confucian humanism. (Tu, 1992, pp. ii–iii)

We in TESOL have a lot to learn from the educational philosophies of Confucius, Mao, and Dewey in developing an understanding of dialogic pedagogy. Their theories must be understood within the social and historical context in which they wrote, as well as in our own TESOL contexts today, whether in China, the United States, Venezuela, Saudi Arabia, or Italy.

LEARNING BY DOING: THE PILGRIMAGE CURRICULUM

One of the methods employed throughout the Pilgrimage Curriculum for the Chinese theological students was to "learn how to do theology by doing theology." They interacted with theological language by attending classes at Union Theological Seminary, reviewing videos of lectures, attending worship services (including from different faiths), going to church conferences, and reading theological texts. They learned word processing. The students developed their English language proficiency by speaking and writing with real audiences. They prepared articles for publication in church journals and speeches for conferences.

Academic papers and conventions were approached through a problem-posing methodology consistent with the idea of learning through doing, using models, and summing up lessons to become more professional language learners. For example, students attended academic presentations on the church in China and developed a critique of positive and negative models of scholarship. Through this discussion, the teacher and students developed criteria for academic excellence. Academic conventions, such as footnotes, were approached with a person who had just finished writing a dissertation, and by editing real academic papers using academic style sheets and manuals.

When I interviewed Zhang Xianyong after he had begun his work in graduate school, I got feedback from him on how well the curriculum had met his needs. Zhang Xianyong stressed the cultural preparation over the linguistic preparation:

> I think I still regard my one semester in New York City to be very valuable. As I told the Theological Education Committee before, I regard the linguistic component as secondary. Clearly the cultural component, adaptation was the primary part of the experience. Of course it is difficult to distinguish between linguistic and cultural, because language is also a part of culture, and in learning a language you are also becoming familiar with the culture.
>
> In particular the access to computers, the libraries and lectures while I was in New York City, were an important part of the experience which I found to be helpful in my further theological studies.[14]

This response indicated the value of immersion in another culture. There is a qualitative difference between reading about life at Columbia University and experiencing it first hand. In fact in New York City, all three students were "students," *xue sheng*, in that they "learned" (*xue*) from "life" (*sheng*).

In general, the field of English as a second language is committed to the importance of practice in language learning and integrating hands-on experiences with speaking and writing. Experiences of learning English through the use of jazz chants, dance movements, and "Simon Says" are a part of elementary school curricula and standard in many adult education programs and university language classes. Although this kind of active learning is standard, the experiential aspect of language learning should not be taken for granted and is critical to dialogic pedagogy.

Gao Ying looked back on her preparation critically. We had had a few lessons on how to use a library using exercises from study skills books, but we didn't practice by physically using the card catalogue or going through the stacks. Gao Ying felt that she needed more practice in how to use a library and how to write a research paper. Exercises are not the same thing as real life, they are not like "eating the pear itself."

English for Academic Purposes

The first semester we introduced American culture; the second semester focused on English for academic purposes, specifically, English for theological purposes. The readings, videos, speakers, trips, and lessons during the first semester concerned American culture. However, many materials used to introduce American culture were ecumenical church publications, for example, the National Council of Churches of Christ policy statement on Native Americans, and a book from Church World Service on

[14]Zhang Xianyong, interview with author, June 19, 1988, at Stony Point, New York, tape recording, after he had completed a semester of graduate studies at Lutheran Theological School of Chicago.

immigration (see Appendix). Attending English-language worship services, particularly hearing sermons, was good preparation for listening to theological lectures in seminaries. Finally, we began work with word processing and using library computers and video machines and tapes the first semester. Li Yading went to the Teachers College Library weekly to watch video movies to improve his listening comprehension. Although a movie like *The Godfather*, as well as the other movies he watched, might not be academic English, it helped his overall listening comprehension and enabled him to better understand lectures.

During the first semester, the students' American Language Program schedules did not permit us to audit a class at Union Theological Seminary; however, the students attended lectures. At Union we heard Phyllis Tribble lecture on feminist interpretations of the Bible. I took notes and went over them with the students after the lecture. On their own, they weren't able to catch much of what she was saying. At Teachers College they heard Shirley Brice Heath, the author of *Ways with Words*, and a panel, "Forty Years of Neglect: Experiences of Puerto Ricans in New York City Schools," which included Maria Canino, from the Board of Regents of the City University of New York (C.U.N.Y.), Isaura Santiago-Santiago, the President of Hostos, and Diana Caballero, a community activist. They heard Paulo Freire, who was a guest speaker in Maxine Greene's class. At Columbia they heard lectures on China. At the Interchurch Center, Franklin Woo initiated a lecture series of China scholars. Our dialogue and critique of the various lectures became the basis for us to pose the question, "What is good scholarship on China?," and to discuss criteria of what constituted good scholarship on China.

Zhang Xianyong, the former English teacher, was able to not only understand, but participate in discussions over the content of the lectures he attended. Gao Ying and Li Yading were able to understand little of the lectures unless the topic was on China, when they could use their background knowledge. I remember when Li Yading was so pleased to be able to follow for the first time the main points of a discussion on China at Columbia. He said that because he could anticipate what they were going to say and he was familiar with the terminology, he could understand most of what was said. Gao Ying understood only some of the points, because her vocabulary was more limited than Li's.

The second semester, with Zhang Xianyong off to the Lutheran seminary, we focused on English for theology. This did not mean that we abandoned the study of American culture; rather, cultural questions came up in the context of discussions over the theological lectures. We were advised to audit Professor Christopher Morse's Fundamentals of Christian Theology class. The course was recommended because Morse's lectures were organized, challenging, and stimulating. The students and I found Professor Morse's lectures to be the most worthwhile part of our spring curriculum.

Professor Morse and Dean Gatch of Union Theological Seminary graciously allowed the students to audit and me to videotape each lecture. The class consisted of about 60 students; it was a required course for all master's of divinity students. The course was not a "catechesis"; Professor Morse stressed in the first session that students would not be penalized for their beliefs. He recognized that there were probably as many as 30 different confessional traditions in the class and hoped that the course would enable each student to come to terms with her/his own tradition in becoming familiar with major, formative doctrines of systematic theology.

Each week I videotaped the lecture (which we all attended) in the morning and then we replayed it at our afternoon tutorial sessions. The goal was for the students to be able to take notes of the main points of the lecture. We used the videotape to work on new vocabulary and to listen for and talk about the key points and key words. We also worked on reading and discussing the assigned readings. Finally, with the help of Brenda Sansom, who was writing her dissertation in Chinese history, we had sessions on study skills, library research and the format of research papers.

Working With Videotaped Lectures

The videotapes were not a substitute for attending the lectures. Presence at the lectures was important to the learning experience. I encouraged the students to get to know other students in the class, to talk to the teaching assistant, and to attend the study sessions. One of the students in our seminar made copies of her "Utrum" paper, written in the form of a medieval proof, so that the students could see how argumentation and counterargumentation were presented. Over the semester Li Yading became friends with a Chinese American student in the class and discussed with her the lectures and readings.

By attending the lecture and then having an opportunity to listen to it again, students were able to understand more, simply from repetition. It was highly motivating to work with the videos. The lectures were not only in theology, the students' own field of study, but were given by an eminent professor at an internationally known academic institution. The students knew that the concepts they were discussing and the vocabulary they were learning would help their future studies. They were indeed "learning warfare from warfare." At first I photocopied my notes for the students to use in outlining and discussing the main points of the lecture. Later they worked from their own notes. Learning how to take notes in a foreign language is important because one's memory is not as strong as it is in the mother tongue. Li Yading commented that even if he thought he understood what was being said, he could not recall it afterward.

Our weekly procedure in the tutorial session was to begin by my writing down on newsprint key terms from the lecture that I thought might be new vocabulary items for the students. We practiced the pronunciation of the terms and translated them into Chinese. Here are examples of vocabulary selected from the lecture by Brenda Sansom:

Brenda: The first one.
Li: Antithetical. Antithetical.
Brenda: Right. Antithetical. Professor Morse said, "We face in our own lives forces that are *antithetical* to God's love and freedom."
Li: Antithetical is ... how to say ... uh ... something contradict with God's will or love.
Brenda: Okay. Contradiction. Or we would say contradictory.
Li: Yes. Contradictory.
Brenda: Or opposed?
Li: Yeah. Opposed.
Shelley: Opposite?
Li: Yes. Opposite.
Brenda: Is that clear?
Li: Yes.
Brenda: What about the next one?
Li: Onslaught.
Brenda: Wait a minute. What do you think, Gao Ying?
Gao: Uh.
Brenda: I'll read the sentence: "Creation is under a constant *onslaught* from the forces that are antithetical to God's love and freedom." Creation is under a constant *onslaught* from these forces. Onslaught. Anybody else? Creation is under a constant *onslaught* from the forces that are antithetical to God's love and freedom.
Li: This word seems familiar.
Brenda: Onslaught would be like an attack. A constant attack.
Li: Oh. Yes! Attack.
Brenda: A constant attack.
Li: Yes or occupy.
Brenda: Yeaaaaaaaaah. (intonation indicates conditional approval or that she's not totally in agreement)
Li: Or assault.
Brenda: Yes. Assault.
Li: Yes. In *The History of the Jews* they often use this word.
Brenda: So you could say during the Anti-Japanese War in China, the Chinese Communists faced an *onslaught* from the Japanese army.
Li: Yes.

Gao: Um hum.
Li: And in a war if an army want to overtake a city you often use this word.

Within the context of "learning by doing," Brenda used a problem-solving approach, giving students a context to see if they could figure out the meaning of the word "antithetical." A "banking pedagogy" approach at this point might have been to present the words and their definitions. Instead of attempting to fill the students' heads with vocabulary, Brenda helped them to work with context in order to figure it out for themselves. When students could not figure out "onslaught," she gave them the definition, but she also gave them time to remember other contexts in which they had seen the word. She also saw to it that both students participated.

After going over the words that Brenda had selected from the lecture, she asked the students if they had any questions about vocabulary. They did, but were unable to say the words they didn't know. Gao Ying suggested that her questions would best be dealt with later, as we listened again to the videotape.

Our typical routine was that after going over some key terms from the lecture, I would ask the students to tell me the main points of the lecture, which I would write in outline form on newsprint. Some lectures lent themselves more to outlining than others:

Brenda: What was the topic of the lecture today?
Gao: Why evil exists.
Li: The doctrine of salvation.
Brenda: Okay. (writes both on newsprint) And as part of the doctrine of salvation he had to discuss about the origin of evil, why evil exists. But the purpose was to go on and talk about salvation. Okay. So. What would you say he started to talk about first. Actually it was kind of difficult to come down with one, two, three.
Li: Yeah! Yeah!
Gao: Yeah, it was.
Brenda: It was really kind of ... well ... in the first part what were the main things he talked about? The main ideas? Well, before he talked about Rachel, what were the main things he said in his introductory part?
Li: He just talked about God is a good creator. Talked about the creation of God and all of these creations is God let everything be. And uh, he also talked about the cross.
Brenda: Yeah, what about the cross?
Li: Cross improves all the life and destiny of Jesus Christ.
Brenda: What did you say?
Li: The cross or crucifixion includes all the life and destiny of Jesus Christ.

Brenda: So how is that significant? What does that mean?
Li: This meaning is the salvation of Jesus Christ is God's plan of eternal salvation.
Gao: Through the cross God reveals the reality of God. God with us.
Brenda: Well, this is what I got from it: that because the cross contains the whole life and destiny of Jesus, the fact of the crucifixion demonstrates that the reality, that God in Jesus was under attack within the good creation. So it demonstrates how much evil there is within the good creation. Because God himself suffered …
Li: Um hm.
Brenda: … and died within the good creation. That the cross demonstrated the extent of evil in the world that God suffered. So the cross is a symbol of the power of death and evil within God's good creation.
Li: Yes.
Shelley: Gao Ying, you got the first part, the cross reveals the reality of God and then the rest of it is "under attack."
Gao: Oh, *under attack*. I wrote T-A-C.
Shelley: Attack.
Gao: Attack.
Shelley: That's good you almost got it. And then "within the good creation."
Brenda: Any other points?
Li: Following that he talked about Christian hope.
Brenda: Christian hope.
Li: Yeah, Christian hope.
Brenda: What did he say about Christian hope?
Li: He talked a lot about Christian hope. Christian hope in early church. And he quoted from Romans 14.
Brenda: What did he say about it? What is the nature of Christian hope? Is it like the world's hope? Ordinary hope? Or is it different from ordinary hope?
Gao: He raises two questions. One of them is for Jewish. For Jewish?
Li: Yes. Two traditions.
Gao: For Jewish, why Mee-ziah [Messiah] doesn't come. And for Christianity, why the Mee-ziah has come, the world is … not the best world, since Mee-ziah has come.
Shelley: (as Brenda writes) Messiah. (pronunciation)
Gao: Messiah.
Shelley: Messiah.
Gao: Messiah.
Shelley: The Messiah.
Gao: The Messiah.
Shelley: Messiah. Why doesn't the Messiah come.
Gao: Why doesn't the Messiah come.
Brenda: So that's the Jewish question: If the world is so bad, where is the Messiah?
Gao: Yeah.
Brenda: And the Christian question, have you got that?

Gao: Why since the Messiah has come, the world is not changed a lot (laughter) something like that. I understood the meaning.
Shelley: That's clear.
Gao: From my original note. For Christianity since the Messiah has come, why is the world in this condition?

Working in this way allowed us to address listening skills specific to hearing a lecture but also other language skills such as pronunciation. Using language in an authentic context does not mean that basic skills are neglected; rather, they are addressed as they arise. Further, we could assess students' skills, such as recognizing that Gao Ying was improving in her ability to understand by reading the notes she made during the lecture.

We worked by playing a section of the video tape at a time, then stopping to outline the main point. We could stop and hear a particular section over and over. This was helpful not only for getting the main points of the lecture, but also for listening for specific information. For example, frequently Professor Morse would make a Biblical citation. It was important for the students to learn how to listen for and jot down Biblical passages so they could look them up.

The students could ask me to stop the tape when they came to a term with which they were unfamiliar. It's difficult for the learner of another language to pick out a new word from a stream of speech unless the word is used over and over again. Video afforded us the means to identify those new words so that I could write them on paper for the students to learn.

Finally, by stopping the video, I was able to give background information and cultural asides. For example in his lecture on eschatology, Professor Morse made a reference to the film *The Day After.* I stopped the tape and explained that it was a fictionalized account of what happens to a family the day after a nuclear bomb is dropped. Whenever Professor Morse made reference to people or places or made a joke, we could stop the tape, explain, and go on.

Often the point of a lecture would be missed, because the students couldn't understand a key word, or an important name, such as "Rachel." While Li and Gao were familiar with Biblical stories in Chinese, they were not used to talking about them in English, and the confusion over proper names led to some mistakes in their rendition of the Biblical stories. For example, if he were speaking Chinese, I don't think Li would confuse Joseph with Rachel's youngest son, Benjamin, as he did in English.

Brenda: Well, what was it? Who is Rachel?
Li: Rachel is, in Genesis, Rachel is the mother of Joseph ...
Brenda: and the twelve tribes of Israel.
Li: Yeah, yeah. Joseph and Joseph is the youngest son.

Shelley: Joseph with the coat of many colors?
Li: Yes, many colors and he was sold to Egypt and Jacob and Rachel was very sad about this youngest son.

Gao was having trouble with the Biblical proper names in English and tried to figure out who was being talked about by asking:

Gao: His father tried to kill him?
Li: No, his brothers tried to kill him.
Shelley: How did Rachel die? Do you remember?
Li: Rachel died because his, how to say that, after he give birth to Joseph he died.
Shelley: Benjamin, the youngest brother.
Li: Oh, yes, Benjamin. Yes, Benjamin.
Shelley: The youngest brother. So she died in *childbirth.*[15]
Li: Yes. I don't know how to say.
Shelley: Childbirth.
Li: Childbirth.
Shelley: She died having a baby.

After a lengthy discussion of who Rachel was and why she was mentioned in connection with Christ's birth, Gao Ying was able to repeat Professor Moore's point:

Gao: In theology we must be very careful ...
Brenda: be careful to what?
Gao: not to pretend to know what we don't know.
Li: Good!
Brenda: Good! Not to give easy answers.
Gao: Um hm.

Sometimes students had problems identifying familiar words because they were slurred together:

Morse: there are such depths of evil in the world. To the question why couldn't God have created things without this annihilating opposition I will throw out some of the answers that have been proposed in the history of philosophy and theology, but I say at the beginning I find none of them persuasive and none of them convincing.
Gao: Nunovum? Nunovum? What's the word? Nunovum?

[15]This tutorial session on April 7, 1988, took place a week before I gave birth to my baby. The fact of my pregnancy lent a weighty authority to what I was saying concerning death in childbirth. Cantonese old ladies would say, "Daih gat lai sih!" (Yale Cantonese romanization) an exclamation to ward off bad luck.

Brenda: None of them. (writes on newsprint)
Li: None of them.
Gao: Oh. None of them.

After Brenda paraphrased Morse, Gao was able to say, "Not powerful to explain."

We attended Professor Morse's class each week and worked with the videotapes for at least 2 hours per week. Li and Gao both felt that this was one of the most valuable activities of the spring semester.

Speaking on the Church in China

As the first students to be sent from Chinese churches to study in American seminaries since 1949, the students were called on to speak to churches, meetings, and conferences almost as soon as they arrived in New York. The students' dialogue with American Christians, as well as Christians from other countries, was important to their pilgrimage. As Li wrote after attending his first conference in the United States:

> I regarded this conference as a good opportunity to learn, to broaden my outlook, to enhance understanding, to make friends, and also to be able to improve my English. Thanks be to God's grace, He's done far more than all that I asked for or thought. And I did experience "How good and pleasant it is for brothers and sisters to dwell together in harmony."[16]

Li's experience in talking to Americans at the conference represented a breakthrough for him in his language development and adjustment to the United States. Written reflection represented further dialogue with Americans, an American readership:

> There are some words in the documents of the conference: "We believe that language is a key to understanding and shaping people's perceptions of themselves. Language is formative.... Our language about God is crucial: it clarifies and colors our views of how God relates to us." Yes. I believe this also. The days of the conference I used the most language and I did the most talking. Beside participating in the plenaries and discussing in groups, I had a lot of time to meet with friends who came from Japan, South Korea, the Philippines, Brazil and Taiwan.[17]

When I told the students that I hoped they would have the opportunity not only to meet people and attend conferences but to speak at confer-

[16]Li Yading, "In the Sound of Jubilee," January 5, 1988.
[17]Ibid.

ences, Gao Ying told me she had been invited to speak at a conference in March. I was delighted and suggested that she start working on her speech immediately and that we could polish the speech for publication. Gao Ying wrote a speech for the Asian Women's Theological Conference in March at Union Theological Seminary.

The Asian Women's Theological Conference was a day-long meeting of about 20 women, including four speakers, all of whom were graduate students or recent graduates from East Coast seminaries. One was a Korean American counselor who spoke about the role of the family and the church in separation and divorce in the oppression of immigrant women. She discussed a woman who was abused by her husband who was a leader in his church. Another Korean woman analyzed an experimental women's church in Korea. A Chinese American woman spoke about discrimination that she faced working as a minister in a hospital. Gao Ying spoke about women in the Chinese church.

I had suggested that she open by acknowledging that she was in a room of pioneers and asking the women to clap for themselves. Gao Ying was shocked at my suggestion. It violated Chinese standards of humility. She felt it was presumptuous to ask the women to applaud their own efforts, as she would be applauding herself. Instead, her speech opened with an expression of solidarity:

> I'm very honored to be able to participate in this Asian women's theological conference. It's a very special time for us as Asian women theologians to come together for reflection and sharing. There are not very many Asian women ministers and theologians and so the time we have together is very precious.[18]

She then introduced her remarks by stating the format. Her introduction clued the group to her topic and prepared them to listen actively. In preparing for the presentation, Gao Ying and I anticipated that many of the women would be hearing about the church in China for the first time and might have misconceptions. Although her topic was "Women Christians and the Protestant Church in China," she began by giving background information about the recent history and current statistics of the church.

Gao Ying then turned to the subject of Christian women, opening by discussing the gains that have been made by women in the church. She talked about the special role of women pastors and lay women, which

---

[18]Gao Ying, "Women Christians and the Protestant Church in China." The text of this speech is what I transcribed from watching the videotape of her speech, delivered to the Asian Women's Theological Network at Union Theological Seminary, New York, March 1988; her speech deviated somewhat from her prepared written text.

provoked later discussion concerning the division of labor of women and men in the church. Her discussion of religious freedom in China also stimulated questions in the discussion to follow. She then talked about the discrimination that women still face in the church and concluded by asking for the women's prayers and support. Gao Ying read her speech in a clear voice and with good pronunciation. As soon as she finished, questions were raised immediately:

Q: I have a question. I have heard that in China Christians are having disadvantages politically. But you mention now religious freedom. When did it change? They say if you are Christian you cannot be a government official, is that true?
Gao: It doesn't mean that. It means if you become Christian you won't be allowed to be a member of the Communist Party.
Q: But in your country, it means a lot. Isn't that true? If you are not allowed to be a member of the ruling party, the Communist party, you are discriminated very badly. Is it a big disadvantage?
Gao: I'm sorry. I don't understand your question.
(Jean Woo translated the question for Gao Ying.)
Gao: Oh, thank you. They can become members of … not party—*jing xie* …
Jean: the Chinese People's Consultative Congress, the consultative body to the national political body
Gao: … and also they can be members of the People's Congress. They are two organizations in China which is the Chinese People's Consultative Congress and the People's Congress.
Q: What's the difference? Can Christian be prime minister in China?
Gao: Prime minister?
Jean: They don't have a prime minister in China.

There was laughter from all the women. At this point, Kwok Pui-lan, a doctoral student at Harvard Divinity School, who was writing her dissertation on women Christians in China, made an explanation of the Chinese political system. She pointed out that because they were a one-party system, the Communist Party was extremely influential.[19]

Another woman commented that it seemed as if the Communists had supported equal work with men. Her question was whether the Communism had helped people be more aware of the need for equality for the sexes. Gao Ying was able to follow and respond to the questions with some help from Jean. One technique that Gao demonstrated in fielding

[19] I learned later from the students, after we replayed the videotape, that technically Kwok was wrong in stating that China was a one-party system. There are actually seven or eight political parties in China. But substantively, Kwok was right that the Communist Party was extremely influential in the government.

questions was that she interpreted and rephrased questions to try to reach her interlocutor. Although Gao Ying didn't understand all the vocabulary, she was able to keep up her side of the conversation, a substantial change from that early session with Dr. Franklin Woo (discussed in chap. 1).

We listened to the videotape of Gao Ying's presentation in class. Looking critically at the tape, Gao realized that she needed to be able to say "National People's Consultative Congress." She also noted that in response to the questions of political rights, she should have stressed that Christians were *citizens* of China. The students pointed out that Kwok was wrong, China was not a one-party system. They also felt that a description of the kinds of discrimination that Christians face at the local level would show the gap between the policy of religious freedom and the reality of cadre at the local level that might still view all religion as backward and reactionary. A viewing of the videotape helped to improve Gao Ying's comprehension of the questions, and also helped her anticipate how to answer questions in future workshops or gatherings.

After the Asian Women's Theological Conference, Gao began to work on a speech that she would deliver to the Presbyterian Women's Conference at Purdue in the summer. The format would be very different: Gao would be given only four minutes to speak before an audience of over five thousand people. There would be no opportunity for discussion.

In preparing for the speech, I suggested that Gao consult with others to get their opinions about what she should say. Li Yading suggested that she make a comparison with the past because it seemed there were very few who understood the historical context. Franklin Woo suggested that she speak about her own opinion and experience. Jean Woo volunteered to edit the speech. She had prepared presentations to the Purdue gathering about the church in China before and knew the audience. Not only did "learning by doing" push Gao Ying to perfect her written and spoken language, it also offered her opportunities to learn from many people as she made her preparations.

After Gao Ying wrote and edited her speech, she asked me to read it into her tape recorder so that she could listen to my voice and practice her speech for pronunciation and intonation. She needed to be able to read her speech in a slow and clear voice so that the large audience would understand her. If the speech were too long, she would be forced to read too quickly to keep to the time limit. We timed the speech and made cuts to keep the speech under four minutes. I didn't get a chance to ask Gao Ying about how her speech went at Purdue until I saw her the following winter:

Shelley: How did the speech at Purdue go?

Gao:	Not anything particular or exciting. It was very short and I got a couple of reflections.
Shelley:	Comments?
Gao:	Comments from other people who said they enjoyed my story.
Shelley:	Were you nervous with 6,000 people?
Gao:	Not because of people, because of English. I didn't have confident[ce] of my English pronunciation. If I spoke in Chinese I wouldn't be nervous at all.
Shelley:	Were you at a table?
Gao:	No, separate folding chairs.
Shelley:	Did they have a spotlight on you?
Gao:	I couldn't see the audience. They could see me. Still some words I couldn't pronounce properly so they couldn't catch.[20]

Some students from San Francisco Theological Seminary asked her to tell her story to a smaller group on campus. It was better because there was reaction from the audience and dialogue. They then asked her to submit her story, which they published in the campus newspaper titled, "My Name Is Gao Ying." Gao thought their title was funny.

As Gao and Li went to seminaries in Chicago and San Francisco, they continued to build bridges between themselves and Christians from all over the world at international gatherings. They each visited more American churches, where they often were called on to speak. This involved getting to know their audiences or readers, and finding out their questions. It also meant reflecting on what is Chinese and what is American, illuminating the universal through particular examples. When Gao Ying spoke about the special role of women pastors in nurturing and caring for women, one of the conference participants exclaimed, "Universal!" It was a statement of solidarity between women.

CONCLUSION: FROM THE SHADOW TO THE SHADE

One of the contradictions in learning a foreign language is that there is a tension between use of simplified and authentic materials, from classroom language to natural spoken language or "immersion" in the foreign language. How do we move from exercises and scripted dialogues to actual *dialogue* in another language? The ESOL language classroom provides a safe place where beginning students can concentrate on "language learning" at their linguistic level.

[20]Gao Ying, interview with author, Gao Ying's apartment in Berkeley, California, January 15, 1989.

A dialogic curriculum gives students opportunities to engage in dialogue with voices from outside the class—learning from diverse voices is critical to the dialogic approach. The anthropological task of "making the strange familiar and the familiar strange" is part of cross-cultural experience, through reflection, discussion and writing, and further reflection. Not all cross-cultural experiences are comfortable. And language learning does not proceed in a straight line, but through twists and turns. Culture shock cannot be, nor should it be, eliminated. But the dialogic classroom mediates the experience. The dialogic feature of "learning by doing" enables students to learn languages by experiencing language use in interaction with a variety of speakers or by participating in a variety of authentic contexts. Within various speech contexts there are predictable events which students can plan for—even in "authentic" contexts, not all speech is spontaneous. Preparation is an important part of dialogic pedagogy or inquiry.

Attending the lectures in Christopher Morse's class was an example of "learning by doing." The course was similar to those that the Chinese theological students would take when they enrolled in graduate schools. However, "learning by doing" also includes a dialectical, recursive process of using "life" to teach "language." Recording actual language and using the recordings in the tutorial enabled me to get to know my students and to assess the difficulties of comprehension—which were cultural as well as linguistic. This goes back to the first feature of the teacher getting to know the needs of the students through repeated investigation. Evelyn Hatch[21] compared language learning to gathering data and analyzing it. Just as there are data gatherers and data analyzers, some language learners tend to learn best through "gestalt," holistic exposure to the language in communication. Others tend to learn best by analyzing bits and pieces of the language. Dialogic pedagogy enables students to work on both "data gathering" and "data analyzing" through a systematic and repeated process.

Finally, in all of the activities, students were motivated to learn English because they knew that this knowledge would be used not only for their own betterment, but for the churches in China.

In representing the China Christian Council at conferences and by speaking to churches, Gao Ying and the others were conscious of their mission to promote goodwill and understanding. This is the fourth feature of dialogic pedagogy, to always ask, "Whom does knowledge serve? How can I learn to better serve?"

---

[21]Unpublished lecture in a contrastive analysis course at UCLA, 1974–1975.

When we enter a new culture and society that speaks another language, we often only see shadows, not the tree itself. Entering a new culture and learning a new language is not easy. It can be troubling and depressing. Although we may take what we think are incremental systematic steps, learning does not proceed in a straight line, but in zigzags. We may learn more about our own culture and our own histories through this experience, particularly if we spend our time in an enclave with our own compatriots. The curriculum I prepared attempted to provide an arena to expose students to a range of voices, to deepen their understanding of American culture and society. The shadow cast by the ginkgo tree takes different forms in the morning, afternoon, and early evening. Depending on the positions of where we stand and the time of day, these shadows may cast different perspectives on how we come to understand or represent the ginkgo tree.

5

Memory: Knowledge for Whom?

[Gingko improves] memory loss, brain function, depression, cerebral circulation, peripheral circulation, oxygenation, blood flow.

—Balch & Balch 1991

The ginkgo tree is apparently mentioned in the oldest Chinese herbal, Shen Non Ben Cao Jing, dating from 2800 B.C. (Michel & Hostford, 1988). Specific reference to the medicinal use of the leaves, however, does not come until 1436 (in Lan Mao's Dian Nan Ben Ciao, which recommends the external use of the leaves for treating skin and head sores, as well as freckles. The first mention of internal use of ginkgo leaves comes in 1505 in a text by Liu Wen-Tai, Ben Cao Pin Hue Jing Yao. In modern Chinese medicine, leaf preparations are recommended as "benefiting the brain" as an astringent to the lungs, and to relieve symptoms of asthma and cough.

—Del Tredici, 1991 pp. 10–11

Our dreams seek Heaven, our deeds plumb Hell. Hell lies about us in our Age: lithely we push into its stench and flame. Suffer us not, Eternal Dead to stew in this Evil—the Evil of South Africa, the Evil of Mississippi; the Evil of Evils which is what we hope to hold in Asia and Africa, in the southern Americas and islands of the Seven Seas. Reveal, Ancient of Days, the Present in the Past and prophesy the End in the Beginning. For this is a beautiful world; this is a wonderful America, which the founding fathers dreamed until their sons drowned it in the blood of slavery and devoured it in greed. Our children must rebuild it. Let then the Dreams of the Dead rebuke the Blind who think that what is will be forever and teach them that what was worth living for must live again and that which merited death must stay dead. Teach us, Forever Dead, there is no Dream but Deed, there is no Deed but Memory.

—Du Bois, 1968, pp. 422–423

WHY IS TEACHING ENGLISH A POLITICAL QUESTION?

If we taught in a world in which all students came to class healthy and with a good breakfast in their stomachs, and our classrooms were equipped with all the materials necessary for learning—art and writing supplies, copy machines and paper, computers, projectors, video cameras and audio tape-recorders, reasonably large classroom libraries, and funds for field trips and other educational experiences—then we could focus on the professional methods of our craft, such as how to make meaningful connections between various content areas or subjects, our students, and their culture(s) and language(s), and how to attend to the connections between the traditional four skills of ESL/EFL (reading, writing, listening, and speaking).

Instead, we work in a stratified system in which relatively few get the benefits of education. Classrooms and school systems reflect the larger contradictions between the haves and have-nots of the world. Our responsibilities as teachers extend beyond the knowledge we share to recognizing and doing what we can to address inequalities:

> It may, however be equally necessary to understand that one of these solutions that lie outside the classroom is the responsibility, at least in part, of the English teacher(s) since it directly concerns linguistic power relations, which are reproduced as language valued. Kandiah is quite right in saying that the best English teaching in the world is not going to change real social inequalities drastically. Yet this does not mean that language teachers are doomed to passivity or to being awns of the socio-economic system. Such a conclusion would be the ultimate alibi or intellectual and moral apathy. (Parakrama, 1995, p. 77)

English is the language of the elites, and we in TESOL hold the keys to the language with the most cultural capital and the highest status. As discussed in chapter 1, sociologists of education such as Pierre Bourdieu consider the question of resources. Who goes to the university? And how does education serve to reproduce the inequities of society?

Teachers in U.S. public schools tell me repeatedly that their teacher preparation courses, however progressive in content, never prepared them to deal with the harsh realities of children coming to school in shorts in winter or having severe dental problems (S. Wong, 1995). And yet many of our students in TESOL in the United States, Australia, and the United Kingdom are children of migrant workers, refugees, and exploited workers. Our students often spend time outside of school helping their parents earn money to keep the family together; for example, in the Washington,

DC area, middle school students may accompany their parents as they work cleaning office buildings (Wong & Grant, 1995).

In addition, because English serves a gatekeeping function, and standardized tests drive the curriculum, we in TESOL find ourselves "teaching to the test." As discussed in previous chapters, we must use learner assessment to guide our instruction (Ekbatani & Pierson, 2000) and to help our students pass writing exams, proficiency tests, reading tests, university entrance exams, and at the same time work to reform the exams (Lynch & Shaw, 2005).

BRANCH 5-1:
THE REVOLUTIONARY IMPLICATIONS OF VYGOTSKY'S WORK FOR TESOL/BE AND MINORITY STUDENT ACHIEVEMENT

Lev Vygotsky was interested in providing an understanding of human consciousness and the development of human thought or cognition and culture. Through engaging in a community of revolutionary social practice, scientific experiments, and revolutionary educational practice, he established a new theory of thought and language. He died tragically of tuberculosis at the age of 37, but his contributions as the chief architect of sociohistorical psychological theory have revolutionary implications.

The historical context in which he worked as a psychologist was the aftermath of the Bolshevik Revolution in Russia in 1917. For intellectuals to work in a period of time of revolutionary change is different from working during a period of "business as usual" during which the power structures are firmly entrenched. Although a very young man, Vygotsky became influential during a time of massive revolutionary change, when a small handful of progressive intellectuals could make a revolution and engage in a massive egalitarian social experiment. He made remarkable theoretical contributions by developing a new theory of Marxist psychology in a short period of time. These contributions would have notable implications for working-class and minority student achievement. Vygotsky was an avid reader in fields as diverse as art, the law, and psychology. He could read Shakespeare in English, and the work of 19th- and 20th-century psychologists and philosophers in French, German and Russian. He was a "Renaissance" person of many creative talents and gifts, like Leonardo da Vinci and other great revolutionaries like Karl Marx, Paul Robeson, and Mao Zedong.

Vygotsky established the first school in Russia for children with mental and physical disabilities who had never gone to school before. The education of exceptional children or children with special needs continues to be a theoretical and practical problem today. In many countries of the world—with the exception of private schools for the wealthy—there are few schools for these children. What is our attitude toward bilingual and second-language education in the education of children with developmental disabilities (Harry, 1992)? Do we take an attitude that only students who are "normal" or "gifted and talented" should learn foreign languages? What if the child is a language minority learner in English speaking countries like the United States or Australia? Do we adopt an English-only perspective because we erroneously believe that using the mother tongue will "confuse" the child? Vygotsky's perspective was that ability is not fixed, that children with development disabilities are capable of learning with social assistance, and that learning precedes development. His perspective that all children can learn and should have the right to participate in society is an egalitarian ideal still not actualized.

Vygotsky understood education as a tool for social transformation—for social emancipation and freedom from want. Today, we in TESOL can similarly view our work if we link our curriculum to practices of democratic community building and economic development. Some may question, "To what extent is Vygotsky different from other progressive educators? Don't all politicians claim to support educational opportunities for all? How can you claim that his work is 'revolutionary'?" Those are good questions. The view of education for all was actually first advanced before the Bolshevik Revolution. The manufacturers or capitalists were the first ruling class to put forward the ideal of extending education beyond the aristocracy to the masses. They extended their vision to "those with property" (although not to slaves and not initially to women). Under industrial capitalism, public education was established.

In reality, two hundred years after the French and American revolutions, there are different resources provided to public schools, depending on the location of the school. If the school is in a poor or working-class neighborhood, there will be fewer resources (books, materials, and a different curriculum) than in the wealthy suburban schools that are largely White. Working-class and minority students are systematically weeded out from making it to tertiary or higher education. Within higher education, there are different trajectories for the children of the elite, who attend the research universities where the most resources are located, and children of the working class and minorities, who go to community or technical two-year colleges. The sorting process by which students are placed in different trajectories (with a few exceptions) occurs through a number of systematic practices:

1. A Eurocentric curriculum in which white is the majority, male is the norm, and contributions of women, working-class, and racial and ethnic minority cultural values and resources are not valued, but rather seen as deficient.

2. Counseling that encourages a disproportionate number of girls and minorities away from college preparatory math and science courses, or that pigeonholes Asians into math and science.

3. Exclusionary and elitist hiring practices that continue the "old boys' network" and transmit low expectations for working-class and minority students as opposed to programs that welcome participation of families who have traditionally been excluded from the institution.

4. Transmission or banking pedagogies rather than dialogic, problem-posing, and community-building education.

5. Ideology of meritocracy, in which reproduction of inequality is justified.

Vygotsky and IQ

One of the weeding-out practices is testing, which has been mentioned in other chapters. Standardized tests come in many forms, claiming to measure attributes that change in the course of a person's lifetime (e.g., academic achievement) and attributes that are supposed to remain static (such as "intelligence"). Both achievement and intelligence tests are gatekeepers, even while what they purport to measure is dubious.[1]

The concept of IQ is suspect. When we grant unmerited value to the idea of an "intelligence quotient" represented by a number, we validate the exclusion of certain minds from the educational arena. We justify providing an impoverished (back-to-basics) education to some, and a stimulating program for the "gifted and talented" to others. As a gatekeeper, IQ testing ensures that the children of the elite go to the university and that those from working-class backgrounds do not. IQ also legitimizes deception. Because of our school system's democratic façade, people think that every child has equal opportunity because the tests are supposed to be "objective." In fact, there isn't equal opportunity.[2] These exams are both racially and class-biased. They are a more accurate measure of family income and parent education.

[1] There is also a growing industry in the United States as there is in Korea and around the world for SAT and TOEFL exam preparation. Students who have paid money to take the courses to learn to pass the exams are at an advantage over students who have no money to hire tutors or pay for private exam courses. TESOL as a field feels the effects of stratification and reproduction of social inequities in the field of education. TESOL is also influenced by the recent trends in higher education toward marketing and management techniques—the privatization and commodification of education. In private schools and elite institutions, the class size is ideal for dialogic, problem-posing education. In the schools for working-class children, the large class size and lack of technological resources, space, and textbooks make communicative, small-group work almost impossible.

[2] Look at OSU. One of the measures by which institutions are rated as being in the "top ten" is by measuring the average SAT scores (college entrance examination scores) of the incoming freshman class. Presumably if the incoming students tested at the top of the exam, the student body is superior to a group of students whose scores are worse on the exam. This sounds very logical, and a parent whose child scores 50 points more than another child will think that her/his child should enter the university.

Vygotsky critiqued the concept of IQ. He believed that it was important to measure both what a child could do independently and what a child could do with the assistance of an adult or more capable peer. What a child could do with assistance today, s/he would be able to do independently tomorrow. This approach of working within the child's zone of proximal development (the difference between what a child can do independently and what a child can do with the assistance of a more capable peer or adult) poses a challenge to a stage theory of development. The concept is revolutionary for education because it emphasizes the *social* and places the burden of education on the teachers, not exclusively on the child ("the child is not ready yet"). The *social* is essential to learning. A child learns through the interpersonal level or plane first and then internalizes individually on the intrapersonal plane.

We must develop the curriculum to challenge, to stimulate, to arouse! As teachers we bring our students from everyday concepts to scientific concepts. Vygotskian curriculum development is to move back and forth from the everyday to scientific and back again through a process of interaction and discovery. (What do we know? What do we want to know? How do we know what we know?) The role of teachers is to give students tools and strategies, to categorize, and to group. Through problem solving, we lead students to develop higher order thinking skills.

Vygotsky pointed out that science tells us that mentally retarded children have difficulty learning abstract concepts. If we design curriculum that reveres the concrete, the here and now, the children will never develop a facility for abstract concepts. The "zone of proximal development" concept challenges us to see IQ and abstract reasoning as being very social—intelligence is not fixed, nor is the level of maturation immutable. By using scaffolding to support problem solving, mentally retarded children can learn abstract concepts.

The Bolsheviks led masses to revolution under the banner "Peace, land and bread." Russia was a very poor country, like China, Vietnam, North Korea, and Cuba—all the countries that attempted to make a socialist revolution.[3] Vygotsky and his colleagues worked in a country of mass illiteracy, as did the Chinese revolutionaries. The work of Vygotsky and his colleagues must be understood within this revolutionary context. He and his colleagues were involved in literacy programs for the isolated rural ethnic groups who were for the first time learning to read. Vygotsky and Luria were asking a very important question: What does literacy have to do with cognition? The questions they struggled with are frontier questions that we need to ask in TESOL today: How can English literacy educa-

[3]The German Social Democrats who had a strong developed and organized proletariat and held seats in Parliament were the likely candidates for the revolution that Marx predicted. According to Lenin, the German Social democrats were dizzyed by their parliamentary successes and voted for war credits, instead of taking an antichauvinist, international proletarian stance to oppose German militarization.

tion—especially reading and writing, including computer literacy—be used as a tool for economic development for the masses of people, for human emancipation, rather than in the interests of multinational corporations?[4]

When I welcome students to the field of TESOL, I emphasize that we need their energy, commitment, and creativity. And there is a lot of work to do! But they must be advocates. Our programs are disproportionately itinerant, and we work in institutional arrangements that don't work and are part of the problem. The attitudes among our colleagues may not be supportive, ranging from attributing the lack of comprehension of an ESL student to willful disobedience (i.e., "She understands when she *wants* to") to a belief that because they were not trained in second language methodology that they are not responsible for a child's learning ("Teaching them English is *your* job") to "I can't deal with him" to an elitist view of "high culture" and language: "Your work is remedial, mine is teaching literature." Due to high-stakes testing, ESOL students may be blamed for pulling down the school's test scores. Schools that have high percentages of English language learners may be in jeopardy of being put under receivership or closed down.

Because of the political aspects of our work, the final characteristic of dialogic pedagogy is the question, "Knowledge for whom?" or "Whom does knowledge serve?" When we look at the larger context of our work as teachers, we can decide how to operate within our classroom. Our interactions in the classroom can blindly mimic the inequities that limit our students in the larger world. Or, those interactions can help students recognize their own worth and to find ways of requiring that recognition from others.

---

[4]In posing these questions I want to separate myself from what Brian Street calls the "autonomous" model of literacy. An autonomous model of literacy urges Third-World countries to follow the Western industrial countries. The problem is that this prescription ignores the history of slavery, colonialism, and imperialism that gave rise to the disparities in wealth and economic development between the "First" and "Third" worlds. It sees the problems of illiteracy, infant mortality, AIDS, divisions and interethnic conflict, poverty, and corruption as "African" problems, rather than in relationship with the development of Europe through colonialism (see Walter Rodneys (1982) *How Europe Underdeveloped Africa*). An ideological model of literacy that Brian Street proposed takes into account the political and economic history of the country in relationship to education and literacy. This model of literacy, as Paolo Freire and Donaldo Macedo (1985) put it, sees "reading the word" as "reading the world." Literacy involves a critical reading of subject positions and *memory* of collective experiences, the submerged histories that the ginkgo helps bring into consciousness. A theory of literacy must be class conscious (As Sartre explained a class *for* itself, not *in* itself), which involves an understanding of what Pierre Bourdieu (1991) called "cultural capital." At the same time, as we pointed out in chapter 4, there is also learning of reading strategies and memory and learning of the small "d" of discourse vocabulary, phrases, and cohesive devices.

Unpacking the question of "Knowledge for whom?" entails being (and helping students to become) a transformative intellectual—a person who challenges inequity, as Vygotsky did, for example, when he taught people with disabilities. It necessitates valuing memory: not just the ability to memorize this week's vocabulary, but rather the memory of one's mother tongue and culture. It helps us to present multiple perspectives on historical and current events, to give our students as many options as possible for them to define themselves, their culture, and their beliefs. English is a "power" language because of its role in the history of colonization. As Concha Delgado-Gaitan in *Protean Literacy* (1996, p. 32) wrote:

> Power has a different meaning beyond counter-hegemonic ends. If people discover how they self-construct cultural meanings and identities within and against the ideological frameworks of mass culture, institutional settings and discourses—then students will have the critical tools with which to act in morally responsible, socially just and politically conscientious ways against individual and collective oppression.

Our goal as teachers is to provide students with access to English and all the personal and professional possibilities that come with the ability to speak English, and to decolonize the teaching of English.

MEMORY

Advertisements attest to the ginkgo pill's powers to restore memory, alertness, and thinking. This chapter begins with a discussion of magic, memory, and language learning and then recounts W. E. B. Dubois's concept of "double consciousness," which is critical for us as language teachers for at least two reasons. First, it helps us to address the problem of language loss—a problem for indigenous students, students from former colonies, and speakers of less prestigious languages. Whether our student's home language is a powerful world language or a language on the verge of extinction, we as teachers must be concerned with memory for the home language and the new language.

Second, the concept of double consciousness helps language teachers work with and between two kinds of discourse—the "little d" discourse and Big "D" Discourse, the discourses of the oppressed and the dominant Discourse (Gee, 1990; Luke, 1995; Pennycook, 1994c). Working between two kinds of discourse involves critical readings of history, culture, and ideology. It involves comparing various genres and perspectives and reaching back to collective memories that are suppressed by dominant discourses. Double consciousness enables language learners to understand where they came from, appreciate those who went before them, and criticize "false consciousness"—those taken-for-granted views of the dominant discourse that lead to self-hatred, and being ashamed of parents and grandparents because they speak English with an accent. Double consciousness is an important concept for ethnic and women's studies that seek a multi-voiced writing of history from the grass roots.

MEMORY AND LANGUAGE LEARNING—IS THERE A MAGIC PILL?

As a junior high school student in Los Angeles memorizing vocabulary for a French quiz, I used to dream of a magic language learning pill that, if swallowed, would enable me to speak French. Later, in Hong Kong, I had a fantasy about the British red telephone booths. Just as mild-mannered reporter Clark Kent would enter a booth to emerge as Superman, I would enter one and "Poof!" emerge in my Cantonese guise. I would speak perfectly accented Hong Kong Cantonese and "pass" for a local. Instead of learning how to write 20 characters one week, only to forget 10 of last week's 20, I would be able to read 10,000 characters and all the Chinese classics that I could only read in English translation—Tang Dynasty poems, *Dream of the Red Chamber, The People's Daily*, Mao's *On Practice* and *On Contradiction*, Lu Hsun, Pa Chin, and Xie Bing Xin.[5] Similarly, as my middle school students in Hong Kong studied for the British School Leaving Certificate Examination, they consumed jars of Maggi, a Swiss chicken bouillon product, believing it had special properties for test taking.

Ginkgo pills are purported to stimulate memory; however, taking ginkgo is no substitute for the commitment involved in learning another language. The features of dialogic pedagogy we have discussed are no "magic" ginkgo pill. Learning to read and write a second language is hard work. At their best, dialogic approaches to TESOL facilitate intellectual discovery, artistic imagination, and creativity. Through the magic present in all academic fields, we in TESOL may be engaged—scientific experiment, oral histories, drama, great literature, mathematics—we can provide meaningful experiences that our students will remember their whole lives (Edminston & Enciso, 2003). But there is nothing "instant" about learning or teaching another language. There is no magic pill that will help us memorize thousands of idiomatic expressions, new vocabulary, dialogues, and texts.

---

[5]Literacy and women: The only Chinese woman author of any stature at the time was Xie Bing Xin who we met in China. She had been a teenager in the May 4th Movement and was famous for her children's books. Today I would add to my wish list of books I wish I could read in Chinese women authors like Wang Anyi and Cheng Nai Sha.

BRANCH 5-2: "WE'RE IN AMERICA, MAMA. SPEAK ENGLISH!"

Lucia: Vámonos, pues.
Maria: I don't want to go with you.
Lucia: ¿Porqué no?
Maria: Because you always talk in Spanish. It sounds stupid. When you speak Spanish, everyone knows we come from Puerto Rico. Why don't you talk to me in English?
Lucia: Tu familia habla español. Debe sentirse orgullosa de tus raíces.
Maria: English is better. All my friends speak English. Anyway, I don't understand Spanish. (Auerbach, 1995a, p. 67)

The preceding dialogue was prepared by Andrea Nash, a teacher in an ESL family literacy project in Boston to pose to parents the problem of cultural change and language loss. For language-minority parents, the challenges posed in this dialogue may be an ongoing battle. For language-minority students who live outside of a home language speech community, parents may find that maintaining the home language is a losing battle. Social forces for language loss may include pressure to speak only English by one's peer group and, sadly, by one's teachers, counselors, and school administrators.

Deficit models on the part of school personnel contribute to the problem. These models assume that language-minority children come from "literacy-impoverished home environments" in which parents do not know English and therefore cannot help their children. Elsa Auerbach critiqued the "transmission model of school practices" (from the schools—to the parents—to the children) in which curriculum developers look at the mainstream model and design curriculum to get minority parents to help their children with homework:

> The danger of this picture is that, under the guise of well-intentioned altruism, it projects a new version of the deficit hypothesis, once again bláming marginalized people for their own marginalization. As a result, it ultimately may drive away the very people it is designed to help, because it focuses on their inadequacies and prescribes solutions for them. (Auerbach, 1995, p. 69)

Dialogic approaches ask the question, "Knowledge for whom?" Andrea Nash and Elsa Auerbach ask us as TESOL educators to be critical of deficit models that all of us who were educated in the mainstream in Western universities are not fully conscious of. Part of the effort of developing double consciousness on our part as teachers is to become aware of the ideological power of English-only ideology and to propose concrete alternatives to transform our schools (Tollefson, 1991).

The dialogic approach develops a community of learners. In family literacy programs, we as TESOL educators can play a dual role, utilizing the model of "double consciousness" proposed by DuBois. On one hand, our job as teachers is to teach literacy, and we are "the experts" in the teaching of reading and writing. But there are many areas in which we know nothing, many areas in which the parents are "the experts." This is particularly true when we do not know the languages or cultural and educational backgrounds of our students. To get to know our students, we need to ask them and also, especially if the students are children, we need to ask the parents. This may mean advocating for the hiring of bilingual school personnel and working to ensure that school resources be invested in arranging for translators so that parents can fully participate in dialogue concerning their children's learning at school (Nieto, 1996).

To honor home languages and cultures, we need to bring bilingual and bicultural models into our classrooms and we need to change the climate—the culture of our classrooms, to foster respect for all languages (Reyes, 1992). It takes effort for parents to support their children's continued home language development— especially if the children are not in bilingual programs at school. Collaboration with parents entails getting to know their own educational backgrounds, their aspirations for their children, and their views of how their children learn best. Parents from diverse language backgrounds can serve as models and support for each other so that they can be better advocates for their children.[6]

Middle- and upper-class mainstream parents work hard to make sure their children are in gifted and talented programs and they work hard to insure if their children have special needs that the schools follow inclusive policies. Being an effective advocate for one's own children involves cultural capital and perseverance. The organization of parents to fight for quality education of their children enables parents to recognize that they are not alone. Dialogic approaches enable parents' creativity, ingenuity, and persistence to be supported by a community of practice.

MEMORY AND LANGUAGE LOSS

Tove Skutnabb Kangas (1988) pointed out that while there are four to five thousand languages in the world, the majority of the fewer than two hundred countries are officially monolingual. This has grave repercussions for the speakers of minority languages:

> Those individuals whose mother tongues do not happen to be official languages in the countries where they live, have to become bilingual (or multilingual). If they want to be able to speak to their parents, know about their history and culture, know who they are, they have to know their mother

[6]See Auerbach (1992) and Gail Weinstein-Shr and Elizabeth Quintero (1995).

> tongue. If they want to get a good education (which is usually not available in their own language, at least to the same extent as in the official language) and if they want to participate in the social, economic and political life of their country, they have to know the official language. (p. 10)

In the United States where there is a strong English-only social movement (Auerbach, 1995) and ideology of assimilation, language loss is a problem. Immigrant parents who are anxious for their children to learn English may not predict that their children could thereby become unable to converse in the home language. Lily Wong-Fillmore (2000) wrote about this problem, "When Learning the Second Language Means Loss of the First." Bonny Norton's case study of two immigrants to Canada poignantly expresses the problem of language loss, particularly for non-White immigrants who are seen as "foreign" and "unassimilatable" (Norton, 1998, 2000). In her study Mai, a Vietnamese woman, is contrasted with Katrina, a Polish immigrant. Mai's 8-year-old nephew and Katrina's 8-year-old daughter are seen by their third-grade teacher as having comparable English language fluency and achievement in content subjects. Katrina's daughter continues to speak Polish at home and has a close family bond. However, language loss leads to deterioration of Mai's family; there's no common language between the Vietnamese and Cantonese-speaking grandparents and the English-speaking grandchildren. Mai's nephews answer in English when spoken to in Vietnamese. To compound the problem, the children rarely see their mother because she works in the factory all the time. They are ashamed of their mother for her heavy accent. Instead of "Mommy," they derisively call her "Money." Because of the dominance of English in the world, we in TESOL must be conscious of the tragic consequences of first language loss (Kouritzin, 1999).

The memory we speak of in dialogic approaches to TESOL is not only memory for the new language, but also memory for the first language. It is what Cummins, Thomas and Collier, Wong-Fillmore, and others call an "additive" rather than a "subtractive" approach to language learning. We don't seek to replace the home language with English, but to add to the already existing linguistic and cultural repertoire of a child (Faltis & Hudelson, 1994).

BRANCH 5-3: DECOLONIALIZING TESOL

"For it does appear that the colonial experience, negative though its impact undoubtedly was in too many ways, also bestowed on the former colonies an unin-

> tended advantage from the point of view of making adequate responses to some of the important problems of our culturally highly complex and variegated modern world.... More particularly, out of the centuries of dialectical interaction between their indigenous cultures and what came in from outside, there emerged an interesting symbiotic nature and outlook, together with language codes."
>
> In the increasingly heterogenizing modern world that the different peoples and cultures are presently in the process of constructing, this would in principle equip them to make more perceptive and meaningful responses to the actual needs of this world than others who do not have this advantage. (Thiru Kandiah, Department of English Language and Literature, National University of Singapore, from Foreword to Parakrama, 1995, p. xxxv)

Thiru Kandiah pointed out that those who have been in the margins have a different perspective that is valuable. Those from the former colonies were forced to learn the language and culture of the colonial masters. The developing creole languages and language codes from colonialism have a unique contribution to make to world literature. Like Du Bois, Kandiah celebrated the dual or double consciousness that emerges from oppression:

> This allows the users of these codes, if my rhetoric might be permitted to draw on the Lankan situation I am familiar with, to access from deep within themselves Shakespeare *and* Sarachchandra, Tolkkaappiyar *and* Chomsky, Western technology *and* inherited craft skills, and so on, with a far more experienced immediacy than is possible to the users of the codes associated with the more considerably monotype Standard Average European culture (to use the Whorfian descriptor) which is home to the dominant academic centres. (Kandiah 1979/81, 1989, 1991b)

Taken one step further, it could be said that the monocultural monolingual speakers who are the most disadvantaged in the world today (Brown, 1998). We should see what we can learn from *The Souls of Black Folk.* At the top of each of Du Bois's chapters he places a few bars from the sacred music of Black people, Negro spirituals. The sorrow song "Follow the Drinking Gourd" was a code. The Drinking Gourd was the Big Dipper. The North Star pointed in the direction of freedom, for the people escaping slavery on the Underground Railroad.

> By the rivers of Babylon,
> There we sat down, yea, we wept
> When we remembered Zion.
> We hung our harps
> Upon the willows in the midst of it.
> For there those who carried us away
> captive required of us a song,
> And those who plundered us required of us mirth,
> Saying, "Sing us one of the songs of Zion!"

How shall we sing the Lord's song
In a foreign land?
If I forget you, O Jerusalem,
Let my right hand forget her skill!
If I do not remember you,
Let my tongue cling to the roof of my mouth—
If I do not exalt Jerusalem
Above my chief joy. (Psalm 137:1–6

The Negro spirituals were the slaves' responses to the question posed by the Jewish slaves held captive in Babylon and forced by their captors to sing a song of Zion: "How shall we sing the Lord's song in a foreign land?" Signifying is one example from African American talk or spoken English (Lee, 1993). In signifying, there are simultaneously two messages: one for the master and one for the Black community (Gates, 1988). We as TESOL educators can take the view of creoles, vernaculars, the speech of the natives and the oppressed as worthless, bad language, and having nothing to teach us. Or we can take the position of Du Bois, Thiru Kandiah, Carol Lee, and Henry Louis Gates, Jr., so that all students, especially those from the monocultural centers, can learn from diverse languages and cultures of the world. We can develop dual, double, multiple consciousness of diverse ways of being in the world. Through dialogic explorations of difference, we can move from dual and double to multiple consciousness and diverse ways of being and doing in the world (Kramsch & von Hoene, 1995).

DOUBLE CONSCIOUSNESS

W. E. B. Du Bois's theory of double consciousness and the transformative role of intellectuals are two concepts that address the question, "Knowledge for whom?" He called on the world to "listen to the striving in the souls of black folk." A historian and sociologist, Du Bois examined the condition of African American people at the beginning of the 20th century, 40 years after slavery ended, and asked why the nation had "not found peace from its sins," why freed men and women had "not found freedom in their promised land." He said the problem of America was the color line. His claim can be extended to Europe and all countries that participated directly or indirectly in slave trade and colonialism. As the colonized have immigrated to the homes of their former colonial masters, there has been a resurgence of racial attacks by skin-heads, neo-fascist, racist, and anti-immigrant political organizations, in the United States, the United Kingdom, Germany, and France.

The color line also persists in U.S. public schools today:

Of every 100 White kindergartners, 88 graduate from high school.

> Of every 100 African American kindergartners, 83 graduate from high school.
>
> Of every 100 Latino kindergartners, 60 graduate from high school.
>
> Of those same kindergartners, 25 Whites, only 12 Blacks and 10 Latinos graduate from college. Dr. W. E. B. DuBois said the problem of the 20th century is the color line. As we close this century, I think we can safely say that the problem of the 21st century will remain the color line, expanded in its definition by adding at least language and income. (David Hornbeck, Philadelphia Superintendent of Schools[7])

We in public education want to extend education to all rather than to allow knowledge, like private property, to be kept only in the hands of the wealthy. We can guard knowledge like the master craftsmen and guilds in feudalism, or we can work to democratize, extend it to serve the masses, work to dismantle the forces in education that reproduce inequity. Posing the question "Knowledge for whom?" helps us consider what our students need in order to succeed; when we pose this question, do our best to answer it, and cause our students to reflect on those answers, we pave the way toward increasing the numbers of formerly disenfranchised people who participate in all levels of education (Walsh, 1996).

In *The Souls of Black Folk*, DuBois (1961) described "double consciousness":

> After the Egyptian and Indian, the Greek and Roman, the Teuton and Mongolian, the Negro is sort of seventh son, born with a veil, and gifted with second-sight in this American world—a world which yields him no true self-consciousness, but only lets him see himself through the relation of the other world. It is a peculiar sensation, this double-consciousness, this sense of always looking at one's self through the eyes of others, of measuring one's soul by the tape of a world that looks on in amused contempt and pity. One ever feels his two-ness, an American, a Negro; two souls, two thoughts, two unreconciled strivings; two warring ideals in one dark body, whose dogged strength alone keeps it from being torn asunder. (pp. 16–17)

BRANCH 5-4: DIALOGIC APPROACHES TO RESEARCH

How can our research *give back* to our students, their families, and their communities? Here are some ways that dialogic research helps you "stay honest." First, by engaging in member checking you can see if what you have recorded

[7]Hornbeck, D. Speech before the National Council of Churches of Christ in the U.S.A, Chicago, November 11, 1998.

rings true or is off the mark. Cross-cultural research (and what work involving second/foreign language teaching is not cross-cultural at least in aim?) can be problematic in several respects: divergent audiences, different expectations, and different perspectives.

- Ask "Whom does knowledge serve?" To answer this question, look at the material basis for inequities. In the United States, the key to understanding inequalities in capital is property—beginning with the European conquest of the indigenous Native American peoples and institution of slavery to segregation practices, differential property values assigned to neighborhoods based on race, differential treatment in providing loans, and so forth. Property taxes fund schools.
- Look at the structural systematic patterns of reproduction—for example, different resources allocated to schools.
- Conduct gender, racial, linguistic, and working-class "audits"—how many students actually come from various backgrounds? Are female students and indigenous students disproportionately placed in certain programs and excluded from others? Look at tracking both between schools and within schools (Yamashiro, 1996).
- Look at the representation from the standpoint of multicultural criteria (Check on Banks & Banks for actual criteria). Is there cosmetic or transformative inclusion? Has the curriculum been sanitized or has it actually drawn on the funds of knowledge from multiple communities? Is there an explicit critique of sexism, racism, classism, or only a vague "diversity" —which sees any thoroughgoing critique of educational practices as "divisiveness?"
- Look at the achievement rates. Look beyond the test scores to community pride, reputation, alumni associations, and projects that give back to the community such as health fairs and students' community service.

One tenet of dialogic approaches to TESOL is that our students' reality is the starting point for curriculum design. This was in the tradition of Chu Hsi (1130–1200), one of China's greatest educators who wrote *Reflections on Things at Hand* (1967). Chu suggested that we learn about the world through first learning about what is in front of us, what is close at hand. Then through reflection, we have a deeper understanding. From the knowledge of immediate experience, the dialogic process enables us to direct our attention from a single to multiple levels of meaning, understanding and consciousness. What are our students' needs and realities? When do they use the language? Can we provide opportunities for them to use the language, successfully? A functional approach to language and literacy asks students to draw on their own resources to develop a metacognitive awareness of language use. At the macro level, we need to investigate the motivation for English language learners. And at this level, there is need for more active intervention and policy work. Bilingual research can help us understand the structures of curriculum so that we can have a closer fit between Vocational English as a Second Language (VESL) and economic development, drawing on the funds of knowledge in the community to create curriculum that enables immigrants to make a greater contribution to community and society. Bilingual research—honoring and utilizing the resource is central to this work.

Many ESOL students have been traditionally excluded from sitting under the ginkgo tree. To understand race and racism is critical for non-White language learners, teachers, and researchers, although race often is not dealt with in methodology textbooks or studies of second-language acquisition. By "race" I mean a "socially constructed" concept of categorization that has no basis in biological reality (Omi & Winant, 1986). Nineteenth- and 20th-century studies of brain size or body shape that attempted to show the superiority of the "White," "Aryan," or Europeans have been discredited (Gould, 1981; Selden, 1999). There are enough differences within any of the so-called "races" with respect to skin color, type of hair, and other features to make biological categorization of the "races" problematic. But while there is no biological basis for "race," racial tagging and racism exist as part of American culture. As Henry Louis Gates, Jr., wrote:

> [Race] pretends to be an objective term of classification, when in fact it is a dangerous trope. The sense of difference defined in popular usages of the term "race" has both described and *inscribed* differences of language, belief system, artistic tradition, and gene pool, as well as all sorts of supposedly natural attributes such as rhythm, athletic ability, cerebration, usury, fidelity and so forth. The relation between "racial character" and these sorts of characteristics as been inscribed through *tropes* of race, lending the sanction of God, biology, or the natural order to even presumably unbiased descriptions of cultural tendencies and differences. (Gates, 1986, p. 5)

Racism is a social fact and a historical reality embedded in our literature, culture, and national consciousness. We are socialized into accepting racial categorizations and racism, the ideology that supported and was engendered by the African slave trade, slavery in the Americas, and colonialism and imperialism in Africa, Asia, Australia and the Pacific, and Latin America and the Caribbean. Racism continues through war, military conquest, institutional racism, inequitable distribution of social and economic resources, and political injustice.

The phenomenon of "double consciousness," looking at oneself through the eyes of the other and "measuring one's soul by the tape of another world," is the situation of an outsider to a language and a culture. It was not the situation of the colonial master who imposed his language and culture on the natives whose land he conquered and occupied. But it is the situation of those who are the former slaves and colonized (Memmi, 1970). *The Souls of Black Folk* speaks to the moral dilemma poised by the being of two worlds. An example of this duality is provided by the hyphenated identity of being Chinese-American or Mexican-American. Hyphenated Americans may find the following dialogue familiar:

> "Real" (read: White) American: "What are you?"
>
> Asian American: American.
>
> White American: But where are you from?
>
> Asian American: California.
>
> White American: But what are you *really*? [Implying that only White people are real Americans.]

The world is divided into "marked" and "unmarked"; "unmarked" is English, White, the Anglo core. Double consciousness is having the awareness that one is measured by the standards of the unmarked Anglo American or the White European American core group. The White "mainstream" is not homogeneous (as much as those of us on the outside may experience their closing ranks with respect to us). Within the White core, there were historic differences between the Irish, the Italians, and the core Anglos. Many Italian Americans or Eastern Europeans experienced bigotry akin to racial prejudice in that their darker skin and hair were associated with "dirtiness," ignorance and inferiority.[8]

Language teaching—especially for children who are of working class origin or racial or cultural minorities—accounts for the issues of double consciousness, and reflects sensitivity to the complexity of racial and other forms of social identity. Racism and colonialism can lead to denigration of one's ethnic, cultural, or racial identity, self-hatred, or being ashamed of one's background. In addition, marginalized students may think that learning academic English is a betrayal of their native language and culture or in conflict with promoting their home language, culture, and community (Ladson-Billings, 2000). If we are unaware of the power relations involved

[8]My colleague Bill De Lorenzo remembers vividly his Catholic school experiences as a working-class Italian American growing up in New Jersey. The Irish nuns discriminated against the Italian students.

in the teaching of English to indigenous students or students who are products of a colonial legacy, we may be in danger of unwittingly participating in cultural and linguistic genocide.

COLLECTIVE MEMORY

> What defines oral history and sets it apart from other branches of history, is ... its reliance on memory rather than texts. Yet oral historians seem reluctant to emphasize what's in people's heads rather than in the Public Record Office. What is memory? Do we hunt it with a questionnaire, or are we supposed to use a butterfly net? (Errante, 2000, pp. 16–27)

Collective memories and memories of the oppressed involve the (re)discovery of indigenous discourses, antiracist, and Black consciousness discourses, anticolonialist discourses, womanist[9] and feminist discourses, gay and lesbian discourses, heteroglossic and hybrid voices, and submerged memories. These memories are submerged because they oppose those in power who want us to forget. These memories are subversive because they challenge us to reevaluate the dominant order and to imagine alternatives to the present inequalities and hierarchical structures that are reproduced through education.

BRANCH 5-5: LITERACY AS A TOOL FOR ECONOMIC DEVELOPMENT

In TESOL our work of English for specific purposes (ESP) is closest to economic development, but often at the adult level the two areas that are most closely tied to English for economic development are vocational ESL (VESL) and ESP. The question for us in public education is how we can develop curriculum that will support economic development for poor and working-class students and their communities (Wong, 2000).

Luis Moll and Jim Greenberg's "funds of knowledge" is an outstanding model of extending Vygotsky's model of tool and symbol into economic development. They take the zone of proximal development out of the schools by going to the sources of household support in the community to design curriculum for literacy. In the community they identify "funds of knowledge," such as carpentry and fixing cars, and incorporate these in an after-school club curriculum. If we only focus on academic achievement in terms of minority students acquiring the power language (acquiring the cultural capital that is valued in schools), we will not look at the political and economic relationships that give rise to the inequalities in education in the first

[9]Dolores Williams (1996), "womanist" refers to African American feminists. It is a reference to Sojourner Truth's question to the White women abolitionists, "Ain't I a woman?"

place. Instead, we must see school transformation as reciprocal—we must incorporate the funds of knowledge from the community into curriculum that will support community and economic development (Osterling, 2001).

This includes oral histories and cultural development (see Hones & Cha, 1999, for the life history and contributions of an elder Hmong leader who is a community liason for an elementary school). The new cultures that ESOL students create will draw on the memories and collective knowledge, values, and tastes of the elders of their communities but will also have an aesthetic of new identities. An example of this is Hmong performance artist Tou Ger Xiong:

> On center stage in the comfortable auditorium of the Oakland Middle School in Lake Elmo, Minnesota, a distant suburb of the Twin Cities, a cheerful blond twelve-year old named Marnie opens the assembly. "We're having a Hmong speaker today. Tou Ger Xiong does it all," she says to the four hundred seventh graders. A muscular young man with an embroidered Asian beanie-type hat springs onto the stage and starts doing push-ups. "Ngo-xiong?" he asks. "What's up?" He gets the children to repeat the question in Hmong.
>
> "How many of you know any Hmong people?" a few hands go up. "We are a four-thousand-year-old-culture. We're the hillbillies of Asia. Heeee-haaaw! Or as we say in Hmong, Cheeee-haaaw!" The students enthusiastically repeat, "Cheee-haaw!" Xiong combines traditional stories, puppets, and embroidered Hmong outfits with rap music, hip-hop, and humor to perform the tale of how his family came to St. Paul from Laos.... In Minnesota, Hmong Americans like Tou Ger Xiong have been engaged in a long term cultural struggle that goes beyond fighting stereotypes. They and other Asian American cultural workers in the Twin Cities and elsewhere are creating new images of Asian Americans and the culture that makes us uniquely American.
>
> Xiong doesn't gloss over the hardships of adapting to life in America, nor does he skirt experiences with racism or Hmong youth gangs. Students laugh as he talks about his first encounters with a flush toilet and when he shares his reaction to the first white people he saw when he was a child: "I saw a tall, big ugly monster with a long nose and yellow hair—my mom told me, 'Don't go too close, he'll bite you.'" His listeners grow quiet as he talks about getting beaten up as a kid. "Other kids called me 'gook' or 'chink,' and said, 'Go back to your country.' They beat me, kicked me, and spit on me. I wondered what was wrong with me—I didn't like being Hmong for a long time. How many of you have ever been called names? How many of you have been hurt by words?" he asks. Hands shoot up from all over in his multiracial student audience. (Zia, 2000, pp. 254–255)[10]

[10]Zia's chapter "Reinventing Our Culture" (pp. 252–280) discusses a Twin Cities KQRS broadcast by a KQRS about a 13-year-old Hmong girl in Wisconsin who allegedly killed her baby after giving birth in a YMCA bathroom. "The broadcast included a recurring fake Asian character named 'Tak,' who made comments in a mock-Asian, pidgin English accent and joked that it would 'take a lot of eggrolls' to pay the criminal fines for concealing a corpse. The radio announcer recommended that Hmong 'assimilate or hit the goddamn road'" (p. 258). *(continued)*

For us as teachers and intellectuals, "Knowledge for whom?" challenges us to uncover submerged memories. These submerged memories challenge us to reconsider to what extent the American and French revolutionary ideals we learned as schoolchildren—liberty, equality, fraternity, and sisterhood—have been realized by all people, rather than only those of property. These memories of indigenous people, African slaves, Chinese coolies, indentured servants, and immigrant workers are important for us in teaching English to speakers of other languages so that our students and our fellow teachers can draw inspiration from and strength from those of "bitter strength" who went before us.[11]

An example of a relatively unknown chapter in American history was the crusade for free elementary education for all immediately after the Civil War. In *The Souls of Black Folk*, DuBois describes the "crusade of New England schoolma'am" who established schools throughout the South for the newly freed slaves and poor White farm workers. Congress formed the Freedmen's Bureau (1861–1872) during the Civil War to organize the fugitive slaves who appeared among the Union armies as soon as they entered the slave-owning states of Virginia and Tennessee. The Freedmen's Bureau was to provide for the resettlement of the formerly enslaved people, and to help them become free workingmen. These people had been deliberately denied education; they escaped to join the Union armies with nothing but the clothes on their backs. The Union army faced a huge refugee resettlement problem—how to feed, clothe, and train the former slaves.

In the first year of the Freedmen's Bureau, Freedmen's Aid societies worked to eliminate physical suffering. The American Missionary Association, sprung from the *Amistad*,[12] various church organizations, the National Freedmen's Relief Association, and the American Freedmen's Union sent clothes, money, schoolbooks, and teachers southward. Seven thousand refugees were removed from congested centers to farms, and they began to build schoolhouses throughout the South. DuBois (1968) described the crusade to build schools as the brave "waving of the calico dresses"

[10]*(continued)* Hmong and Asian American community response included initiating the Community Action Against Racism, a loose coalition that rallied Africans and African Americans who remembered previous insensitive comments aired about the murder of a Somali cab driver; they protested and demanded that the radio station apologize. The chapter discusses Hmong community issues, including marriage, oppression of women and girls within the community, and the role of identity and hybridity in Asian American art and culture—adoptees and Hapa, or Hawaiian for "half" or mixed race and heritage.

[11]The word for "coolies" may be derived from the Chinese characters *ku li. Ku* means "bitter" and *li* means "strength."

[12]The Amistad Revolt (1839–1842) began as a shipboard uprising, or mutiny, by captives from Sierra Leone. What began off th coast of Cuba carried itself to the United States—where an intense legal, political, and popular debate ensued over the slave trade, slavery, race, Africa, and ultimately, America itself. See: http://amistad.mysticseaport.org/main/overview.html

through the battlefields, as New English women dared to travel through the areas devastated by the Civil War to plant schools for freed slaves and poor Whites alike:

> The annals of this Ninth Crusade are yet to be written—the tale of a mission that seemed to our age far more quixotic than the quest of St. Louis seemed to his. Behind the mists of ruin and rapine waved the calico dresses of women who dared, and after the hoarse mouthings of the field guns rang the rhythm of the alphabet. Rich and poor they were, serious and curious. Bereaved now of a father, now of a brother, now of more than these, they came seeking a life work in planting New England school houses among the white and black of the South. They did their work well. In that first year they taught one hundred thousand souls and more. (p. 31)

The New England schoolteachers' crusade has parallels in the literacy campaigns following the Bolshevik Revolution in Russia and campaigns in China, Cuba, and Nicaragua (McKay, 1993). Transformative intellectuals seek to raise literacy as a means for the oppressed to become conscious of their condition, and to be better able to participate in their own liberation and the building of a new society. Literacy for the masses is a means toward humanization and selfhood. This stance toward knowledge runs counter to the Southern plantation owners (or in the case of China and Russia, the feudal aristocracy), who saw that illiteracy would keep poor White farm laborers divided from the former slaves:

> The opposition to Negro education in the South was at first bitter, and showed itself in ashes, insult, and blood; for the South believes an educated Negro to be a dangerous Negro. And the South was not wholly wrong; for education among all kinds of men always has had, and always will have, an element of danger and revolution, of dissatisfaction and discontent. Nevertheless, men strive to know. Perhaps some inkling of this paradox, even in the unquiet days of the Bureau, helped the bayonets allay an opposition to human training which still today lies smouldering in the South, but not flaming. Fisk, Atlanta, Howard and Hampton [13] were founded in these days, and six million dollars were expended for educational work, seven hundred and fifty thousand dollars of which the freedmen themselves gave of their poverty. (pp. 35–36)

Times of war have often provided cracks or openings for the development of social movements of oppressed peoples. Sometimes war has in-

[13] Fisk, Atlanta, Howard and Hampton are the African American institutions for higher education that were formed when African Americans were not allowed to attend the White Universities. They educated the first generation of African American professionals and continue today to play an important role in the education of African Americans.

creased expectations and provided a broader perspective through travel, causing a rise in the consciousness of the oppressed. For example, during World War I, Chinese workers dug trenches and contributed to the Allied war effort in France. These workers were radicalized when at the end of the war their contribution was forgotten. The Treaty of Versailles, supported by U.S. President Wilson, signed over German-controlled areas in China to Japan. Many of the Chinese workers and students in France, including Premier Zhou Enlai (Chou En-lai) and Chen Duxiu, the first General Secretary of the Chinese Communist Party, consequently formed a branch of the Chinese Communist party in France. Similarly African American soldiers who contributed to efforts in World War I by doing the most denigrating work, digging trenches, returned to the cities of the North such as Chicago, not as welcomed heroes, but to race riots and lynchings. A disproportionate number of African Americans were sent to the front, were injured, and gave their lives in World War II, the Korean War, the Vietnam War, and the war in Iraq (see Cruse, 1969).

DOUBLE CONSCIOUSNESS, NOT ASSIMILATION

> The history of the American Negro is the history of this strife—this longing to attain self-conscious manhood, to merge this double self into a better and truer self. In this merging he wishes neither of the older selves to be lost. He would not Africanize America, for America has too much to teach the world and Africa. He would not bleach his Negro soul in a flood of white Americanism, for he knows that Negro blood has a message for the world. He simply wishes to make it possible for a man to be both a Negro and an American, without being cursed and spit upon by his fellows, without having the doors of Opportunity closed roughly in his face. (Du Bois, 1968, p. 17)

Through the development of double consciousness a person has a sense of identity and continuity with the past, a sense of wholeness—uniting the two cultural worlds—and DuBois wants "neither of the older selves to be lost." The ginkgo must help us and our students remember not only the voices in the new language, but the voices of our past, our families, and the communities. For example, reclaiming African cultural traditions, enables black authenticity and selfhood for liberation for all those of African descent (Sutherland, 1997) If we lose our past, we lose our selves. The quest for identity in learning a new language must be connected to our former selves.

In asking the question "Knowledge for whom?" the teacher might be cautious in adopting certain methods that might be successful with students whose home culture and language is highly valued in the schools and who will not likely "lose" their home language. For example, in teaching English as a foreign language in France, it may be entirely appropriate to "fine" students for speaking their native language in class, but in English-speaking countries with indigenous children such as Maori or Hopi, fining children contributes to linguistic genocide.

Another example is Suggestopedia, which may be a successful and appropriate method of teaching students who already speak prestigious languages. Through Suggestopedia, also known as the Lozanov method of foreign language teaching, students take on a new identity when they learn the language through using a new name (Bancroft, 1983). The taking on of a new identity releases inhibitions. Students also sit in comfortable chairs as if they are in a parlor and listen to classical music. This approach is fine if the students do not have to choose between their identities.

Now picture these techniques (fining students for speaking their home language or requiring them to adopt a new identity) if you are a TESOL instructor teaching Indian telecommunications workers. If you teach them how to replace their Indian accents with American accents and how to develop a fictional American identity to talk to American customers, you may unwittingly be a tool in a system of multinational corporations' exploitation of labor. Many Indian communication service workers are encouraged to adopt an American or British accent and guise so that First-World customers will believe that they talking to a representative in the United States or Britain. By "outsourcing" to telecommunications companies in India, U.S. and British corporations avoid paying workers in their own countries a minimum wage and instead pay Third-World workers in former colonies an annual salary of $3,000 for taking as many as 100–150 calls a day.[14]

"Knowledge for whom?" asks us to consider the social, political, and economic positions of our students as we choose our teaching methods. How might English language education contribute to democratic participation in self-rule, self-determination, and elimination of exploitation? Our curriculum must support community and economic development. Questions of voice, identities, and taking on a new name in learning English must be addressed by asking, "Whom does knowledge serve? How can it improve our students' lives and the lives of their families and the community? How can curriculum support world peace and combat social and economic injustice?" (Vásquez, 2003).

---

[14]The multinational corporations that use Third-World workers for their customer service lines might argue that they are providing Third-World workers with a better than average wage for that part of the world. It is a complicated issue because English allows these people to get jobs. At the same time, Third-World workers are being asked to deceive callers through developing fictitious first world identities, which indicates that the corporation is attempting to hide its source of workers—pretending to use Americans, for example. These corporations maintain high profits through this deception.

BRANCH 5-6: KNOWLEDGE FOR WHOM: CURRICULUM FOR PEACE

Because of the international character of our work in TESOL, peace and human relations are essential components to dialogic curriculum. We may have in the same school students who have family members or friends fighting on opposite sides of a war. Students who themselves have no personal experiences of animosity will have parents who have been historic enemies. As ESOL teachers, we can utilize dialogic approaches to address historic wounds. ESOL student journalism can address issues of violence and war. A good example is the *Silver International* a Montgomery High School ESL student newspaper, sponsored by Joe Bellino. On the pages of *Silver International*, students have addressed tough issues of war and peace. An Ethiopian student and an Eritrean student wrote articles that were published side by side to address the problem of how high school students should tackle the problem of their parents being enemies. A Salvadorean student wrote about his refugee experience, which encouraged a Cambodian student to write an article about his experiences. The stories and personal narratives of one student will support the development of another student's writing (Bellino, 2005).

Subscribe to the Print Version of Silver International for a year!
To Subscribe, fill out this form, cut and mail to:

Silver International
Montgomery Blair High School
51 E. University Blvd.
Silver Spring, MD 20901

Prices: $5 for one subscription (3 issues a year).
10 or more subscriptions are $1.50 per subscription (3 issues a year).

If you are subscribing from outside the U.S. contact us for price information at SilverInternational@mbhs.edu

The United Nations General Assembly resolution 53/243 outlined eight action areas of a program of action for a culture of peace (Adams, 2000, p. 5). These areas are helpful for us in TESOL as we design curriculum for peace to address the question "Knowledge for whom?":

1. Culture of peace through education.

2. Sustainable economic and social development.
3. Respect for all human rights.
4. Equality between women and men.
5. Democratic participation.
6. Understanding, tolerance, and solidarity.
7. Participatory communication and the free flow of information and knowledge.
8. International peace and security (peace diplomacy, peacekeeping, disarmament, and military conversion).

In approaching peace education, teacher-educators Toh Swee-Hin and Virginia Floresca-Cawagas (2000) pointed out the importance of three key pedagogical principles in peace education: holism, dialogue, and critical empowerment. They highlighted the "interconnectedness of multiple issues with the problems of violence" (Toh & Floresca-Cawagas, 2000). Building on the work of peace educators internationally and using print media and electronic communication, such as the Internet, as tools to exchange, sustain, and amplify efforts of peace education, we in TESOL have an important role to play in developing a culture of peace.

It is very important, when TESOL, Inc. as an international organization of English language professionals is based in the United States with three quarters of our membership in the United States that we actively take up the cause of peace and promote international understanding. The U.S. government is the major military power in the world. We who are TESOL professionals and U.S. citizens have a very special role to play in countering antiforeign and chauvinistic sentiments among our compatriots and creating a climate of support for our students.

> In public, at conferences, for example, I insist that my full name appears on my name tag. In a society that cannot accommodate names that come from "other" cultures, this can be a frustrating exercise. It is no wonder that many Black children will anglicize their names to avoid playground taunts … and much worse. We are still fighting colonialism. Friends ask me why I don't just drop my non-African names. It would be a good idea, but not a practical one. In reality, my reason has nothing to do with practicality, it has to do with my own identity. For better, for worse, my names locate me in time and space. It gives me a sense of my own history that I not only share specifically with a generation of people in Africa, but also with all Africans in the Diaspora. ("Felly" Nora Nkweto Felicitas Mfula Simmonds, 1998, p. 36)

Curriculum design begins with the realities of our students—which may be distinct, hybrid, mixed identities, born of various significant heritages in their lives and not necessarily homogeneous (Pao, Wong, & Teuben- Rowe, 1997). As TESOL professionals getting to know the cultural background of our students we should not essentialize (Kubota, 2002). We cannot ignore realities of racism, war, colonialism, and economic hardships. "Knowledge for whom?" means that English is not to supplant or replace the home language and culture. Dialogic approaches encourage the bridging of the old to the new and comparing and contrasting the different ways with words between home, playground, and the school.

BRANCH 5-7: REMEMBERING AND RECLAIMING HERITAGE LANGUAGES AND CULTURES

Bilingual programs are an important institutional corrective to language loss. In the strongest models of bilingual education, the two-way immersion model, the first language is given status in the schools as a medium of instruction, and students from both the majority (i.e., English) and the minority language (i.e., Spanish) become proficient in both languages. Cultural capital is measured in knowledge of L1 as well as L2. This is an institutional remedy for the social inequality and the associated family problems for racial and ethnic minorities.

Two-way bilingual programs are most effective with 50% Anglophones and 50% Francophones. Where there are as many as 12 to 40 languages in a single school it is also critical to support and honor the home languages and cultures of language minority students. Through creativity this is possible even when teachers don't know the primary languages of their students. David and Yvonne Freeman (2001, p. 158) cited six strategies to support the development of home languages and cultures:

1. Ensure that environmental print reflects students' first languages.
2. Supply school and classroom libraries with books, magazines, and other resources in languages in addition to English.
3. Have bilingual students read and write with aides, parents, and other students who speak their first language.
4. Encourage bilingual students to publish books and share their stories in languages other than English.
5. Allow bilingual students to respond in their primary languages to demonstrate comprehension of content taught in English.
6. Use videotapes produced professionally or by the students to support academic learning and raise self-esteem.

We honor home languages and cultures by providing space for them in our classrooms and schools. This requires creativity, advocacy, and a long-term perspective. Begin by conducting a linguistic audit of the languages and dialects your students speak. Develop a network, starting with the students in your classroom. Ask the students to bring in examples of environmental print in their languages and ask parents, older brothers and sisters, and other family members to use different languages to label the various objects in your classroom (e.g., fish tank, desk, calendar, etc.). With the Internet, it may be possible to order books and other materials in students' home languages. Local social service programs for refugees may have material in students' home languages that could be brought into the classroom. Stores that cater to these populations might even have magazines for sale and videos that can be rented and shared with students.

TRANSFORMATIVE INTELLECTUALS

As ELT professionals, the answer to the question, "Knowledge for whom?" is tied to Prator's question, "What are the aims of instruction?" We begin with needs analysis to determine the kinds of discourse our students will be required to interpret, analyze, and generate. We then design our curriculum and instruction based on analysis of the purposes for which our students need to know English (Crandall, 1993). As English language specialists, we begin with discourse with a "small d" and investigate the genres that students will need in their professional, vocational, or academic fields. One way is to design "sheltered workshops" or seminars for second-language learners alongside the courses they take in the field. Criteria to select good courses are: (a) Is the course a required course in the major? (b) Is the instructor known for being a good lecturer? (c) Is the course a "foundational" course that will introduce key principles, theories, and terminology?

English for special purposes (ESP) researchers have interviewed instructors and students about the kinds of assignments and writing and reading needed in the field of study. They have also probed what constitutes quality scholarship in the various areas and looked for model examples of research. Needs analysis can also be conducted with native-language surveys and interviews. The dialogic approach puts needs of the students at the heart of syllabus design and will explore a variety of avenues to understand the actual English language or discourse that students need to acquire.

Posing the question "Knowledge for whom?" also has a component in working with discourse with a capital "D" in which language is mediated by ideology (Gee, 1990, 2001). "Whom does knowledge serve?" is an ethical and political question. This question may assist in language learning because students are motivated to learn, not only for themselves, but for their families, their communities, and for a better world (Edelsky, 1991; John-Steiner, Panofsky, & Smith, 1994). Essential to "Knowledge for whom?" is to remember where you came from. For Chinese intellectuals since the May 4th movement of 1919, the movement to save China from foreign powers and corrupt warlords, to lead China from semicolonialism and semifeudalism, was a part of one's historic mission. For the Chinese theological students, the question "Knowledge for whom?" was an essential component of the dialogic curriculum. An English language curriculum that supported them as they brought greetings from the churches in China to churches in the United States was an encouragement to them to reaffirm their faith ("for the least of my sisters and brothers") and support for their commitment to study abroad to assist in the development of the churches in China. The immediacy of being asked to represent Chinese Christians enabled them through "learning by doing" to carry out their pilgrimage and mission. "Knowledge for whom?" was critical for them to keep in mind as orientation for their work as bridge people—to be ambassadors of friendship and goodwill and peace between the people of the China and the United States.

In their quest to learn English, there was no danger that Gao Ying, Li Yading, and Zhang Xianyong would forget Chinese. They were highly educated, literate and accomplished writers in their first language, adult professionals in their late twenties and early thirties. Although their proficiency in writing Chinese could decline, even to the point of forgetting how to write a few characters, "language loss" was never a serious problem. However "Knowledge for whom?" was a critical feature in dialogic pedagogy to help these three students become transformative intellectuals.

Posing the question "Knowledge for whom?" asks students to draw meaningful connections between the classroom and their own families and communities. We invite students to reflect on their own memories in relation to their elders, peers, and the next generation—the significant people in their lives—present, past, and future. Dialogic approaches link the individual quest to sift for and uncover significant memories to the search for social or group memories.

Going Beyond the "Heroes and Holidays" Approach to Multicultural Curriculum

Along with encouraging the development of transformative intellectuals and helping teachers to ensure that classroom methods do not further oppression, the question "Knowledge for whom?" encourages us to be critical of historical perspectives that tell only the oppressor's view of history. We need to go beyond the "Foods, Facts and Fiestas" (Ovando & Collier, 1985) approach to multicultural education. A focus on holidays can provide a superficial understanding of culture and historical perspectives (Lee, Menkart, & Okazawa-Rey, 1998).

As Thanksgiving neared, the Chinese theological students and I discussed the American Indians. I shared a cartoon that raised the question of what the Native Americans might have thought of the coming of the Pilgrims. In the following excerpt from that discussion,[15] Gao Ying became involved in the dialogue, despite her limited vocabulary. She followed instructions, and asked for clarification when she wasn't sure where she should read. She also successfully indicated which words she needed help with. In this section of tape there is a lot of "teacher-talk." The dominant voice is mine; Li Yading is silent.

Shelley: Who's talking in this cartoon? Are there Pilgrims talking or only the Indians?
Zhang: Only the Indians.
Shelley: What's the first comment?
Zhang: "The food is very good."
Shelley: Actually, historically, the Indians taught the Pilgrims how to cook the new foods, so that's not accurate. How about the second one? The second comment, "Hey, I've got a news flash for you—they're *not* summer people!" What does it mean to be summer people? What do you think?
Zhang: Warm hearted?
Shelley: No. People who come in the summer who are tourists. If you live in a resort area, a beach area, the people who come in the summer are summer people.... He's saying they're not here for summer camp. They're coming permanently.
Zhang: They're here to settle down.
Shelley: Yes, they're here to settle down. What's the next comment? The third one. Can you read that Gao Ying?
Gao: The third one.
Shelley: Yes. They're not ...
Gao: They're not?
Shelley: Uh huh. They're not ...
Gao: They're not leaving. Why should we let King James. King James?
Shelley: Yes.
Gao: Dum?
Shelley: Dump.

[15]Tape recording of class session November 24, 1987. All the passages from this section were transcribed from the same session.

Gao: Dump ... dump all of his mis ... mis?
Shelley: Misfits.
Gao: Misfits. Misfits on us?
Shelley: Okay. What's a misfit?
Gao: fits
Shelley: Okay. A fit is suitable. A misfit is someone who doesn't fit, is unsuitable. So a misfit could be
Gao: the opposite meaning
Shelley: Yes, the opposite meaning. Now why should we let King James *dump* all of his misfits on us? Now, who's King James?
Zhang: King of England.
Shelley: Now why should we allow him to give us all his criminals, and all of the rejects of English society.
Gao: Rejects.
Shelley: (goes to the board and writes) Okay reject means we don't want them,
Gao: uh hum
Shelley: go away
Gao: uh hum.
Shelley: That's a verb. It's also a noun. The people who you "reject" are "rejects." So um, the people who came from England a lot of time were criminals. And were rejects. They were not liked in English society and that's why they were asked to go to the new world. Now this particular.... Now who is saying that today? [silence] Who has a similar statement today? [6-second pause of silence] Are there any Americans who say we shouldn't allow—Have you followed the news about the Cuban prisoners?

I recounted to them at length the negotiations between Cuba and the United States to allow some Cubans to immigrate to the United States in exchange for returning some of the mentally ill Cubans who entered the United States with the boat people in the early 1980s.

Shelley: And so the American government said that Fidel Castro was using this as an opportunity to get rid of all of the rejects of his society, all of the criminals of his society and a number of them went to prison when they got to the United States, some of them for crimes they committed in the United States, some were crimes they had committed in Cuba. And um, when the news um, hit the Cuban prisoners in prison, they took hostages [writes "hostage" on the board]. So there are two prisons that have a big riot [writes "riot"] now. And they have set fire to the prison. Gao Ying, do you know prisoners?
Gao: No.
Shelley: Oh. [writes "prisoners"]
[Zhang translates].
Gao: Oh, prison.

In playing back the tape, I was struck by the length of my digression and the fact that there was no pause on the tape between "they have set fire to the prison" and "Gao Ying, do you know prisoners?" She responded immediately to my question. It indicated a tremendous ability on her part to be able to follow along, even if she didn't understand every word. This was a strong example of her ability to tolerate ambiguity.

BRANCH 5-8: MEMORY, RACE, COLONIALISM, AND LANGUAGE TEACHING

> This world divided into compartments, this world cut in two is inhabited by two different species. The originality of the colonial context is that economic reality, inequality, and the immense difference of ways of life never come to mask the human realities. When you examine at close quarters the colonial context, it is evident that what parcels out the world is to begin with the fact of belonging to or not belonging to a given race, a given species. In the colonies the economic substructure is also a super-structure. The cause is the consequence; you are rich because you are white, you are white because you are rich. This is why Marxist analysis should always be slightly stretched every time we have to do with the colonial problem. (Fanon, 1963, p. 39)

> Everything up to and including the very nature of pre-capitalist society, so well explained by Marx, must here be thought out again. The serf is in essence different from the knight, but a reference to divine right is necessary to legitimize this statutory difference. In the colonies, the foreigner coming from another country imposed his rule by means of guns and machines. In defiance of his successful transplantation, in spite of his appropriation, the settler still remains a foreigner. It is neither the act of owning factories, nor estates, nor a bank balance which distinguishes the governing classes. The governing race is first and foremost those who come from elsewhere, those who are unlike the original inhabitants, "the others." (Fanon, 1963, p. 40)

Another example of a dialogic approach is a unit on the theme of intolerance and genocide for bilingual Spanish-English fifth graders from Santa Barbara, California (Jennings & Pattenaude, 1999). While dialogic curriculum is open-ended, it requires as much (if not more) preparation as other ESOL/bilingual curriculum. It requires a great deal of thought to facilitate student voices, especially if students have different levels of proficiency in the second language. Texts and materials (film, videos, photos, realia) and guest speakers and field trips are carefully selected around a theme which integrates language arts and generally a content area such as science, social studies, or mathematics. A photographic essay, *The Children We Remember* (Abells, 1983) which the teacher read to the students in English and Spanish, was selected to introduce the children to the Holocaust. The photos show synagogues burning, the Star of David patches that Jews were forced to wear and starving children helping each other. The text states, "The Nazis hated the children because they were Jews." They are open-ended in that there is room for the students to bring in and create materials, around which the language experience unfolds. What are the key components to dialogic treatment of holidays and other cultural accouterments?

1. Create an awareness of the history as viewed by all the participants. The Santa Barbara children thought about the Jewish children, similarly to thinking about the dropping of the bomb on Hiroshima through the eyes of Hibakusya, the survivors of the blast. We must recognize their efforts to work for international understanding and peace by making sure that we never forget the horrors of the atomic bomb. We need to see history through the eyes of those who have been enslaved, discriminated against, victims of war. (Takaki, 1993)
2. Ask the students to interview different people about key historical events, creating questions that help students to find out about perspectives that are outside the mainstream. For example, the Chinese theological students were asked to commemorate Thanksgiving by asking three different Americans about the treatment of Native Americans.
3. The experience of students, being exposed to, criticizing, and confronting racist or chauvinist ideology, is important.
4. We don't want to expose students (of any age) with problems and not talk about what we can do to change things. This is the most important part. The difference in following through on this last point is the difference between piling on more oppression and showing the way out.
5. Knowing the depth of racism, sexism, poverty, we must do something and we must take concrete steps. We must affirm even the small steps we take. Otherwise we can lose to despair. Memory of those who struggled for justice in the past is critical. There are ebbs and flows in social movements, and change does not occur in steady, incremental steps.

Besides the cartoon, I also handed out an op-ed column, "The Seasonal Symbolic Indian Mocks the Native American Reality." [16] We attended a Thanksgiving dinner and program at the National Council of Churches that featured Native Americans sharing their experiences about the treatment of Indians on the reservations and in urban areas. Zhang Xianyong asked

[16] Hirschfelder (1987). Arlene B. Hirschfelder is an education consultant with the Association on American Indian Affairs, based in New York, and the author of numerous school texts on this subject. Her book *Happily May I Walk* (Scribner's) won the 1987 Carter G. Woodson award from the National Council for Social Studies.

one of the Native Americans, Owanah Anderson, who works for the Episcopal Church, for suggestions of books to read to learn about Native American experience. She suggested *House Made of Dawn* and *The Way to Rainy Mountain* by N. Scott Momaday, a Navajo who won a Pulitzer Prize. She also suggested Vine Deloria, Jr., who has written 10 books of protest literature, including *God Is Red.*

We also read the policy statement on Native Americans written by the National Council of Churches that provides a history of Native Americans and is critical of the role that churches played in colonizing.[17] I made handouts and transparencies for an overhead projector of a list of words and expressions that I thought the students needed to know to understand the policy statement. Here is a brief sample:

subjugate	political rights and prerogatives
residing	explicitly
essential	viability, viable
occupancy	harmony
ensure	attributable solely, attribute
imposes	fiduciary

Finally, the assignment I gave them was to interview three Americans about the meaning of Thanksgiving and to see what they had to say about Indians. Gao Ying talked to her hostess, a retired teacher and author of four books on techniques for homemaking. Her hostess, who was kind to Gao Ying, told her that "they thank God for harvest and that they made Indian friends who taught them to plant corn. Later the Indians were killed and they moved to other places." Gao Ying was surprised when her hostess said that the government gave the Indians lots of money but that they became alcoholic and squandered it. Gao Ying also talked to the librarian at the Children's Library where she was volunteering, who told her that after a cold and terrible winter they thanked God. She said because so many "Americans" came, the Indians didn't like it and fought them. Zhang reported that he had spoken to Ken Guest, who said that White people should say they were sorry and should do something for the Indians. He also talked to someone's 5-year-old daughter who couldn't answer about the Indians, but said that Thanksgiving was a harvest festival for God.[18] Although Li Yading did not participate very much in the discussion in class, here is the last paragraph from an essay he later wrote titled "Indian—Real

[17]National Council of the Churches of Christ in the U.S.A., "A Policy Statement on Indian Affairs adopted by the Governing Board, November 4, 1978."

[18]My notes from our class, November 24, 1987.

American" that reflected the complexities of what he was learning about Native Americans:

> With the increase of the immigrants, they separated and went their own way at last because different culture and different value concept. New colonists became more and more greedy. They had forgotten all but the desire for the land. They relied on guns to conque[r] Indian who only had the spears and arrows. They brutal massacred the "barbarous Indian" in this bloody war. Gradually, Indian lost their rights to share the nature. Indian who had spreaded whole continent of America were limited a few small "reservations." Millions and millions Indian were reduced to a few ten thousand. They haven't been swallowed or destroyed by the wild beasts and the natural calamity during the long history. But they are facing an extinct danger in the world with modern civilization. The reason of this situation is that Indian were regarded as a sub-human by certain white people. These people compelled Indian to submit by the "legal form" (signed the agreement) by illegal form (occupied by force), or resorted to all kinds of fraud. In short, they didn't treat Indian as human. But Indian are human after all. Since they are human, they ought to enjoy all the rights which the human have. American always is claimed to be a country of freedom, democracy and human right. Since it is so, when they spent the Thanksgiving Day with boundless joy, shouldn't they ask some questions about Indian, who? where? why? when? (or shouldn't they ask five-w on Indian problem?) (Li, 1987)

Posing the Question, "Knowledge for Whom?"

Both Mao and Freire challenge intellectuals to commit themselves to the service of the people by asking the question "Knowledge for whom?" Freire's answer to the question "Knowledge for whom?" was "for the oppressed":

> This pedagogy makes oppression and its causes objects of reflection by the oppressed, and from that reflection will come their necessary engagement in the struggle for their liberation. And in the struggle this pedagogy will be made and remade. (Freire, 1970, p. 33)

Mao's (1970) answer, also in a Third-World context, was "for the workers, peasants and soldiers" (p. 262). Maxine Greene (1988) answered the question from an American context, within an advanced capitalist society:

> The aim is to find (or create) an authentic public space, that is, one in which diverse human beings can appear before one another as, to quote Hannah Arendt, "the best they know how to be." Such a space requires the provision

> of opportunities for the articulation of multiple perspectives in multiple idioms out of which something common can be brought into being. (p. xi)

The theology students who came from a Third-World country and were therefore accountable to that reality, were in dialogue with Americans from an advanced capitalist country. The cross-cultural exchange took place across political and economic systems. One striking contrast was the material wealth in the United States. Initially, it was difficult for them to see the disparity between the haves and have-nots in the United States because as Zhang Xianyong pointed out, "Even the beggars dress better than Chinese workers."

It was also difficult for them to see the inequities in power because of the developed democratic institutions and freedoms of assembly, protest, and expression, or what the Italian theoretician Antonio Gramsci called rule not by coercion but through ideological "hegemony." Gramsci (1971) pointed out that in advanced capitalist societies, "The relationship between intellectuals and the world of production is 'mediated' by the whole fabric of society and by the complex of superstructures, of which the intellectuals are, precisely, the 'functionaries'" (p. 12). For Gramsci, the dominant group exercised its hegemony through "civil society" or private institutions in the superstructure and "direct dominion" through "political society," or the state (p. 12).

In advanced capitalist societies one of the problems is to hear what Maxine Greene called the "submerged voices." In looking at American society and the quest for the opening of what she called public space, she traced works of women and "strangers"—African Americans and immigrants—voices that have been subjugated and silenced. Greene (1988) identified the tension between those voices and the opening of public space:

> The matter of freedom, then, in a diverse society is also a matter of power, as it involves the issue of a public space. There have been voices, as we have seen, articulating the connections between the individual search for freedom and appearing before others in an open place, a public and political sphere.... How, in a society like ours, a society of contesting interests and submerged voices, an individualist society, a society still lacking an in-between, can we educate for freedom? And, in educating for freedom, how can we create and maintain a common world? (p. 116)

The tension between diversity and creating a common world is a problem for all teachers with students from varied backgrounds. How do you introduce new culture without negating home culture? How do you encourage the development of selfhood? I felt the tension on two levels. One was concerning the relationship of the students to American culture. The aim was, as Gao Ying put it, to learn to accept cultural differences while retaining your own cultural identity:

> Every international student will face culture shock in some form or another. However, it is a good experience, and can be challenging and stimulating. You will perhaps find you are not only learning about the new culture but learning about yourself too. In the sense that you are adapting your behavior to American culture, but you are not being assimilated. In another word you "are accepting of cultural differences while retaining your own cultural identity." I have identified my own cultural identity through the American culture.[19]

The other level was how to introduce American society. The tension between diversity and common ground is reflected in the question, "What is American?" The students saw the conflict when they asked Americans to tell them the significance of Thanksgiving. Gao Ying found children's books in the library that reflected an uncritical approach that ignored the injustices done to Native Americans. The struggle for submerged voices to be heard goes on in the American context in civic and political society. The church is one sphere among many where the question "for whom?" is being posed.

The quest for common ground is a theme with which the students were familiar. Philip Wickeri entitled his dissertation "Seeking the Common Ground: Protestant Christianity, the Three-Self Movement and China's United Front" (1984) because the Chinese phrase "seek the common ground while reserving differences" was applied to relationships between Buddhists, Christians, and Moslems in China and believers from other parts of the world, to relationships among members of different religions in China as to relationships between believers and nonbelievers in China. He explained that

> "seeking the common ground" provides the means whereby men and women holding different world views can co-operate in matters of common concern, and at the same time retain their particular understandings of faith. (1984, p. iii)

For the students, "seeking the common ground" represented their mission in coming to the United States to study in seminaries. During their study here they would be representatives of the Chinese church. Their

[19]Gao Ying, "Culture Shock," presentation to international students at San Francisco Theology School and General Theological Union, fall 1989.

study would help them to be better representatives in the future. In the tradition of the May 4th movement (1919), the students had a mission to study not for their own betterment alone, but to develop skills that they could take back to China to help the Chinese people. This was their patriotic duty and part of their heritage as Chinese intellectuals.

The question "Knowledge for whom?" encouraged the development of the students' own theological voices by posing the commitment question clearly. Students were in the public arena, speaking not as individuals but as representatives of the Chinese churches. The students were challenged to academic excellence through the dialogic method by developing a cultural and linguistic appreciation for their audiences. For example, the students reflected on and worked with the questions that Americans had asked them about China and the church. They were motivated to do their best, because they knew that they were representatives and statespersons for the church in China and their work would make a difference for China. There can be no empowerment or academic excellence without risk taking. Speaking and writing must have real-life consequences.

The students made a greater contribution to theological reflection and discussion in their talks and writings by remaining true to their own cultural context and identity. The dialogic process was essential for the students to maintain their cultural integrity in an alien environment. In this way they were not only enriched by the discussions at the academy, but enriched the academy by offering it their own experiences and theology.

WHERE THE GINKGO TREE GROWS: KNOWLEDGE FOR WHOM?

The human practice of restricting the pursuit of knowledge to an elite few is as old as ancient history. But human history, however long to us humans, is not as old as the oldest living things on earth. Ginkgo biloba is the oldest species of tree known. The ginkgo grew long before there were schools and before knowledge became "private property." It grew long before one group of humans became the rulers and oppressed others. Marxists argue that the restriction of knowledge to the rulers of society occurs first under slave society. It does not occur in primitive communal societies where there is no surplus labor. Socialist feminists argue that the origins of patriarchy occur with division of labor and the origin of surplus value. We do not need to go back to the ancient civilizations such as the Aztecs or Egyptians or Chinese to see the restriction of knowledge in the service of the slave-owning ruling classes. In contemporary history, African slaves in the United States were forbidden to read. Yet there were slaves who dared to learn to read and write, and to pass on that knowledge to others. Their struggle for knowledge, literacy, and liberation is documented in the form of the slave narratives and oral history.

In the nut of the ginkgo tree is a recurring question that emerges where there are dialogic openings. The ginkgo tree grows where this question is posed. I've called this question "Knowledge for whom?" or "Whom does knowledge serve?" Asking the question "Whom does knowledge serve?" helps teachers to avoid replicating oppressive social structures in the classroom. It also helps teachers and students to become transformative intellectuals—people who can make a difference in the world (Nieto, 1996). Finally, it helps teachers to ensure that information presented about cultures reflects multiple perspectives. It is said that the winners get to write history; whether a person is deemed a "terrorist" or a "freedom fighter" depends on the perspective of the person doing the writing. When we consider "Knowledge for whom?" we allow our students the chance to engage with the complexities that can lead to drastically different conceptions of an action, reflected by the terms "terrorist" and "freedom fighter." When students have these understandings, they can develop their own perspectives. This helps students to maintain double consciousness because they have access to enough information to find an understanding that is congruent with their own perspectives—to be true to their own heritage even while they engage with learning English.

There is no magic memory pill that enables us to learn a foreign language. It is simply hard work! Likewise, there is no magic formula for creating a dialogic classroom. Like learning a foreign language, creating a dialogic classroom is slow. Progress zigzags as we struggle with new situations. Like learning a foreign language, creating a classroom is a social experience; we are not the sole creators of the classroom. We depend on our students, and we are influenced by the school and the community. Teaching is socially mediated. Yet over time, trying a new strategy here and finding a new resource there, we can improve the dialogic nature of our classroom and help our students use their English skills to help themselves, their families, and their communities.

6

Conclusion

In this book we have located dialogic methodological approaches historically as communities of practice. In one sense, dialogic pedagogy is as old as the ginkgo tree. In ancient China and ancient Greece were the Confucian and Socratic dialogues. Both Confucius and Socrates had a humble attitude toward the pursuit of knowledge in their philosophic and ethical investigations. Their dialogues were clearly examples of learning in community and problem posing rather than what Freire called "banking education."[1] Although the classical examples of dialogic pedagogy are readily available for study—one can find translations of Plato's record of the Socratic dialogues and the Confucian Analects in libraries around the world—it is not as easy to locate dialogic approaches in TESOL today.

Within the field of TESOL/bilingual/second and foreign language education, the teachers whose classroom practices are similar to examples featured in this book might not call their methodology "dialogic." Instead they might identify their teaching as falling broadly under critical pedagogy (Benesch, 2001) or critical applied linguistics (Pennycook, 2001), participatory or emancipatory, sociocultural, critical multiculturalism (Kubota, 2004), the instructional conversation (Goldenberg, 1991), or social constructivist. It is also possible, depending on where they studied and the professional activities in which they have been engaged, that they might describe their work with such diverse labels as "intercultural," TESOL for social responsibility, feminist, "antiracist," communicative language teaching, "eclectic," or possibly even "postmethodological." A notable exception is a

[1]The original Confucian dialogues as recorded in the Analects were examples of open-ended questioning rather than a transmission-oriented, banking pedagogy. This was in contrast to the Confucian education and the civil examination system and Confucian ideology, which maintained order for centuries under feudalism.

middle school teacher who Lorrie Stoops Verplaetse (2000) called "dialogic." In this teacher's science class, language-minority students excelled academically. "Mr. Wonderful: Portrait of a Dialogic Teacher" describes a teacher whose problem posing and questioning techniques were highly interactive, enabling English language learners to participate at exceptionally high levels of frequency and cognition.

In this book we have attempted to introduce and characterize a new emerging dialogic trend through comparing it to the dominant approach communicative language teaching (CLT) and the other major approaches in TESOL during the last century, notably grammar translation and the audiolingual method. We drew from the work of Clifford Prator, who put forward three questions or cornerstones to assist in determining appropriate TESOL methodology. These questions were the basis for understanding the history of various approaches to TESOL methodology:

1. What is known about the nature of the language?
2. What is known about the nature of the learner?
3. What are the aims of instruction?

DIALOGIC INTERPRETATIONS OF THE NATURE OF LANGUAGE

This book has introduced linguistic schools of thought that support dialogic interpretations of the nature of language. It did not discuss in depth any one of the number of theories presented, but attempted to situate the authors of dialogic theories in relationship to each other. Reading this book is a poor substitute for reading the original works of the various theorists and linguists. My aim was to make concepts and theories accessible in such a way that readers would want to read the primary sources for themselves: Freire, Vygotsky, and others who have contributed to the "dialogic tool kit."

Halliday and Hasan's (1985) framework for analyzing language, text and context as a social semiotic or system of meaning and Bakhtin's dialogics (Bakhtin & Holquist, 1981; Bakhtin, 1986) stand in sharp contrast to sender–receiver models of communication, such as the computer metaphor "input–output," which has dominated the field of second-language acquisition. For Bakhtin there is always present a multiplicity of meaning, rather than a mathematical code in which $a = 1$. Bakhtin's contribution is to utilize the *utterance* as the unit of analysis to show the workings of language in the world. Rejecting a formal or an abstract conception of language, through *the utterance* the Bakhtin Circle grounded its Marxist philosophy of language in social intercourse, through dialogue that is historically constituted and deeply ideological (Vološinov, 1973). For Bakhtin, the *nature* of language is *dialogic*. This understanding of language through the utterance places the individual and freedom in responsiveness to others. This provides a moral, relational plane of dialogism, which we have also seen in Confucius in the concept of *ren*, in John Dewey's emphasis on moral education, and in pedagogies of liberation such as those of Mao and Freire. In dialogue one speaks in the words of others. One is always a product of culture, a culture bearer. As Marx said, we are stamped with the birthmarks of the old order.

For Bakhtin, as we discussed in chapter 4, we use language that we have heard from other voices, and these voices are in turn discursive products of their historical positions and their membership in various social groups. These voices are also stratified, and support both complicity in hierarchical, unequal power relations and resistance and challenges to the established order. They manifest themselves in speech genres, stylized, predictable formats or scripts. And yet there is the potential for uniqueness, creativity, and authorship within each utterance. Heteroglossia exists as a force for change and diversity. The ongoing centrifugal and centripetal forces that unify and stratify all language and cultures illuminate each other. This occurs through parody, double voicing, a shift in inflection, or a gesture. The possibilities for variation, novelty, exist within each utterance, but are also proscribed by the traditions of culture.

DIALOGIC APPROACHES TO THE NATURE OF THE LEARNER

To answer "What is known about the nature of the learner?," dialogic approaches draw from sociocultural or sociohistorical psychology, notably the work of Lev Vygotsky, which draws from interdisciplinary knowledge bases from sociology, anthropology, political economy, or the social sciences, as well as arts and the humanities. Cultural psychology, in contrast to cognitivism, explores the development of mind, rather than brain and physiological functions (Bialystock & Hakuta, 1994; Wertsch, 1985). Cultural psychology is critical of "scientific" accounts of second-language acquisition (SLA) that look at culture as a "factor" that could be taken out of the equation (Kozulin, 1990).

In "Methodology for the Human Sciences," Bakhtin (1986, pp. 159–172) explained that the difference between natural and human sciences is that the subject of investigation in natural sciences is a thing, an object, whereas the subject of investigation in the human sciences is another subject, a living consciousness who can "talk back" to the scientist. In a more precise formulation, the "object of human sciences is a text, in the broad sense of signifying matter, and humans as producers of texts" (Todorov, 1984, p. 17). Bakhtin elaborated this distinction through pointing out:

> Mathematics and natural sciences do not acknowledge discourse as an object of inquiry. The entire methodological apparatus of the mathematical and natural sciences is directed toward mastery of *reified objects* that do not reveal themselves in discourse and communicate nothing of themselves.... In their practice, knowledge is not bound to the reception and interpretation of discourses or signs coming from the very object to be known.
>
> In the human sciences ... there arise specific problems of establishing, transmitting, and interpreting the discourse of others (for example, the problem of sources in the methodology of the historical disciplines). And of course in the philological disciplines, the speakers and his or her discourses are the fundamental objects of inquiry. (Bakhtin, "Discourse in the Novel," from the *Dialogic Imagination*, trans. M. Holquist, as cited by Todorov, 1984, p. 15)

We seek to know an *object* in natural science like physics. We seek to know a *subject* in social science. The theme of the object of research was a major programmatic theory advanced in 1921 by Vološinov in *Marxism and the Philosophy of Language*[2]:

> The human sciences are the sciences of humans in their specificity, and not the sciences of a voiceless thing and a natural phenomena. Humans in their human specificity are always expressing themselves (speaking) that is always creating a text (though it may remain in potential). Where human being is studied outside of the text and independently of it we are no longer dealing with the human sciences (but with human anatomy or physiology, etc.). Physical and chemical bodies exist outside human society as well, whereas the products of ideological creation develop only within it and for it. (Vološinov/Bakhtin, as cited in Todorov, 1984, p. 17)

In TESOL the distinction between natural and human sciences is important for us to remember when we ask how humans learn a second or additional language. The difference between "what works" in a physics experiment is very different from "what works" in a classroom experiment, in that weights and pulleys and fulcrums are objects and tools, but students are subjects, tool makers. As Volsinov/Bakhtin stress, human beings are creators of *text*.[3] One of the important implications for us in TESOL is to support authorship in our students. If our students view themselves as

---

[2]There is some controversy as to whether Bakhtin was the author of *Marxism and the Philosophy of Language* and Vološinov and V. N. Medvedev his disciples, who published the book under their names. Both Vološinov and Medvedev died under Stalin in 1936 and 1938. It is clear that Bakhtin was a part of the circle and influential to the development of the theoretical positions. There are continuity and development between the understanding of discourse and ideology in *Marxism and the Philosophy of Language* and Bakhtin's last writings on methodology of the human sciences (Moraes, 1996).

[3]See the James Lantolf (1996) critique of positivism in SLA theory construction.

authors and text makers of meaning, who they are, their personal histories, and a sense of their audience are critical to how they craft their texts. Authorship involves self and audience in dialogic interaction. It also involves self identity in relation to discourses of social groups and appropriating discourses as members of communities.

The difference between "knowledge of the thing" and "knowledge of the person" is that our reflections and our praxis concerning "knowledge of the person" in teaching methodology are a moral question. Teaching methodology can be seen as the sum set of our responsible acts, rather than what is often thought of as merely a technical question. The moral dimension of teaching highlights the significance of posing the fourth feature of dialogic inquiry, "Who does knowledge serve?" or "Knowledge for whom?" (Johnston, Juhász, Marken, & Ruiz, 1998).

Sociocultural approaches to the development of mind or thought look at learning as being a social process, connected through dialogic interaction or learning in community. Knowledge is not "in one's head" but is revealed through social practice or activity. Cognition is embodied in activity that is both physical and artistic, such as weaving, playing a violin, doing T'ai Chi chuan, or embodied discursively such as in telling a joke or writing a letter. In all these activities, as we discussed in chapter 3, what we value as "quality," our "taste" or sense of the aesthetic, is intertwined with our culture and history. Our sense of timing, use of tools, the way we mark our steps, direct our gaze, move our fingers, are all prescribed by the culture. In all these things we take our cues from others, often more expert than ourselves. Knowledge and cognition are distributed socially through networks and funds of knowledge that are part of the language of social groups, rather than being solely "in one's head."

Because dialogic pedagogy is concerned with the question "Knowledge for whom?," the areas of ethnic studies and women's studies and cultural studies enable us to become more aware of how racism, androcentrism, patriarchy, and other oppressive ideologies affect the interpretation of the "nature of the learner." In TESOL, critical discourse analysis analyzes the intersections of discourse and power in relationship to historically produced structural inequalities and ideological hegemony. Poststructural feminist and critical-race approaches to TESOL have encouraged us to question "essentialist" views of the nature of the learner that unconsciously adapt male-as-norm standards. There is also no universal "woman" learner, but particular women, stamped with particular histories, caste, class, and racial and ethnic backgrounds.

Critical of seeing European cultures as God-like and indigenous cultures as sinful, contemporary liberation theologies and local theologies of context have questioned the traditional negative views of syncretism, which was deemed as capitulating to the devil. Similarly, recent research in social identity and language learning has looked at theoretical constructs such as hybridity, creoles, and heteroglossia to interrogate, re-vision, and transform traditional ethnic and racial categories (Gutierrez, Rymes, & Larsen, 1995; Luke, 2000; Pao, Wong, & Teuben-Rowe, 1997). Queer theory has challenged us to go beyond "nature" as we theorize the "nature of the learner" (Pinar, 1998) and to see the complex ways that identity, sexuality and emotion intersect in learning how to teach (Evans, 2002). Transgendered perspectives encourage us to consider how blurring or mixing the categories "blue is for boys" and "pink is for girls" might be liberating to both those who feel at home with those categories and those who are oppressed by them (Feinberg, 1998).

Phillipson (1988, 1992) analyzed the nature of the learner from the standpoint of linguistic imperialism. As language teachers, we cannot be blind to the economic inequalities and the market forces that make our students want to learn English.

The inherent inequalities in who knowledge serves reproduce social inequalities between the former colonial masters in the English-speaking centers and the former colonized in the periphery. This has implications for English language teaching methodology. For example, the following five tenets were originally given approval at the British Commonwealth Conference on the Teaching of English as a Second Language held at Makerere, Uganda in 1961:

1. English is best taught monolingually.
2. The ideal teacher of English is a native speaker.
3. The earlier English is introduced, the better the results.
4. The more English is taught, the better the results.
5. If other languages are used much, standards of English will drop. (Phillipson, 1988, p. 349)

These five tenets became widely accepted in the English language teaching (ELT) profession, although "linguicism," which promotes one language at the expense of others, runs counter to the UNESCO 1953 recommendations on the use of the mother tongues in education (Phillipson, 1988). Challenging established tenets and myths concerning the nature of the learner is so important to us in TESOL today (McLaughlin, 1992). In English-speaking centers, where it is often believed by mainstream teachers that speaking the home language will "hold back" or retard English language learning, it is important for ESOL teachers to educate fellow teachers, other staff, and parents about the dangers posed by language loss or a subtractive approach to the second language (Samway & McKeon, 1999; Wong-Fillmore, 1993). These assumptions of

English language teaching methodology that privilege knowledge transmitted from the centers over the periphery must be challenged so that textbooks, methodology, and experts from the United Kingdom or the United States are not automatically seen as the most "up-to-date, scientific, professional and effective"—in short, superior to locally constructed knowledge (Canagarajah, 1999; Lin, 1999).

These historic problems of methodology, including the unquestioned export of American and British TESOL methods, textbooks, and experts from the English-speaking center countries to the periphery, have made some question the concept of methods itself, calling for a "postmethodology."

METHODOLOGY OR POST-METHODOLOGY?

The concept of "methods" has been criticized from various vantage points. Kumaravadivelu (1994, 2001) correctly pointed out the need to

> Reconfigure the relationship between the theorizers and the practitioners of method. As conceptualizers of philosophical underpinnings governing language pedagogy, theorizers have traditionally occupied the power center of language pedagogy while the practitioners of classroom teaching have been relegated to the disempowered periphery. (1994, pp. 28–29)

Pennycook (2002) pointed out:

> The Method concept has played a role in the gendered division of the workforce, a hierarchically organized division between male conceptualizers and female practitioners. (p. 65)

The unequal power relationship between theorizers and practitioners of method reflects a number of dimensions of inequality:

Center	Periphery
Native speaker	Nonnative speaker
Male	Female
Colonial master	Colonized, descendants of slaves
Settlers' English	Indigenous people's English
University researcher	Classroom teacher

Posing the question "Knowledge for whom?" entails opening up the heretofore elite-controlled domains of philosophy, theorizing, and knowledge construction to those who have been denied access to participation in research and scientific inquiry in the past. Kumaravadivelu is quite right to call for a reconceptualization of the relationship between theorizers and practitioners. But the major problem that must be addressed in the traditional separation of theory and practice is the exclusion of the practitioner from participation in knowledge construction (Clarke, 1994). Brian Morgan (1998, p. 64) pointed out:

> The boundary between theory and practice has become increasingly blurred, however. It is not acceptable to speak of theorizing as a contingent or "situated" activity; that is, concepts or even "intuitions" generated from the unique circumstances that characterize each ESL classroom Moreover, the arbitrary separation of those who theorize and those who teach is being increasingly challenged.

Teacher research, in which teachers reflect on their own practice and share their insights about teaching methodology with others in the field, is a very important means by which practitioners join the ranks of the theorists, and thereby enrich theory construction (Allwright & Bailey, 1991; Edge & Richards, 1993; Johnson & Golombek, 2002).

van Lier (1994) developed a theory of practice that places classroom research at the center:

> The theory of practice I advocate is based on the approach Bourdieu worked out over many years of research and reflection (Thompson, 1991). It attempts to do justice to the practical character of pedagogy and the complexity of decisions and influences that shape a practitioner's work inside and outside classrooms. This theory places classroom research in the center, but at the same time actively researches the relationships between one's own classroom and other classrooms, and between what is done in class to what happens elsewhere. (p. 6)

By making classroom practice the starting part for inquiry, and drawing connections between one classroom and others, or one context and others, van Lier emphasized the importance of collaboration and learning in community. By proceeding from questions generated from classroom practice, teacher research theorizes language learning and teaching methodology "from the inside out" (Lytle & Cochran-Smith, 1993):

> It would be erroneous ... to perceive practical psychology as an application of previously established theories. The relationship should be reversed, with practice selecting its own psychological principles and ultimately creating its own psychology. (Kozulin, 1990, as quoted in van Lier, 1994, p. 7)

If methodology is constructed as a rigid prescription for classroom behavior or a series of prescribed codified procedures, it should be challenged. This was Prator's purpose in putting forth his three questions. What is our understanding of the nature of the learners, the language, and the aim of instruction? We must particularly question methodology if it comes unexamined from the center to periphery—from ESL to EFL, from the descendants of settlers or slave owners to the descendants of indigenous people or slaves, from "native speakers" to "nonnative speakers," from men to women.

We must look at English language teaching from the standpoint of the larger global inequalities in the world which are reflected in the varying positions of power for our students (Willett, Solsken, & Wilson-Keewan, 1998). If our students are working two or three jobs to make ends meet, if they come to school with dental problems or need glasses, a methodology that ignores these student realities is bound to fall short of the mark (Wong & Grant, 1995). As van Lier (1994) pointed out:

> If we want our practice to transform our students' reality and educational trajectory, then our theory of practice must examine what it takes for such a transformation to become real. Inevitably at some point, our investigations will take us beyond the classroom into the wider institutional and social contexts in which our work and our students' world unfolds. (p. 6)

In discussing the significance of the methods–postmethods debate, Bell (2003) pointed out that "post-method need not imply the end of methods but rather an understanding of the limitations of the notion of method and a desire to transcend those limitations" (p. 334). He suggested that "method and post-method can also be seen as inevitable and necessary dialectical forces: the one imposing methodological coherence, the other deconstructing the totalizing tendency of method from the perspective of local exigencies" (Bell, 2003, p. 334). If we place our students' realities at the center of curriculum design and instruction, the search for guiding principles to support their learning can be seen as a way of reclaiming methodology, from a series of narrow codified prescriptions, to an evaluation of which tools and resources will enable us to better understand how to support our students' language learning.

> Method has important meanings in philosophy which I think we can usefully reclaim. A method is a way of bringing together what we think we are doing and how we are doing it: *meta* + *hodos* = about the way; the way about the way. (Berthoff, 1981, p. 4)

Method or way in Chinese can be translated to convey a prosaic, technocratic interpretation of methodology or, from the standpoint of philosophy and ethics, "the way" or "the meaning of life" (Fig. 6.1).

Fang fa 方法 , fang shi 方式 , fa zhi 法制, or ban fa 辦法 method, way versus dao de 道德 the way, the meaning of life

Translations of “method” or “the way” 方法 / 方式 /法治/辦法 * mean the same, and can be used interchangeably and yet mean more or less the same.

FIG. 6.1. Translation as a way to understand “method.”

Dialogic approaches, rather than seeing the two translations of method—the technocratic and the philosophical—as mutually exclusive, would draw from both, depending on the nature of the learners, the nature of the language, and the aim of instruction. A similar tension was posed by Prator almost four decades ago in his article “Cornerstones of Method.”

LANGUAGE TEACHING: AN ART OR A SCIENCE?

One of the recurring debates in TESOL methodology is whether language teaching is an art or a science. Whatever position one takes in the debate, the results of the dialogue have shown the complexity of teaching and the importance of a multifaceted approach to TESOL. Prator wrote about this issue in his “Cornerstones of Method” article:

> Language teaching must be both an art *and* a science. To the extent that it remains an art, it permits the individual teacher to exercise such personal gifts as s/he may be endowed with. To the extent that it can be related to a science or sciences and thus itself become an applied science, it can be developed in a coherent way, be given continuity and be taught.
>
> The most successful teacher will always be something of an artist. But the art will be enhanced rather than destroyed if it is exercised within a framework of scientifically established guidelines. Therein lies the possibility of faith. (Prator, (1979, “Cornerstones of Method,” p. 6)[4]

Since Prator’s time, perhaps the most significant change in the debate is the changing definition of science, with philosophy of science causing the reevaluation of scientific “truth” and providing a critique of positivism

[4]“Cornerstones of Method,” although first published in 1979, was written while Prator was on sabbatical in 1964–1965.

(Harding, 2000). Analysis of what scientists do and analysis of scientific discourse have also challenged traditional views of science (Lemke, 1990). One such transforming event in the field of TESOL was the "Great Debate" at the 1996 TESOL Convention in Long Beach, California. Prator's question "Is Language Teaching an Art or a Science?" was taken up and debated by five panelists.

Moderator David Nunan explained that when the theme of the Long Beach convention "the Art of TESOL" had been announced, a number of his fellow board members had objected that "TESOL was a science, not an art." The animated debate in the boardroom prompted him to suggest that they hold a Great Debate as a featured event. Nunan opened the debate with a quote from Hatch:

> In art the emphasis is on how and what is expressed. In teaching, it has to be placed on what is learned, not just what is expressed. What's art got to do with it? What does it matter? What matters is advancing the debate about what students are learning, and rich and articulate representations of educational activities—whether we call them research, criticism or art—can do that. (Hatch, 1994, as quoted in Nunan, 2000, p. 8)

Elana Shohamy and Diane Larsen-Freeman were charged with arguing the position that TESOL was a science. Henry Widdowson was assigned the position that TESOL was an art, and Dick Tucker was asked to comment on all the papers and the relative contributions of science and art to TESOL. A recurring theme in all papers was that although traditional definitions of art and science dichotomized them into discrete entities, art and science were shown to be interconnected. Shohamy pointed out that critiques of science by practitioners have led to new definitions of science:

> While the positivist view of science included standardization, replication, and objectivity, it is now perceived as a limited way of understanding the world. The new paradigm, an interpretative one, originates in the realization that the contexts of social science vary from one situation to another, and are dynamic and fluid. It is socially and culturally constructed and represented by various means and forms—numerical, verbal, qualitative and quantitative.
>
> Science no longer needs to be guarded from "foreign elements" as these are viewed as enriching it. It continues to seek truth, but it is realized there is no *single* truth, but multiple truths, multiple sources of knowledge, determined by interpretative communities. (Shohamy, 2000, p. 12)

Shohamy's interpretive perspective on research presented goals that are achieved through dialogic means:

> The goals are not to find consistency, to prove, to disprove, and to predict. Rather, the goals are to interpret, understand and gain insights into specific contexts as exemplified between the researcher and that which is researched, often in a form of a dialogue. (Shohamy, 2000, p. 12)

In arguing that TESOL was an art and a craft, Henry Widdowson cautioned:

> But notice that to talk of TESOL as art does not mean that it is simply a matter of untrammeled individual creativity that teachers are born not made and that's that. Artists are made by knowing about their craft and so are teachers. Leonardo da Vinci did not become an artist at birth and neither did David Nunan. Of course some artists are better than others. But even those with instinctive gifts need to have them informed by a conscious awareness of the principles, the theoretical principles of their craft. (Widdowson, 2000, p. 15)

Widdowson's call for an examination of theoretical principles is consistent with his metaphor of teaching as a craft. The sociocultural metaphor of apprenticeship (Rogoff, 1990) has been used to show how craftsmanship is developed in weaving and student teaching. Indeed, during feudalism, the guild system of apprentice, journeyman, and master craftsman was the way all learning, from ironwork to copying sacred texts, from carpentry to baking, was passed from one generation to the next.

Diane Larsen Freeman's defense of science dispelled stereotypes such as that science was "objective," "analytical," "sterile," "predicting and controlling," "omniscient," "arrogant," "absolute," and "dispassionate." She quoted a chemist who explained that "science deals with mystery" and quoted computer scientist John Holland, who used meteorology to explain that "prediction and control" were not the essence of science:

> The weather never settles down. It never repeats itself exactly. It's essentially unpredictable more than a week or so in advance. And yet we can comprehend and explain almost everything that we see up there. We can identify important features such as weather fronts, jet streams, and high-pressure systems. We can understand their dynamics. We can understand how they interact to produce weather on a local and regional scale. In short, we have a real science of weather—without full prediction. And we can do it because prediction isn't the essence of science. The essence is comprehension and explanation. (Holland as quoted by Larsen-Freeman, 2000, p. 19)

Larsen-Freeman argued, as she has elsewhere (Larsen-Freeman, 1997) that chaos/complexity theory as an example of scientific inquiry into complex adaptive systems may be of interest in understanding science and second-language acquisition:

> Chaos/complexity science has also shown that reductionist thinking, which has been the most powerful tool in the "hard" sciences for the past 400 years, is inadequate for dealing with the dynamics of complex, nonlinear systems. (Larsen-Freeman, 1997, p. 19)

In defending TESOL as a science, Larsen-Freeman also argued for the importance of science as "curiosity and awareness and about learning to look." These are all qualities that reflect an attitude of inquiry in teaching:

> Like scientists, teachers approach practice with theories on how teaching and learning are supposed to work. Their theories-in-action (Schon, 1983) may or may not be explicit, but they are what drives and shapes in a fundamental way what teachers do in the classroom. (Larsen-Freeman, 2000, p. 20)

Like Shohamy, in defense of TESOL as science, Larsen-Freeman pointed out the importance of taking a perspective that science is *social* and is comprised of a discourse community. Whether or not teacher research is viewed as science and advances the knowledge in the field "hinges on what is meant by knowledge" (Larsen-Freeman, 2000, p. 20). If, like Shohamy, we take an interpretive rather than positivist view of science, teacher research may be the most important area for the development of dialogic approaches to TESOL. Larsen-Freeman quoted Marilyn Cochran-Smith and Susan Lytle (1993):

> We think that with teacher research, knowledge will accumulate as communities of school-based and university-based teachers and researchers read and critique one another's work, document and perhaps disseminate their responses, and create a network of citations and allusions, and hence begin to build a different kind of "interpretive universe" (p. 59)

G. Richard Tucker summarized the Great Debate by asking us to look at the broader challenges facing TESOL in public policy. Our field has a professional responsibility to work for language policies and educational policies that support English language learners around the world. From a policy perspective, Tucker argued that TESOL professionals must be scientists:

> We must continue, for example, to document effective practice, to document the contributions of competing social, political, economic, and pedagogical factors on the processes and the products of teaching and learning. We must aim, I believe for accuracy, systematicity and accessibility in our findings. We must encourage work that is contextualized and that is collaborative—work that draws upon a broad range of models and analytical tech-

> niques, our questions and our agenda should determine the methods that we choose and not vice versa. (Tucker, 2000, p. 26)

To reach our audience, Tucker argued that policy must be proposed in a style that best advocates for ESOL students which combines "the elegant simplicity and power with which Carl Sagan has unlocked ... the mysteries of the universe" and the precision, elegance and simplicity of the artist:

> We must describe the needs of the children and of the adults who desperately seek access to educational, social and economic opportunities, not in the arcane and jumbled jargon so characteristic of academia, but with the precision, the elegance and the simplicity of an artist. Only then can we hope to reach and to affect those responsible for the formulation of public policy. In the past, we have not been very effective in telling our stories, and while it is easy to blame the close-minded, bigoted listener, surely we—the tellers—must bear much of the blame. (Tucker, 2000, p. 26)

Dialogic inquiry is one way to incorporate the voices of students and their families and teachers in proposing public policies. Educational policies cannot be dictated successfully from the top down. Grass-roots efforts to incorporate the experiences and realities of students and teachers in setting research agendas and educational policy require grass-roots organizing and a bottom-up approach. School change can only take place through specific concrete policies and practices that are political (Ricento, 1998).

WHAT DOES THIS MEAN FOR TEACHERS?

Dialogic pedagogy can only "take root" and grow if it makes sense to other teachers. It becomes a living community of practice if others are challenged to take up the question "knowledge for whom." The goal is for the ideals of life, liberty, and the pursuit of happiness to become real possibilities in the lives of our students—all our students. In considering Prator's three cornerstone questions and in taking into account the contexts from which we draw our students—their communities but also the school as an institution—teachers may be able to make a difference in the lives of their students.

WHAT ARE YOUR VISIONS FOR THE FUTURE?

Dialogic approaches are not designed to replace strategic teaching methodologies such as the communicative approach, which is the major paradigm in TESOL. It should be clear from the review of teaching methods in chapter 1 that the communicative approach has much to offer. It provides students with information they need about the language they are learning, as well as authentic materials to work with and the opportunity to become strategic users of a second language.

The overall purpose of dialogic pedagogy is to reach the students who have been traditionally excluded, to make our classrooms a place where all students are able to learn, to keep students from falling between the cracks. Dialogic pedagogy succeeds in this goal through recognizing the significant factors that affect learning. All the realities of a student's life, from how easy it is to obtain food through how he or she is treated in school to teachers' expectations of a student—all these factors affect the learning process. Many of those factors have political and economic roots. With dialogic pedagogy, we engage the whole student and we strive to find out what motivates and interests him or her. We attempt to bring into our classroom those ideas, experiences, and people who will spur our students' interests. We also recognize the challenges our students face, and we support our students in handling those challenges, and where possible we try to change those challenges.

This is not easy. Nor is dialogic pedagogy a "pie in the sky" kind of approach. First of all, the status quo is very strong and likely to remain so. Change is not easy when so many of those who are in charge have a vested interest in maintaining the present system with all of its oppressive elements intact.

Yet teachers can be a powerful force for change, not just in the lives of individual students but in the teaching and learning community and in larger communities. Dialogic pedagogy offers the tools for understanding and communicating about the conditions of a particular learning situation. We can start in our own classrooms, and over time we build relationships with other teachers and create the type of school-based changes that truly benefit students. Ultimately, after all, we must reach beyond the doors of our own classrooms. Our students move on to other teachers. Students, especially those who are disenfranchised, need more than a single understanding and compassionate teacher in their educational careers, and this is why we need schoolwide change in the long run (Gebhardt, 2005).

Trees don't grow from the top down. They begin as small seeds, and they establish roots. Over time, the roots go deep into the ground. As the roots grow downward, the tree begins to grow upward. At first it is slender, slim. Over time it fills out and occupies a large amount of space, but this process takes years.

Dialogic pedagogy begins the same way—in single classrooms, in the adapting of an idea here and an idea there, to establish the roots. Each year, dialogic teachers try something new or gain some new understanding about their students that they incorporate into their teaching. Eventually, dialogic pedagogy may grow beyond a single classroom and become the impetus for schoolwide and even systemwide change: True educational reform is organic.

Appendix

An excerpt from the Pilgrimage Curriculum

In 1987, three students from Nanjing Union Theological Seminary arrived in the United States:

> Ms. GAO Ying,[1] age 34, from Beijing, graduated from Nanjing Seminary in 1985. Interested in sociology and religion, she spent a year at the Community Church and the Academy of Social Sciences in Shanghai. After a year of English study in New York City, Ms. Gao enrolled at the San Francisco Theology School in California in 1988. She graduated with a master's of art degree in 1991.
>
> Mr. LI Yading, age 32, from Fuxin, Liaoning Province, graduated from Nanjing Seminary in 1985. Interested in church history, he traveled China as a research assistant to gather data on churches in China. After a year of English study in New York City, Mr. Li enrolled in Garrett-Evangelical Theological Seminary in Evanston, Illinois, in 1988. He completed a master's degree at Garrett in theological studies and a second master's at Fuller Seminary in Pasadena, California, in cross-cultural studies.
>
> Mr. ZHANG Xianyong, age 28, from Changzhou, Jiangsu Province, graduated from the Nanjing Teachers University in 1982. He taught English at the Television University in Huaiyin. Interested in the history of Christian thought and Chinese intellectual history, he graduated from the graduate program of Nanjing Seminary and was married in 1987. After 3 months of English study in New York City, Mr. Zhang entered the Lutheran School of Theology in Chicago 1988. He completed his master's degree in 15 months and returned to Nanjing Theological Union to teach. He later pursued a doctoral degree in theology in Switzerland.

[1] I capitalize the surnames here for emphasis for readers not familiar with the Chinese practice of placing the surname or "last" name first. Later in the text, the surnames appear first, following the Chinese practice.

They were the first Chinese theological students to visit the United States after 1949, and were fulltime students (20 hours a week) at the American Language Program at Columbia University. In addition to their American language classes, I was hired by the National Council of Churches to prepare the students for advanced work in theology.

Mackey and Mountford, the authors of *English for Specific Purposes*, explained that "special" in English for special purposes (ESP) should be construed as *specific*. In order to design effective courses, the teacher needs to identify what genres will be used so that the language of the classroom approximates what the student will use in the field. For example, the Pilgrimage Curriculum included my accompanying the students in auditing a course at Union Theological Seminary. We attended and videotaped each class and then met in a seminar (a sheltered tutorial) to view the tape again.

I titled my dialogic curriculum "Pilgrimage: An American Journey." The theme "pilgrimage" was a spiritual journey in a foreign land. In learning about American culture and society, the students were called on to reflect on questions such as: What was distinctively American? What was Chinese? Universal? Particular? What did it mean to be part of the human family?

Another sense of pilgrim is one who travels to a shrine or holy place as a devotee. The curriculum I developed explored a number of personal journeys through literature and visits with people. Cognizant of the fact that American culture was not monolithic, I wanted the students to meet Americans from diverse walks of life. They worshiped at Canaan Baptist Church in Harlem and heard the gifted African American preaching of Dr. Wyatt T. Walker. They met with community organizers from the Asian Americans for Equality in New York Chinatown. They attended a Native American commemoration of Thanksgiving at the National Council of Churches in the U.S.A. In addition, the students' own journeys and experiences in America provided the starting point for dialogic reflection.

GOALS OF THE DIALOGIC CURRICULUM

1. To identify, analyze, and interpret American society and reflect upon cross-cultural experiences through observation, participation, and readings and to articulate that experience in English through speaking and writing.
2. To develop study skills for graduate school in theology: understanding lectures and note-taking, use of the library, writing academic papers, computers and word processing.

3. To identify and try out various learning strategies to facilitate language learning. To experience learning through active participation in determining topics, designing questions for investigation and research, and looking for resource people and materials.

PROBLEM POSING AND THE PILGRIMAGE CURRICULUM

Dialogic approaches to language teaching emphasize both the "product" and the "process" in learning another language—not only the "product." Rather than emphasizing a set of material to be learned, students learn strategies for language learning and reflect on "how to be good language learners."

The first goal was to introduce the students to American culture. Aware that American society is made up of diverse communities, I designed a multicultural curriculum to expose students to New York City—the academic communities at Columbia University and Union Theological Seminary and many other communities in the New York metropolitan area, including New Jersey and rural communities in upstate New York. In addition, within any community there are different perspectives. I hoped to expose the students to some of the voices that called for social justice and liberation. At the same time, I was also aware that it was impossible to introduce my students to all the voices that were important in the American experience. The intention instead, through the dialogic feature of problem posing, was to ask the question "What is American?" in various situations so that the students could themselves experience and reflect on some of the diversity in American culture.

Often international students studying in intensive English programs or ESL classes in the United States complain about the lack of contact or quality of contact with native speakers of English. Yet interaction with native speakers has been found to be a most valuable means of learning a language (Christison & Krahnke, 1986). Students interacted with Americans from diverse walks of life in the following contexts:

1. American family: Students were matched with host families for holidays and some weekends in church and home settings.
2. Community service: One of the students volunteered at a library. All visited community projects such as soup kitchens and community organizations.
3. Churches and ecumenical organizations and agencies: Students visited many member churches of the National Council of Churches of Christ, brought greetings from Christians in China, and attended both Conservative and Orthodox Jewish services. They visited the Catho-

lic Maryknoll Fathers in Larchmont, New York, and the Huttite Christian community in New Paltz, New York. They also participated in church meetings and conferences in different parts of the United States.

4. Field trips: Students visited museums, parks, attended concerts, and made visits to particular communities, such as Harlem, Chinatown, Little Italy, the New Jersey suburbs, and outlying areas.

The dialogic mode opened up for inquiry not only American culture but the student's own experiences as pilgrims or sojourners, including the literature on cultural adaptation and culture shock and differences between American and Chinese culture. In attempting to anticipate the problems that the students might come up against, I realized that there was no way that all the situations that they faced could be addressed by any curriculum. In fact, the more I read of the literature, the more I became convinced that the goal was not to prevent culture shock, but rather to make *sense* of it. The role of the teacher as a tutor is to assemble materials concerning the problem, provide some examples or models of exemplary work in the area, and engage the students in collectively investigating the problem. A problem-posing approach poses the question, but doesn't provide all the possible answers.

An essential aspect to problem posing is that although the teacher is responsible for designing the curriculum, the goals are set in such a way that the students themselves participate in determining topics and designing questions for investigation and research.

Here is an example from one of the first classes with the Chinese theological students, in which they identified questions for investigation and research related to the first goal of the curriculum.

Interdisciplinary Approaches to New York City

During one of the first classes, I used an exercise I adapted from Columbia Teachers College Professor Heidi Jacobs's course on interdisciplinary curriculum:

> The teacher directs the students' attention to a wastebasket. If a scientist looked at a wastebasket s(he) might ask the chemical composition of the wastebasket. If a historian looked at a wastebasket, s(he) might ask who invented the wastebasket or when wastebaskets started to be made of plastic. Teacher asks the students what an anthropologist might ask, or an artist, or studying the wastebasket from the perspective of literature or philosophy. What could a physical education teacher do with a wastebasket?

Teacher writes wastebasket on the board and spokes with the various disciplines and writes down some possible questions.

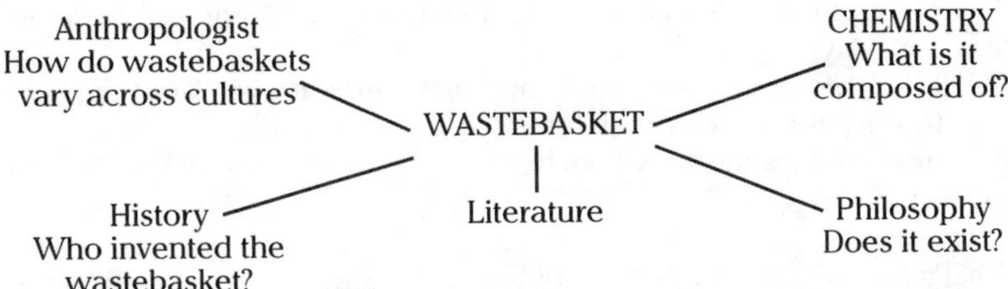

Teacher explains: Not all disciplines are universal. Certain disciplines such as History and Philosophy are found in universities around the world. Others, such as Sociology, are relatively new disciplines and are not as universal. Lenin wrote about Marx's contributions from the standpoint of Philosophy, Political-Economy and History. During the Cultural Revolution American academic disciplines such as Sociology were seen as bourgeois disciplines. What is the situation today? What are the subjects taught in primary and secondary schools? Teacher comments on academic disciplines at American Universities. List the typical disciplines at American universities and comment on the subjects in the public schools.

Teacher then writes N.Y. on the blackboard and spokes on the wheel. Asks students to cite disciplines that they are interested in exploring and writes those on the spokes. Ask everyone to brainstorm questions about N.Y. from these different perspectives and write them down for homework.[2]

Interestingly enough, of the three students, only Gao Ying handed in the homework according to the instructions, from the standpoint of various disciplines. Although the questions appeared to be direct translation from the Chinese, they clearly reflected questions within the different disciplines she selected. She selected:

Anthropology:

1. What is the influence of the nationalism of the American on giving production and culture of develop of the New York City.
2. How did the mankind give the social develop to throw [develop] the Man's culture in the long history of the manking [mankind].
3. How did understand social satuation [situation] the plackman [Blackman] of the New York City to throw [develop] the different culture of the manking [mankind].

[2]From the Pilgrimage Curriculum.

Social Sciences:
1. What is the characteristic of the New York City different from the other city of the United States?
2. How did many people of the different culture of background live in the New York City?
3. Why have the many poor people and high crime in the New York City. How to solve this serious social problems.
4. What reason does the New York become the pluralistic culture of city?

History:
1. What's the influence of the War Between the States of the United States on develop of the New York City.
2. What's the history reason that why all kinds of people to come New York city to try to live in the world.

Philosophy:
1. What's the view of value of people of the New York City?

Zhang Xianyong submitted two lists of questions. The one that concerned the "Big Apple" reflected the interdisciplinary approach of our class session, but was not organized according to the given assignment within various disciplines:

1. What is the transportation in N.Y. City?
2. Do New Yorkers prefer sky-kissing buildings?
3. How people with different backgrounds and from various countries live together here?
4. What's the unemployment rate?
5. Who is the first builder of the city?
6. What's the average income per person in New York City?
7. How many Christian denominations here?
8. Who is the most famous poet of the city?
9. Who writes the best book or article about the city?

The second, about the United States, was more based within the field of Zhang's interests, intellectual and cultural history and religious studies:

1. What is the women's liberation movement in 60s–70s? (It's beginning, process, leaders and the place in the U.S. history.)
2. Theological education in the States? (including Roman Catholics)
3. What's the function of Interchurch Center (Riverside Drive 475)? (Its limit and relation with other mainline churches and small sects or denominations.)
4. U.S. education in the Post Dewey period?
5. Academic climate in today's US?

6. If I want to know more about M. Mead or other sociologists and anthropologists in the States, which are basic books to read?
7. U.S. people's attitude towards religion?

From the standpoint of the desire to teach language, this assignment gave students an occasion to use their writing skills, so it was possible to become aware of the language skills with which they felt comfortable, as well as possible next steps for each student in relation to learning English. The students adapted the assignment to their own interests and goals. Their responses yielded rich data about their interests, and it was an excellent problem to consider in relation to their goals as English learners.

For a full copy of the Pilgrimage Curriculum I prepared for the Chinese Theological Students, please see my web site at George Mason University.

Glossary

Given as: Pin yin/Wade Giles or Cantonese English spelling (Chinese characters): English translation or identification.

Anhui 安徽 : Anwei Province

Beijing 北京 : Peking, the capital of China

Baoyu/Pao-yu 寶玉 : a character in the classic novel, *Dream of the Red Chamber*

Bajin/ Pa Chin 巴金 : author of the novel *The Family*, a critique of the feudal family structure

Changzhou 常州 : Changhow in Jiangsu (Kiangsu) Province

Ci ping gong she 茨坪公社 : Ci Ping Commune

Chen Duxiu 陳獨秀 : Ch'en Tu-hsiu, the first General Secretary Chinese Communist Party

Dazibao 大字報: "big character poster"

Deng Xiaoping 鄧小平 : Teng Shiao-ping, veteran leader of China

Deng Yanda 鄧演達 : left wing Kuomingtang (KMT) theoretician

Ding Guangxun 丁光訓 : Bishop K. H. Ting

Du Weiming 杜維明 : Tu Wei-Ming, the author of Confucian thought: *Selfhood as Creative Transformation*

Dongbei 東北 : the Northeast of China (formerly know as Manchuria)

Enping/Yanping 恩平 : one of the four districts

Facai/Faat Tsai 髮菜/發菜 : a black, hairy-looking moss

Folaishan 佛來山 : a mountain located in Shandong province

Fuxin 阜新 : a city in Liaoning Province

Gan /Gon1 乾 : dry

Gao Ying 高英 : Chinese theological student

Geming 革命 : revolution

Guangdong 廣東 : Kwangtung province

Guangxi 廣西 : Kwangshi province

Guangzhou 廣州 : the city of Canton

Guiyang 貴陽 : Kweiyang, the capital city of Guizhou

Guizhou 贵州 : Kweichow Province

Guo min dang 國民黨 : Kuomintang (KMT)

Guo Peilan 郭佩蘭 : Kwok Pui-lan, Harvard Divinity School PhD candidate from Hong Kong

Han 漢族 : the majority Chinese nationality

Hong Lou Meng 紅樓夢 : *The Dream of the Red Chamber*, a famous Chinese novel

Huaiyin 淮陰 : a city in Jiangsu (Kiangsu) Province

Huang Jianping 黃建平 : Zhang Xianyong's wife

Hubei 湖北 : Hopeh Province

Jiao/Chiao 教 : to teach

Jiang Qing 江青 : Chiang Ching, Chairman Mao's wife, one of the "Gang of Four"

Jiangsu 江蘇 : Kiangsu Province

"Jook sing" or Zhu sheng/Zuk1 sing1 竹昇 : Empty bamboo

Kaiping/Hoiping 開平 : ("open peace") a district, where many Chinese Americans came from

Kang 炕 : northern Chinese bed built on a stove

Kunming 昆明 : the capital city of Yunnan province

Kongbu 恐怖 : horrible

Kong Zi/Kungze 孔子 : Confucius

Lao ge ming gan bu 老革命幹部 : old revolutionary cadet

Leng/laang5 冷 : cold

Li Yading 李亞丁 : a Chinese theological student

Li Xinghua 李興華 : a pastor of Ping Jing

Lin Biao 林彪 : a former defense minister

Liu Zongren 劉宗仁 : the author of *Two Years in the Melting Pot*

Lu Xun 魯迅 : Lu Hsun, a famous 20th-century author

Mao Zedong 毛澤東 : Mao Tse-tung, the late chairman of the Chinese Communist Party

Miao 苗族 : a national minority

Wu yong / Mou4 jung6 無用 : useless

Mo Ruxi 莫如喜 : Gao Ying's teacher

Mu yang ren 牧羊人 : shepherds

Nainai 奶奶 / Yen Yen 仁 仁 : grandmother (Toishan/Taishan dialect)

Nanjing 南京 : the city of Nanking ("southern capital")

Pang Enmei 龐恩美 : a senior woman pastor at Shanghai Community Church

Ping Jing 平菁大隊 : Ping Qing Brigade

Re/Jit6 熱 : hot

Ren /Jen 仁 : the Confucian virtue—benevolence, humanity, "learning to be human"

Ren min bi 人民幣 : Chinese currency (RMB)

San yi/Sam Yahp 三邑 : three villages, the three districts, Chinese American

Situ Tong 司徒桐 : Gao Ying's teacher

Shi/Sap1 濕 : Wet

Si yi/SzeYup 四邑 : Say yap or Seyup or Sei Yahp—the four districts (where most Chinese Americans came from, including Taishan or Toishan)

Taishan/Toishan 台山 : a place where many Chinese Americans came from

Tian feng/Tien Feng 天風 : *Heavenly Wind*, a Christian journal

Tang ren/Tohng yahn 唐人 : People in the Tong Dynasty; generally refers to Chinese nowadays

Wang Yuanhua 王元華 : the author of *People's Daily* article on tradition

Wu Yaozong 吳耀宗 : Y. T. Wu, Three-Self Movement leader

Xinwei 新衛大隊 : Xinwei Brigade

Xinhui/Sunwui 新會 : one of the four districts, famous for oranges

Xu Guozhang 許國璋 : a famous Chinese author of English textbook

Xu Rulei 徐如雷 : Prof. Hsu at Nanjing Theological Union

Xue/hsueh 學 : to learn

Yangzi 揚子江 : Yangtze River

Yen Yen 仁 仁 : Toishan dialect for grandmother, uses the same character as *ren*, the Confucian virtue

Yi 彝族 : a Chinese minority

Yin-yang 陰陽 : Taoist cosmological concept, the characters mean dark and bright

Yun er/Won-yee 雲耳 : a black fungus which is different from Mu er 木耳

Zhai/Tsai 齋 : vegetarian food

Zhang Xianyong 張賢勇 : Chinese theological student

Zhang Zai/Chang Tsai 張載 : a neo-Confucian scholar (1020–1077)

Zhao Zhiguang 趙志廣 : Chinese theological student

Zhejiang University 浙江大學 : Chekiang University

Zhengxie 政協 : Chinese People's Consultative Congress

Zhou Chao 周朝 : Chou Dynasty

Zhou Enlai 周恩來 : Chou En-lai, late Premier of the People's Republic of China

Zhongshan 中山 : Chungshan, birthplace of Dr. Sun Yat-sen, father of modern China

References

Abells, C. (1983). *The children we remember.* New York: Greenwillow Books.

Aljaafreh, A., & Lantolf, J. P. (1994). Negative feedback as regulation and second language learning in the zone of proximal development. *Modern Language Journal, 78*, 465–483.

Allwright, D., & Bailey, K. (1991). *Focus on the language classroom: An introduction to classroom research for language teachers.* New York: Cambridge University Press.

Anthony, E. M. (1963). Approach, method, and technique. *ELT Journal, 63*(67).

Anzaldùa, G. (1987). *Borderlands: The new mestiza = La frontera/Gloria Anzaldu'a*. San Francisco: Spinsters/Aunt Lute.

Apple, M. (1996). *Cultural politics and education*. New York: Teachers College Press.

Apple, M. W. (1982). *Education and power*. Boston: Ark Paperbacks an imprint of Routledge & Kegan Paul.

Asher, J. (1969). The total physical response approach to second language learning. *Modern Language Journal, 53*, 3–17.

Asher, J. (1982). *Learning another language through actions*. Los Gatos, CA: Sky Oaks Productions.

Atwell, N. (1987). *In the middle: Writing, reading, and learning with adolescents.* Portsmouth, NH: Heinemann.

Au, K. H. (1980). Participation structures in a reading lesson with Hawaiian children. *Anthropology and Education Quarterly, 11*, 91–111.

Au, K. H. (1990). Changes in a teacher's views of interactive comprehension instruction. In L. Moll (Ed.), *Vygotsky and education: Instructional implications and applications of sociohistorical psychology* (pp. 271–286). Cambridge: Cambridge University Press.

Au, K. H., & Kawakami, A. J. (1985). Research currents: Talk story and learning to read. *Language Arts, 62*(4), 406–411.

Auerbach, E. (1989). Toward a socio-contextual approach to family literacy. *Harvard Educational Review, 59*(2), 165-181.

Auerbach, E. (1992). *Making meaning, making change: Participatory curriculum development for adult ESL literacy*. [Washington, DC] McHenry, IL: Center for Applied Linguistics and Delta Systems.

Auerbach, E. (1994a). Deconstructing the discourse of strengths in family literacy. *Journal of Reading Behavior, 27*(4), 643–661.

Auerbach, E. (1994b). Participatory action research. *TESOL Quarterly, 28*(4), 693–697.

Auerbach, E. (1995a). From deficit to strength: Changing perspectives on family literacy. In G. Q. Weinstein-Shr, Elizabeth (Ed.), *Immigrant learners and their families: Literacy to connect the generations* (pp. 63–76). McHenry, Illinois: Center for Applied Linguistics and Delta Systems.

Auerbach, E. (1995b). The politics of ESL classroom: Issues of power in pedagogical choices. In J. W. Tollefson (Ed.), *Power and inequity in language education* (pp. 9–33). Cambridge: Cambridge University Press.

Bakhtin, M. M. (1986). *Speech genres and other late essays* (V. W. McGee, Trans.). Austin: University of Texas Press.

Bakhtin, M. M., & Holquist, M. (1981). *The dialogic imagination: Four essays*. Austin: University of Texas Press.

Balch, J. F., & Balch, P. A. (1991, February). Prescription for nutritional healing. *Better Nutrition for Today's Living*.

Balderrama, M., Texeira, M. T., & Valdez, E. (2004). Una lucha de fronteras (A struggle of borders): Women of color in the academy. *Race, Gender, & Class, 11*(4), 135–154.

Bellino, J. (2005). "I'm a writer now!" The who, where, and when of an ELL newspaper. Retrieved June 23, 2005 from http://www.writingproject.org/cs/nwpp/print/nwpr/2192

Balmuth, J. (1968). Introduction: Marx and the philosophers. In R. Freedman (Ed.), *Marxist social thought* (pp. xxv–xxxiv). New York: Harcourt, Brace and World.

Bancroft, W. J. (1983). The Lozanov Method and its American adaptations. In J. W. Oller & P. A. Richard-Amato (Eds.), *Methods that work: A smorgasbord of ideas for language teachers* (pp. 101–112). Rowley, MA: Newbury House.

Banks, J. (1994). *Multiethnic education: Theory and practice*. Boston: Allyn Bacon.

Banks, J. (1996). *Multicultural education, transformative knowledge and action: Historical and contemporary perspectives*. New York: Teachers College Press.

Bartholomae, D., & Petrosky, A. (1986). *Facts, artifacts and counterfacts: Theory and method for a reading and writing course*. Upper Montclair, NJ: Boynton/Cook.

Baugh, J. (1999). *Out of the mouths of slaves: African American language and educational malpractice*. Austin: University of Texas Press.

Bautista, M. L. S. (1994). Toward intellectualization: Filipino as a pedagogical idiom for teaching literature. In *Teacher talk and student talk: Classroom observation studies at De La Salle University* (pp. 115–131). Manila: De La Salle University Press.

Belcher, D. D., & Hirvela, A. (2001). *Linking literacies: Perspectives on L2 reading–writing connections*. Ann Arbor: University of Michigan Press.

Belden, J. (1970). *China shakes the world*. New York: Monthly Review Press for American journalistic accounts of the Chinese Revolution.

Belenky, M. (1986). *Women's ways of knowing*. New York: Basic Books.

Bell, D. M. (2003). Method and postmethod: Are they really so incompatible? *TESOL Quarterly, 37*(2), 325–336.

Bellino, J. (1991). Double entry reading Logs: A Reading, thinking, writing connection. *WATESOL Newsletter*.

Benesch, S. (1999). Thinking critically, thinking dialogically. *TESOL Quarterly, 33*(3), 573–580.

Benesch, S. (2001). *Critical English for academic purposes: Theory, politics, and practice*. Mahwah, NJ: Lawrence Erlbaum Associates.

Berk, L. E., & Winsler, A. (1995). *Scaffolding children's learning: Vygotsky and early childhood education*. Washington, DC: National Association for the Education of Young Children.

Bernauer, J. (1987). Michel Foucault's ecstatic thinking. In J. Bernauer & D. Rasmussen (Eds.), *The final Foucault* (pp. 45–82). Cambridge, MA: MIT Press.

Berthoff, A. E. (1981). *The making of meaning: Metaphors, models, and maxims for writing teachers.* Montclair, NJ: Boynton/Cook.

Bialystock, E., & Hakuta, K. (1994). *In other words: The science and psychology of second language acquisition.* New York: Basic Books.

Blackwell, A. G., Kwoh, S., & Pastor, M. (2002). *Searching for the uncommon common ground : New dimensions on race in America.* New York: W. W. Norton.

Boas, F. (1928). *Anthropology and modern life.* New York: Norton.

Bourdieu, P. (1991). *Language and symbolic power* (G. Raymond & M. Adamson, Trans.). Cambridge, MA: Harvard University Press.

Bourdieu, P. , & Passeron, J. S. (1977). *Reproduction in education, society, and culture.* Beverly Hills, CA: Sage.

Bowen, J. (1972). *A history of Western education* (Vol. 1). New York: St. Martins Press.

Boyd, W., & King, E. J. (Eds.). (1973). *The history of Western education.* New York: Barnes and Noble.

Braine, G. (Ed.). (1999). *Non-native educators in English language teaching.* Mahwah, NJ: Lawrence Erlbaum Associates.

Brown, W. (1998). Injury, identity, and politics. In A. F. Gordon & C. Newfield (Eds.), *Mapping multiculturalism* (pp. 149–166). Minnesota: University of Minnesota Press.

Bruner, J. (1962). Introduction. In *Thought and language. By Lev Vygotsky* (pp. v–xiii). Cambridge: MIT Press.

Bruner, J. (1983). *Child's talk: Learning to use language.* New York: W. W. Norton.

Bruner, J. (1985). Models of the Learner. *Educational Researcher, 14*(6), 5–8.

Bruner, J. (1986). *Actual minds, possible worlds.* Cambridge, MA: Harvard University Press.

Bruner, J. (1990). *Acts of meaning.* Cambridge, MA: Harvard University Press.

Bruner, J. (1996). *The culture of education.* Cambridge, MA: Harvard University Press.

Brutt-Griffler, J., & Samimy, K. (1999). Revisiting the colonial in the postcolonial: Critical praxis for nonnative English-speaking teachers in a TESOL program. *TESOL Quarterly, 33*(3), 413–432.

Bull, L. (2000). Walking with peace education: An indigenous journey. *Journal of Curriculum Studies, 2*(1), 65–83.

Butts, R. F. (Ed.). (1955). *A critical history of Western education.* New York: McGraw Hill.

Calkins, L. M. (1983). *Lessons from a child: On the teaching and learning of writing.* Portsmouth, NH: Heinemann.

Calkins, L. M. (1986). *The art of teaching writing.* Portsmouth, NH: Heinemann.

Cameron, D. (1992). "Respect, please!": Investigating race, power, and method. In D. Cameron, E. Frazer, P. Harvey, M. B. H. Ramption, & K. Richardson (Eds.), *Researching language: Issues of power and method* (pp. 113–130). London and New York: Routledge.

Canagarajah, A. S. (1999). Resisting linguistic imperialism in English teaching. Oxford: Oxford University Press.

Canale, M., & Swain, M. (1980). *Approaches to communicative competence.* Singapore: SEAMEO Regional Language Centre.

Carter, R., & Long, M. N. (1990). Testing literature in EFL classes: Tradition and innovation. *ELT Journal, 44*(3), 215–221.

Carter, R., & Long, M. N. (1991). *Teaching literature* (Vol. 44). New York: Longman.

Cazden, C. (1988). *Classroom discourse: The language of teaching and learning.* Portsmouth, NH: Heinemann.

Cazden, C. (1992). *Whole language plus: Essays on literacy in the United States and New Zealand*. New York: Teachers College Press.

Celce-Murcia, M. (1998). Making informed decisions about the role of grammar in language teaching. *Foreign Language Annals, 18*(4), 297–301.

Celce-Murcia, M., Dornyei, Z., & Thurrell, S. (1995, December). Communicative competence: A pedagogically motivated model with content specifications. *Issues in Applied Linguistics, 6*(2), 5–35.

Celce-Murcia, M., & Prator, C. (1979). An outline of language teaching approaches. In M. C.-M. A. L. McIntosh (Ed.), *Teaching English as a second or foreign language* (pp. xv, 389). Rowley, MA: Newbury House.

Chen, J. (1990). *Confucius as teacher: Philosophy of Confucius with special reference to its educational implications*. Beijing: Foreign Language Press.

Chin, F. (1991). *Donald Duk: A novel*. St. Paul, MN: Coffee House Press.

Chomsky, N. (1957). *Syntactic structures*. The Hague: Mouton.

Chomsky, N. (1959). A review of Skinner's Verbal behavior. *Language, 35*, 26–58.

Chomsky, N. (1972). *Language and mind*. New York: Harcourt Brace Jovanovich.

Chomsky, N., & Macedo, D. (2000). Beyond a domesticating education: A dialogue. In D. Macedo (Ed.), *Chomsky on MisEducation*. New York: Rowan and Littlefield.

Chow, T. (Zhou, C.). (1967). *The May Forth movement: Intellectual revolution in modern China*. Stanford, CA: Stanford University Press.

Christie, F. (1999). Genre theory and ESL teaching: A systemic functional perspective. *TESOL Quarterly, 33*(94), 759–763.

Christison, M. A., & Krahnke, K. J. (1986). Student perceptions of academic language Study. *TESOL Quarterly, 20*(1), 61–81.

Chu, H., & Lu, T. C. (1967). *Reflections on things at hand*. (W. T. Chan, Trans.). New York: Columbia University Press.

Clark, K., & Holquist, M. (1984). *Mikhail Bakhtin*. Cambridge, MA: Belknap Press of Harvard University Press.

Clarke, M. (1994). The dysfunctions of the theory/practice discourse. *TESOL Quarterly, 28*(1), 9–25.

Clay, M., & Cazden, C. B. (1990). A Vygotskian interpretation of Reading Recovery. In L. Moll (Ed.), *Vygotsky and education: Instructional implications and applications of sociohistorical psychology* (pp. 206–223). New York: Cambridge University Press.

Cochrane-Smith, M., & Lytle, S. L. (1993). *Inside/outside: Teacher research and knowledge*. New York: Teachers College Press.

Cole, M., & Scribner, S. (1978). Introduction: Biographical Note on L. S. Vygotsky. In M. Cole, V. John-Steiner, S. Scribner, & E. Souberman (Eds.), *Mind in society: Development of higher psychological processes*. Cambridge, MA: Harvard University Press.

Collins, J., & Blot, R. (2003). *Literacy and literacies: Texts, power and identity*. New York: Cambridge University Press.

Collins, P. H. (1991). *Black feminist thought : Knowledge, consciousness, and the politics of empowerment*. New York: Routledge.

Cortes, C. (1986). The education of language minority students: A contextual interaction model. In *Beyond language: Social and cultural factors in schooling language minority students* (pp. 3–33). Los Angeles: California State University Evaluation, Dissemination, and Assessment Center.

Coughlan, P., & Duff, P. (1994) Same task, different activities: Analysis of a second language acquisition task from an activity theory perspective. In J. P. Lantolf & G. Appel (Eds.), *Vygotskyan approaches to second language research* (pp. 173–193). Norwood, NJ: Ablex.

Crandall, J. A. (1993). Content-centered learning in the United States. *Annual Review of Applied Linguistics, 13,* 111–126.
Crawford, J. (1998). Endangered Native American languages. In B. Burnaby & T. Ricento (Eds.), *Language and Politics in the United States and Canada: Myths and Realities*. Mahwah, NJ: Lawrence Erlbaum Associates.
Cruse, H. (1969). *Crisis of the Negro intellectual.* New York: Morrow.
Cummins, J. (1986). Empowering minority students: A framework for intervention. *Harvard Ed Review, 56*(1), 18–36.
Cummins, J. (2000). This place nurtures my spirit: Creating contexts of empowerment in linguistically diverse schools. In R. Phillipson (Ed.), *Rights to language: Equity, power and education*. Mahwah, NJ: Lawrence Erlbaum Associates.
Curran, C. A. (1976). *Counseling learning in second languages*. Apple River: IL: Apple River Press.
Darder, A. (1991). *Culture and power in the classroom: A critical foundation for bicultural education.* New York: Bergin & Garvey.
Dawson, R. (1981). *Confucius*. New York: Hill and Wang.
deBeaugrande, R. (1997). Theory and practice in applied linguistics: Disconnection conflict or dialect? *Applied Linguistics, 18*(2), 279–313.
De Guerrero, M. (1996). Krashen's i + 1 and Vygotsky's ZPD: Really two very different notions. *TESOL-GRAM Puerto Rico TESOL Newsletter, 9*.
Delgado-Gaitan, C. (1996). *Protean literacy: Extending the discourse on empowerment.* London: Falmer Press.
DeLorenzo, W., Wong, S., Motha, S., Teuben-Rowe, S., Frye, D., Harden, S. J., Malaev, L., & Spezio, K. (1998, March 16–22) *Emergent literacy strategies for ESOL readers*. Workshop. TESOL '98, 32nd Annual Convention, Seattle.
Delp, L., Outman-Kramer, M., Schurman, S. J., & Wong, K. (2002). *Teaching for change: Popular education and the labor movement*. Los Angeles: UCLA Center for Labor Research and Education.
Delpit, L. (1988). The silenced dialogue: Power and pedagogy in educating other people's children. *Harvard Ed Review, 58*, 280–298.
Delpit, L. D. (1995). *Other people's children : Cultural conflict in the classroom*. New York: New Press: Distributed by W. W. Norton.
Del Tredici, P. (1991). Ginkgos and people, a thousand years of interaction. *Arnoldia, 51*, 2–15.
Dewey, J. (1973). *John Dewey's lectures in China*. Honolulu: University of Hawaii Press.
Dewey, J. (1997). *How we think*. Mineola, NY: Dover Publications, Inc.
Di Bello, L., & Orlich, F. (1987, July). How Vygotsky's Notion of "Scientific Concept" May Inform Contemporary Studies of Theory Development. *The Quarterly Newsletter of the Laboratory of Comparative Human Cognition, 9*(3).
Diaz-Rico, L. T. (1998). Towards a just society: Recalibrating multicultural teachers. In R. Chavez & J. O'Donnell (Eds.), *Speaking the unpleasant: The politics of (non)engagement in the multicultural terrain*. Albany: SUNY Press.
Diaz-Rico, L. T. (2004). *Teaching English learners*. Boston: Pearson.
Dobb, M. (1968). *Studies in the Development of Capitalism*. New York: International Publishers.
Dubin, F. & Kuhlman, N. (Eds.). (1992). *Cross-cultural literacy: Global perspectives on reading and writing*. Englewood Cliffs, NJ: Regents/Prentice Hall.
DuBois, W. E. B. (1961). *The souls of black folk*. Grennwich, CT: Fawcett Publications (originally published 1903).
DuBois, W. E. B. (1968). *The autobiography of W. E. B. DuBois*. New York: International.

Dunn, W. E., & Lantolf, J. P. (1998). Vygotsky's zone of proximal development and Krashen's "i + 1": Incommensurable constructs; incommensurable theories. *Language Learning, 48*(3), 411–442.
Edelsky, C. (1991). *With literacy and justice for all.* London: Falmer Press.
Edelsky, C., Altwerger, B., & Flores, B. (1991). *Whole language: What's the difference?* Portsmouth, NH: Heinemann.
Edge, J. & Richards, K. (Eds.) (1993). *Teachers develop teachers research: Papers on classroom research and teacher development.* Oxford: Heinemann.
Edminston, B., & Enciso, P. (2003). Reflections and refractions of meaning: dialogic approaches to reading with classroom drama. In J. Flood, D. Lapp, J. R. Squire, J. M. Jensen, (Ed.), *Handbook of research on teaching the English language arts* (2nd ed., pp. 868–880). Mahwah, NJ: Lawrence Erlbaum Associates.
Ekbatani, G., & Pierson, H. (2000). *Learner-directed assessment in ESL.* Mahwah, NJ: Lawrence Erlbaum Associates.
Ellis, R. (1994). *The study of second language acquisition.* Oxford: Oxford University Press.
Errante, A. (2000). But sometimes You're not part of the story: Oral histories and ways of remembering and telling. *Educational Researcher, 29*(2), 16–27.
Evans, K. (2002). *Negotiating the self: Identity, sexuality and emotion in learning to teach.* New York: Routledge Falmer.
Fairclough, N. (1989). *Language and power.* London: Longman.
Fairclough, N. (1992). *Critical language awareness.* London: Longman.
Faltis, C., & Hudelson, S. (1994). Learning English as an additional language in K-12 schools. TEXOL Quarterly, 28(3), 457–468
Fanon, F. (1963). *The wretched of the earth.* New York: Grove Press.
Fanselow, J. (1987). *Breaking rules: Generating and exploring alternatives in language teaching.* New York: Longmans.
Feinberg, L. (1998). *Transliberation: Beyond pink or blue.* Boston: Beacon Press.
Figueroa, P. (1991). *Education and the social construction of "race."* London: Routledge.
Flower, L. S., & Hayes, J. R. (1981). A cognitive process theory of writing. *College Composition and Communication, 32*, 365–387.
Foucault, M. 1972). The archeology of knowledge. New York: Pantheon.
Franklin, E. (Ed.). (1999). *Reading and writing in more than one language: Lessons for teachers.* Alexandria, VA: Teachers of English to Speakers of Other Languages.
Franklin, E. A. (1989). Encouraging understanding the visual and written works of second-language children. In P. Rigg & V. G. Allen (Eds.), *When they don't all speak English: Integrating ESL students into the regular classroom* (pp. 77–95). Urbana, IL: National Council of Teachers of English.
Freedman, R. (1968). *Marxist Social Thought.* New York: Harcourt, Brace and World.
Freeman, D. (1996). Redefining the relationship between research and what teachers know. In K. Bailey & D. Nunan (Eds.), *Voices from the language classroom: Qualitative research in second language education* (pp. 89-122). Cambridge, England: Cambridge University Press.
Freeman, D., & Johnson, K. (1998). Special topic issue: Research and practice in English language teacher education. *TESOL Quarterly, 32*(3).
Freeman, D. E., & Freeman, Y. S. (2001). *Between worlds: Access to second language acquisition* (2nd ed.). Portsmouth, NH: Heinemann.
Freeman, Y. S., & Freeman, D. E. (1992). *Whole language for second language learners.* Portsmouth, NH: Heinemann.
Freire, P. (1970). *Pedagogy of the oppressed.* New York: Herder and Herder.
Freire, P. (1985). *The politics of education: Culture, power and liberation* (D. Macedo, Trans.). Granby, MA: Bergin & Garvey.

Gallimore, R., & Tharp, R. G. (1990). Teaching mind in society: Teaching, schooling, and literate discourse. In L. C. Moll (Ed.), *Vygotsky and education: Instructional implications and applications of sociohistorical psychology* (pp. 175–205). New York: Cambridge University Press.

Gass, S. M., Mackey, A., & Pica, T. (Eds.). (1998). *The role of input and interaction in second language acquisition.* (Vol. 82).

Gates, H. L., Jr. (1986). Writing "race" and the difference it makes. In H. L. Gates (Ed.), *Race, Writing, and Difference* (pp. 1–20). Chicago: University of Chicago Press.

Gates, H. L., Jr. (1988). *The signifying mondy: A theory of Afro American literacy criticism*. New York: Oxford University Press.

Gebhardt, M. (2005). School reform, hybrid discourses, and second language literacies. *TESOL Quarterly, 33*(94), 187–210.

Gee, J. (1990). *Social linguistics and literacies: Ideology in discourses.* London: Falmer Press.

Gee, J. P. (2001). Identity as an analytic lens for research in education. *Review of Research in Education, 25*, 99–125.

Geertz, C. (1983). *Local knowledge: Further essays in interpretive anthropology.* New York: Basic Books.

Gieve, S. (1998). Comments on Dwight Atkinson's "A critical approach to critical thinking in TESOL": Another reader reacts. *TESOL Quarterly, 32*, 123–129.

Gilligan, C. (1993). *In a different voice: Psychological theory and women's development.* Cambridge: MA: Harvard University Press.

Gitlin, A. (1991). *Teachers' voices for school change.* New York: Teachers College Press.

Goldenberg, C. N. (1991). *Instructional conversations and their classroom application.* Washington, DC: National Center for Research on Cultural Diversity and Second Language Learning, U.S. Department of Education Office of Educational Research and Improvement, Educational Resources Information Center.

Goldstein, T. (2004). Performed ethnography for critical language teacher education. In B. Norton & K. Toohey (Eds.), *Critical pedagogies and language learning* (pp. 311–326).

Goodman, K., Goodman, F., & Flores, B. (1979). *Reading in a bilingual classroom.* Roslyn, VA,: National Clearinghouse for Bilingual Education.

Gould, S. J. (1981). *The mismeasure of man.* New York: Norton.

Gramsci, A. (1971). *Selections from the prison notebooks of Antonio Gramsci* (Q. Hoare & G. N. Smith, Eds.). New York: International.

Grant, R., & Wong, S. (2003). Barriers to literacy for language-minority learners: An argument for change in the literacy education profession. *Journal of Adult and Adolescent Literacy, 46*(5), 386–394.

Grant, R., & Wong, S. (2004). Forging multilingual communities: School-based strategies. *Multicultural Perspectives, 6*(3), 17–23.

Green, J., Franquiz, M., & Dixon, C. (1997). The myth of the objective transcript: Transcribing as a situated act. *TESOL Quarterly, 31*(1), 172–176.

Greene, M. (1986). In search of a critical pedagogy. *Harvard Educational Review, 56*(4).

Greene, M. (1988). *Dialetic of freedom.* New York: Teachers College Press.

Guiterrez, K., Rymes, B., & Larson, J. (1995). Script, counterscript and underlife in the classroom: James Brown versus *Brown v. Board of Education. Harvard Educational Review, 65*(3), 445–471.

Gutirrez, K. D., & Stone, L. D. (2000). Synchronic and diachronic dimensions of social practice: An emerging methodology for cultural-historical perspectives on literacy learning. In C. D. Lee & P. Smagorinsky (Eds.), *Vygotskian perspectives on literacy research: Constructing meaning through collaborative inquiry.* Cambridge; New York: Cambridge University Press.

Hakuta, K. (1986). *Mirror of language: The debate on bilingualism*. New York: Basic Books.
Haley, M. H., & Austin, T. Y. (2004). *Content-based second language teaching and learning*. Boston: Pearson.
Hall, J. K. (2002). *Teaching and researching: Language and culture*. Harlow: Longman.
Hall, J. K., & Eggington, W. (2000). *The sociopolitics of English language teaching*. Clevedon; Buffalo [N.Y.]: Multilingual Matters.
Hall, J. K., & Verplaetse, L. S. (2000). *Second and foreign language learning through classroom interaction*. Mahwah, NJ: Lawrence Erlbaum Associates.
Hall, J. K., Vitanova, G., & Marchenkova, L. (2004). *Dialogue with Bakhtin on second and foreign language learning*. Mahwah, NJ: Lawrence Erlbaum Associates.
Halliday, M. A. K. (1973). *Explorations in the function of language*. London: Arnold.
Halliday, M. A. K. (1975). *Learning how to mean: Explorations in the development of language*. London: Arnold.
Halliday, M. A. K. (1985). *Introduction to functional grammar*. London: Arnold.
Halliday, M. A. K., & Hasan, R. (1985). *Language, context and text*. Geelong, Australia: Deakin University Press.
Halliday, M. A. K., McIntosh, A., & Strevens, P. (1964). *The linguistic sciences and language, class and power in language teaching*. London: Longmans.
Handea, M. (2000). Modes of student participation in an elementary-school science classroom: From talking to writing. *Linguistics and Education, 10*(4), 1–27.
Haney, W. (1993). Testing and minorities. In E. L. Weiss & M. Fine (Ed.), *Beyond silenced voices: Class, race ad gender in the United States schools*. Albany, NY: State University of New York Press.
Hansen, J. G., & Liu, J. (1997). Social identity and language: Teeoretical and methodological issues. *TESOL Quarterly, 31*(3), 567–576.
Harding, S. (1987). *Feminism and methodology: Social science issues*. Bloomington: Indiana University Press.
Harding, S. (2000). Gender, development, and post-englightenment philosophies of science. In U. Narayan & S. Harding (Eds.), *Decentering the center: Philosophy for a multicultural, postcolonial and feminist world* (pp. 240–261). Bloomington: Indiana University Press.
Harklau, L. (1994). Tracking and linguistic minority students: Consequences of ability grouping for second language learners. *Linguistics and Education, 6*(3), 217–244.
Harry, B. (1992). *Cultural diversity, families, and the special education system: Communication and empowerment*. New York: Teacher's College Press.
Hawkins, M. R. (2004). Researching English language and literacy development in schools. *Educational Researcher, 33*(3), 14–25.
Heath, S. B. (1983). *Ways with words: Language, life and work in communities and classrooms*. Cambridge, England: Cambridge University Press.
Hegel, F. (1969). *Hegel: Texts and commentary* (W. Kaufmann, Trans.). Garden City, NY: Doubleday Anchor Books.
Heller, M., & Martin-Jones, M. (2001). Introduction: Symbolic domination, education and linguistic difference. In *Voices of Authority: Education and linguistic difference* (pp. 1–28). Westport, CT: Ablex.
Hirschfelder, A. B. (1987, November). The seasonal symbolic Indian mocks the Native American reality. *Los Angeles Times*, p. 7.
Hodge, R., & Kress, G. (1988). *Social semiotics*. Ithaca, NY: Cornell University Press.
Hones, D. C. & Cha, C. H. (1999). *Educating new Americans: immigrant lives and learning*. Mahwah, NJ: Lawrence Erlbaum Associates.
hooks, b. (1981). *Ain't I a woman : Black women and feminism*. Boston: South End Press.

hooks, b. (1994). *Teaching to transgress : education as the practice of freedom.* New York: Routledge.

Hu, S. (1963). *The Chinese Renaissance.* New York: Paragon.

Hudelson, S. (1984). Kan yu ret and rayt in ingles: Children become literate in English as a second language. *TESOL Quarterly, 18*, 221–238.

Hudelson, S. (1986). ESL children's writing: What we've learned, what we're learning. In P. Rigg & D. S. Enright (Eds.), *Children and ESL: Integrating perspectives* (pp. 23–54). Washington, DC: TESOL.

Hymes, D. (1974). *Foundations in sociolinguistics: An ethnographic approach.* Philadelphia: University of Pennsylvania Press.

Hyon, S. (1996). Genre in three traditions: Implications for ESL. *TESOL Quarterly, 30*(4), 693–722.

Igoa, C. (1995). *The inner works of the immigrant child.* New York: Saint Martin's Press.

Jennings, L., & Pattenaude, I. (1999). Oye y escucha mi voz—Hear and see my voice: Responding to intolerance and genocide. *Multicultural Perspectives, 1*(1), 30–36.

Jespersen, O., & Bertelsen, S. Y. (1912). *How to teach a foreign language.* London, New York: S. Sonnenschein.

Johnson, K. E., & Golombek, P. R. (Eds.). (2002). *Teachers' narrative inquiry as professional development.* New York: Cambridge University Press.

Johnston, B., Juhãsz, A., Marken, J., & Ruiz, B. R. (1998). The ESL teacher as moral agent. *Research in the Teaching of English, 32*, 161–181.

John-Steiner, V., Panofsky, C. P., & Smith, L. W. (Ed.). (1994). *Sociocultural approaches to language and literacy: An interactionist perspective.* Cambridge: Cambridge University Press.

John-Steiner, V., & Souberman, E. (1978). Afterword. In M. Cole, V. John-Steiner, S. Scribner, & E. Souberman (Eds.), *L. S. Vygotsky. Mind in society: Development of higher psychological processes.* Cambridge, MA: Harvard University Press.

Jordan, D. F. (1988). Rights and claims of indigenous people: Education and the Reclaiming of identity. In J. Skutnabb-Kangas (Ed.), *Minority Education* (pp. 189–222). Clevedon, England: Miltilingual Matters.

Kachru, B. B. (1986). The power and politics of English. *World Englishes, 5*(2–3), 121–140.

Kachru, B. B. (1995). World Englishes: Approaches, issues, and resources. In H. D. Brown (Ed.), *Readings on second language acquisition* (pp. 229–261). Upper Saddle River, NJ: Prentice Hall Regents.

Kiang, P. N. (1996). Southeast Asian and Latino parent empowerment: Lessons from Lowell, Massachusetts. In C. E. Walsh (Ed.), *Education Reform and social change: Multicultural voices, struggles and visions* (pp. 59–69). Mahwah, NJ: Lawrence Erlbaum Associates.

Kinginger, C. (2001). i + 1 = ZPD. *Foreign Language Annals, 34*(5), 417–425.

Kouritzin, S. (1999). *Face[t]s of first language loss.* Mahwah, NJ: Lawrence Erlbaum Associates.

Kozol, J. (1991). *Savage inequalities : Children in America's schools.* New York: Crown.

Kozulin, A. (1990). *Vygotsky's psychology: A biography of ideas.* Cambridge, MA: Harvard University Press.

Kramsch, C. & von Hoene, L. (1995). The dialogic emergence of difference: Feminist explorations in foreign language learning and teaching. In D. Stanton & A. Stewart (Eds.), *Feminisms in the academy* (pp. 330–357). Ann Arbor: University of Michigan Press.

Krashen, S. D. (1985). *The input hypothesis: Issues and implications.* New York: Longman.

Krashen, S. D., & Terrell, T. D. (1985). *The natural approach: Language acquisition in the classroom*. Englewood Cliffs, NJ: Alemany Press/Regents/Prentice Hall.

Kress, G. (1989). *Linguistic process in sociocultural practice.* Oxford, English: Oxford University Press.

Kress, G., & Hodge, R. (1979). *Language as ideology.* London: Routledge and Kagen Paul.

Kubota, R. (2004). Critical multiculturalism and second language education. In B. Norton & K. Toohey (Eds.), *Critical pedagogies and language learning* (pp. 30–52). Cambridge, New York: Cambridge University Press.

Kubota, R. (2002). Marginality as an asset: Toward a counter-hegemonic pedagogy for diversity. In L. Vargas (Ed.), *Women faculty of color in the white college classroom* (pp. 293–307). New York: Peter Lang.

Kumaravadivelu, B. (1994).The postmethod condition: (E)merging strategies for diversity. In L. Vargas (Ed.), *Women faculty of color in the white college classroom* (pp. 293–307). New York: Peter Lang.

Kumaravadivelu, B. (2001). Toward a postmethod pedagogy. *TESOL Quarterly, 35*(4), 537–560.

Lado, R. (1964). *Language teaching : a scientific approach*. New York: McGraw-Hill.

Ladson-Billings, G. (2004). New directions in multicultural education: Complexities, boundaries, and critical race theory. In J. A. Banks & C. A. McGee Banks (Eds.) *Handbook of research on multicultural education* (2nd ed.). San Francisco: Jossey-Bass.

Lantolf, J. (2000). *Sociocultural theory and second language learning.* Oxford: Oxford University Press.

Lantolf, J. P. (1996). SLA theory building: Letting all the flowers bloom. *Language Learning, 46*(4), 713–749.

Lantolf, J. P., & Appel, G. (Eds.). (1994). *Vygotskian approaches to second language research.* Norwood, NJ: Ablex.

Lantolf, J. P., & Pavlenko, A. (1995). Sociocultural Theory and Second Language Acquisition. *Annual Review of Applied Linguistics, 15,* 108–124.

Larsen-Freeman, D. (2000). An attitude of inquiry: TESOL as a science. *Journal of the Imagination in Language Learning, 5,* 18–21.

Lather, P. A. (1991). *Getting smart : Feminist research and pedagogy with/in the postmodern.* New York: Routledge.

Lau, D. C. (1979). *Confucius: The Analects (Lun yu)*. Hong Kong: The Chinese University Press.

Lave, J., & Wenger, E. (1991). *Situated learning: Legitimate peripheral participation.* Cambridge: Cambridge University Press.

Lee, C. D. (1993). *Signifying as a scaffold for literary interpretation: The pedagogical implications of an African American discourse genre.* Urbana, IL: National Council of the Teachers of English.

Lee, C. D., & Smagorinsky, P. (Eds.). (2000). *Vygotskian perspectives on literacy research*. Cambridge: Cambridge University Press.

Lee, S. J. (1996). *Unraveling the "model minority stereotype": Listening to Asian American youth*. New York: Teachers College, Columbia University.

Lee, E., Menkart, D., & Okazawa-Rey, M. (1998). *Beyond heroes and holidays: A practical guide to K–12 anti-racist, multicultural education and staff development.* Washington, DC: Network of Educators on the Americas.

Lefebre, H. (1969). *The sociology of Marx* (N. Guterman, Trans.). New York: Vintage Books.

Lemke, J. (1990). *Talking science.* Norwood, NJ: Ablex.

Lemke, J. (1995). *Textual politics.* London: Taylor & Francis.

Leung, C., Harris, R., & Rampton, B. (1997). The idealised native speaker, reified ethnicities, and classroom realities. *TESOL Quarterly, 31*(3), 543–560.

Levy, M. (1968). *The family revolution in modern China.* New York: Vintage Books.

Li, Y. (1987, November–December). *Indian—Real American.* Unpublished essay.

Li, Y. (1988, January 5). *In the sound of Jubilee.* Journal entry.

Lin, A. (1999). Doing English lessons in the reproduction or transformation of social worlds. *TESOL Quarterly, 33*(3), 393–412.

Lin, A. M. Y. (2001a). Resistance and creativity in English reading lessons in Hong Kong. In B. A. S. Comber, A. (Eds.), *Negotiating Critical Literacies in classrooms* (pp. 83–100). Mahwah, NJ: Lawrence Erlbaum Associates.

Lin, A. M. Y. (2001b). Symbolic domination and bilingual classroom practices in Hong Kong. In M. Heller & M. Martin-Jones (Eds.), *Voices of Authority: Education and linguistic difference.* Westport, CT: Ablex.

Lippi-Green, R. (1997). *English with an accent : language, ideology, and discrimination in the United States.* New York: Routledge.

LoCastro, V. (2001). Large classes and student learning. *TESOL Quarterly, 35*(3), 493– 496.

Los Angeles County Commission on Human Relations. (2001). *Compounding the tragedy: The other victims of September 11th, 2001.* 2001 Hate Crime Report. Los Angeles, CA: Author.

Lucas, C., & Borders, D. G. (1994). *Language diversity and classroom discourse.* Norwood, MA: Ablex.

Luke, A. (1986). Linguistic stereotypes, the divergent speaker and the teaching of literacy. *Journal of Curriculum Studies, 18*(4), 397–408.

Luke, A. (1995–1996). Text and discourse in education: An introduction to critical discourse analysis. *Review of Research in Education, 21*, 3–48.

Luke, A. (1996). Genres of power? Literacy education and the production of capital. In R. Hasan & G. Williams (Eds.), *Literacy in society* (pp. 308–338). London: Longman.

Luke, A. (2000). Producing new Asian masculinities. In C. Barron, N. Bruce, & D. Nunan (Eds.), *Knowledge and discourse: Towards ecology of language* (pp. 78–92). Harlow, England: Longman.

Luke, A., Kale, J. Singh, M.G., Hill, T. & Daliri, F. (1994). Talking difference: Discourses on Aboriginal identity in a grade on classroom. In D. Corson (Ed.), *Discourse and power in educational organizations* (pp. 211–324). Cresskill, NJ: Hampton Press.

Luke, C., & Gore, J. (1992). *Feminism and critical pedagogy.* New York: Routledge.

Lynch, _., & Shaw, _. (2005). Portfolios, power and ethics. *TESOL Quarterly, 29*, 263–297.

Lyons, C. A., Pinnell, G. S., & DeFord, D. E. (1993). *Partners in learning: Teachers and children in Reading Recovery.* New York: Teachers College Press.

Maguire, M. (1999). A bilingual child's choices and voices: Lessons in noticing, listening, and understanding. In E. Franklin (Ed.), *Reading and writing in more than one language: Lessons for teachers* (pp. 115–140). Alexandria, VA: TESOL.

Mama, R., & Romney, M. (2001). *Pearls of Wisdom.* Brattleboro, VT: Pro Lingua Associates.

Mao, T. (1971). *Selected readings from the works of Mao Tse-tung.* Peking: Foreign Languages Press.

Mao, Z. D. (1967). On practice. In *Selected Works of Mao Tse-tung* (Vol. 1, pp. 295–309). Peking (Beijing): Foreign Languages Press.

Mao, Z. D. (1971). *Selected readings from the works of Mao Tse-tung.* Peking: Foreign Languages Press.

Marchenkova, L. (2005). Language, culture, and self: The Bakhtin-Vygotsly encounter. In J. K. Hall, G. Vitanova & L. Marchenkova (Eds.), *Dialogue with Bakhtin on second and foreign language learning: New perspectives* (pp. 171–188). Mahwah, NJ: Lawrence Erlbaum Associates.

Martin, J. (1993). Genre and literacy—Modeling context in educational linguistics. *Annual Review of Applied Linguistics, 13*, 141–172.

Martin, L. H., Gutman, H., & Hutton, P. H. (1988). *Technologies of the self: A seminar with Michel Foucault.* Amherst: University of Massachusetts Press.

Marx, K. (1906). *Capital: A critique of political economy* (S. Moore, E. Aveling, & E. Untermann, Trans.). New York: Random House.

Marx, K., & Engels, F. (1939). *The German ideology.* New York: International.

Matsuda, M. (1991). Voices of America: Accent, antidiscrimination law, and a jurisprudence for the last reconstruction. *Yale Law Journal, 100*(5), 1329–1407.

Matsuda, M. (1996). *Where is your body?: And other essays on race, gender and the law.* Boston: Beacon Press.

McClanahan, A. J. (1986). *Our stories, our lives: A collection of twenty-three transcribed interviews with elders of the Cook Inlet Region.* Anchorage, Alaska: The CIRI Foundation.

McDermott, R. P. (1987). Achieving school failure: An anthropological approach to illiteracy and school stratification. In G. D. Spindler (Ed.), *Education and cultural process: Anthropological approaches* (2nd ed., pp. 173–209). Prospect Heights, IL: Waveland Press, Inc.

McGroarty, M. (1993). Cooperative learning and second language acquisition. In D.D. Holt (Ed.), *Cooperative learning: A response to linguistic and cultural diversity* (pp. 19–46). McHenry, IL: CAL Center for Applied Linguistics and Delta Systems, prepared by the ERIC Clearinghouse on Languages and Linguistics.

McKay, S. L. (1991). Variation in English: What role for education? In M. L. Tickoo (Ed.), *Languages & Standards: Issues, attitudes, case studies, RELC Anthology* (Vol. 26). Singapore: SEAMO.

McLaughlin, B. (1987). *Theories of second-language learning.* London: Edward Arnold.

McLaughlin, B. (1992). *Myths and misconceptions about second language learning: What every teacher needs to unlearn.* Santa Cruz, CA: National center for Research on Cultural Diversity and Second Language.

McLaughlin, D. (1994). Toward a dialogical understanding of literacy: The case of Navajo print. In B. J. Moss (Ed.), *Literacy across communities* (pp. 85–120). Cresskill, NJ: Hampton Press.

McLellan, D. (Ed.). (1977). *Karl Marx: Selected writings.* Oxford: Oxford University Press.

McNamara, T. (1997). What do we mean by social identity? Competing frameworks, competing discourses. *TESOL Quarterly, 31*(3), 561–567.

Mehan, H. (1979). *Learning lessons: Social organization in the classroom.* Cambridge, MA: Harvard University Press.

Memmi, A. (1970). *The colonizer and the colonized.* Boston: Beacon Press.

Michaels, S. (1981). "Sharing time": Children's narrative styles and differential access to literacy. *Language in Society, 10*, 423–442.

Molinsky, S. J., & Bliss, B. (2001). *Side by Side: Book 2, Vol. 2.* New York: Longman.

Molinsky, S. J., & Bliss, B. (2001). *Side by Side.* Upper Saddle River, NJ: Prentice Hall Regents.

Moll, L. (Ed.). (1990). *Vygotsky and education: Instructional implications and applications of sociohistorical psychology.* Cambridge: Cambridge University Press.

Moll, L., & Greenberg, J. B. (1990). Creating zones of possibilities: combining social contexts for instruction. In L. C. Moll (Ed.), *Vygotsky and education: Instructional implications and applications of sociohistorical psychology.* (pp. 175–204). Cambridge: Cambridge University Press.

Moraes, M. (1996). *Bilingual education: A dialogue with the Bakhtin circle*. Albany: State University of New York Press.
Moraga, C., & Anzaldùa, G. (1981). *This bridge called my back: Writings by radical women of color*. Watertown, MA: Persephone Press.
Morgan, B. (1998). *The ESL classroom: Teaching, critical practice, and community development*. Toronto: University of Toronto Press.
Morgan, L. H. (1877). *Ancient society*. New York: Holt.
Motha, S. (2003). "I tell because I know, I know because I tell: Storied power in second language teaching." *Educational Practice and Theory, 24*(2), 5–21.
Murray, D. E. (1992). *Diversity as resource: Redefining cultural literacy*. Alexandria, VA: Teachers of English to Speakers of Other Languages.
Murray, D. M. (1984). *Write to learn*. New York: Holt, Rinehart, and Winston.
Muspratt, S., Luke, A., & Freebody, P. (Eds.). (1997). *Constructing critical literacies: Teaching and learning textual practice*. Cresskill, NJ: Hampton Press.
Nakanishi, D. T., & Hirano-Nakanishi, M. (1983). *The education of Asian and Pacific Americans: Historical perspectives and prescriptions for the future*. Phoenix, AZ: Oxford Press.
Nakanishi, D. T., & Yamano Nishida, T. (1995). *The Asian American Educational Experience: a sourcebook for teachers and students*. New York: Routledge.
Narayan, U., & Harding, S. (2000). *Decentering the center: Philosophy for a multicultural, postcolonial, and feminist world*. Bloomington, IN: University Press.
Nauman, S. E., Jr. (1978). *Dictionary of Asian philosophies*. Secaucus, NJ: Citadel Press.
Nelson, C. (1999). Sexual identities in TESOL: Queer theory and classroom inquiry. *TESOL Quarterly, 33*(3), 371–392.
New London Group (1996). A pedagogy of multuliteracies: Designing social futures. *Harvard Educational Review, 66*, 60–92.
Newmann, F., & Holzman, L. (1993). *Lev Vygotsky: Revolutionary scientist*. New York: Routledge.
Ngùgì, wa T. (2003). The language of African literature. In R. Harris & B. E. Rampton (Eds.), *The language. ethnicity and race reader* (pp. 69–84). (Originally published in 1981 in Ngùgì wa Thiong'o Decolonizing the mind. London: Heinemann, pp. 1984–1933). London: Routledge.
Nieto, S. (1996). *Affirming diversity: The sociopolitical context of multicultural education*. White Plains, NY: Longman.
Noddings, N. (1986). Fidelity in teaching, teacher education, and research for teaching. *Harvard Educational Review, 56*(No. 4).
Norton, B. (1997). Language, identity and the ownership of English. *TESOL Quarterly, 31*, 409–430.
Norton, B. (1998). Rethinking acculturation in second language acquisition. *Prospect: A Journal of Australian TESOL, 13*, 4–19.
Norton, B. (2000). *Identity and language learning: Gender, ethnicity and educational change*. New York: Longman.
Nunan, D. (1999). *Second language teaching and learning*. Boston: Heinle & Heinle.
Nunan, D. (2000). The great debate: Is TESOL an art or a science. *Journal of the Imagination in Language Learning, V*, 8–9.
Oakes, J. (1985). *Keeping track: How schools structure inequality*. New Haven, CT: Yale University Press.
Ochs, E. (1988). *Culture and language development: Language acquisition and language socialization in a Samoan village*. Cambridge: Cambridge University Press.
Odlin, T. (Ed.). (1994). *Perspectives on pedagogical grammar*. Cambridge: Cambridge University Press.

Ohta, A. S. (2001). *Second language acquisition processes in the classroom learning Japanese*. Mahwah, NJ: Lawrence Erlbaum Associates.
Olsen, L. (1997). *Made in America: Immigrant students in our public schools*. New York: New Press.
Olsen, T. (1978). *Silences*. New York: Delacorte Press/Seymour Lawrence.
Omi, M., & Winant, H. (1986). *Racial formation in the United States*. New York: Routledge.
Osterling, J. P. (2001). Waking the sleeping giant: Engaging and capitalizing on the sociocultural strengths of the Latino community. *Bilingual Research Journal, 25*(1&2), 59–89.
Ovando, C. J., & Collier, V. P. (1985). *Bilingual and ESL classrooms: Teaching in multicultural contexts* (2nd ed.). Boston: McGraw-Hill.
Oxford, R. (1990). *Language learning strategies: What every teacher should know*. New York: Newbury House.
Pagano, J. *Exiles and communities: Teaching in the patriarchal wilderness*. Albany: SUNY Press.
Pakir, A. (1999). Connecting with English in the context of internationalisation. *TESOL Quarterly, 33*(1), 103–113.
Pao, D., Wong, S., & Teuben-Rowe, S. (1997). Identity formation for mixed heritage adults: Implications for educators. *TESOL Quarterly, 31*(3), 622–631.
Parakrama, A. (1995). *De-hegemonizing language standards: Learning from (post) colonial Englishes about "English."* New York: St. Martin's Press.
Pavlenko, A. (2001). *Multilingualism, second language learning, and gender*. New York: Mouton de Gruyter.
Pavlenko, A. (2004). Gender and sexuality in foreign and second language education: Critical and feminist approaches. In B. Norton & K. Toohey (Eds.), *Critical pedagogies and language learning* (pp. 53–71). Cambridge: Cambridge University Press.
Pennycook, A. (1994a). Critical pedagogical approaches to research. *TESOL Quarterly, 28*(4), 690–693.
Pennycook, A. (1994b). *The cultural politics of English as an international language*. London: Longman.
Pennycook, A. (1994c). Incommensurable discourses? *Applied Linguistics, 15*, 115–138.
Pennycook, A. (1995). English in the world/The world in English. In J. W. Tollefson (Ed.), *Power and inequality in language education* (pp. 34–58). Cambridge: University of Cambridge Press.
Pennycook, A. (2001). *Critical applied linguistics: A critical introduction*. Mahwah, NJ: Lawrence Erlbaum Associates.
Pennycook, A. (2002). Method, interested knowledge and politics. In V. a. S. Zamell, R. Spack (Eds.), *Enriching ESOL pedagogy* (pp. 45–71). Mahwah, NJ: Lawrence Erlbaum Associates.
Perez, B., & Torres-Guzmán, M. E. (1992). *Learning in two worlds: An integrated Spanish/English biliteracy approach*. New York: Longman.
Perry, T. & Delpit, L. (Eds.). (1998). The real Ebonics debate: Power, language and the education of African-American children. Boston: Beacon Press.
Peyton, J., & Reed, L. (1990). *Dialogue journal writing with nonnative English speakers: A handbook for teachers*. Alexandria, VA: TESOL.
Peyton, J. K. (Ed.). (1990). *Students and teachers writing together: Perspectives on journal writing*. Alexandria, VA: TESOL.
Peyton, J. K. (1993). *Dialogue journals in multilingual classroom: Building language fluency and writing skills through written interaction*. Norwood, NJ: Ablex.

Peyton, J. K., Jones, C., Vincent, A., & Greenblatt, L. (1994). Implementing writing workshop with ESOL students: Visions and realities. *TESOL Quarterly, 28*(3), 469–488.

Phillipson, R. (1988). Linguicism: Structures and ideologies in linguistic imperialism. In J. Cummins & T. Skutnabb-Kangas (Eds.), *Minority education: From shame to struggle* (pp. 339–358). Clevedon: Multilingual Matters.

Phillipson, R. (1992). *Linguistic imperialism*. Oxford: Oxford University Press.

Phillipson, R., & Skutnabb-Kangas, T. (1996). English only worldwide or language ecology? *TESOL Quarterly, 30,* 429–452.

Pica, T. (1987). Second-language acquisition, social interaction, and the classroom. *Applied Linguistics, 8,* 3–21.

Pierce, B. N. (1995). Social identity, investment and language learning. *TESOL Quarterly, 29,* 9–31.

Pinar, W. (Ed.). (1998). *Queer theory in education*. Mahwah, NJ: Lawrence Erlbaum Associates.

Platt, E. J. (1995, Fall). Challenges to the input/output model in second language acquisition. *Sunshine State TESOL Journal, 1*(12), 38–44.

Platt, E., & Brooks, F. B. (1994). The "acquisition-rich environment" revisited. *Modern Language Journal, 78,* 497–511.

Power, E. J. (Ed.). (1962). *Main currents in the history of education*. New York: McGraw-Hill.

Prator, C. (1968). The British heresy in TESL. In J. Fishman, C. Ferguson, & J. Das Gupta (Eds.), *Language problems in developing nations* (pp. 11–30). New York: John Wiley & Sons.

Prator, C. (1979). The cornerstones of method. In M. Celce-Murcia & L. McIntosh (Eds.), *Teaching English as a second or foreign language* (pp. xv, 389). Rowley, MA: Newbury House.

Proulx, E. A. (1996). *Accordion crimes*: Fourth Estate.

Rai, M. (1995). *Chomsky's politics*. London: Verso, New Left Books.

Ramirez, M., & Castenada, A. (1974). *Cultural democracy, bicognitive development and education.* New York: Academic Press.

Rassias, J. (1983). New dimensions in language training: The Dartmouth College experiment. In J. W. Oller & P. A. Richard-Amato (Eds.), *Methods that work: A smorgasbord of ideas for language teachers* (pp. 363–374). Rowley, MA: Newbury House.

Reid, J. M. (1993). *Teaching ESL writing*. Englewood Cliffs, NJ: Regents/Prentice Hall.

Ricento, T. (1998). National language policy in the United States. In T. Ricento & B. Burnaby (Eds.), *Language and politics in the United States and Canada: Myths and realities* (pp. 85–112). Mahwah, NJ: Lawrence Erlbaum Associates.

Richard-Amato, P. A. (1988). *Making it happen: Interaction in the second language classroom* (2nd ed.). New York: Longman.

Richards, J. C., & Rodgers, T. S. (1986). *Approaches and methods in language teaching: A description and analysis*. Cambridge: Cambridge University Press.

Rigg, P., & Enright, D. S. (Eds.). (1986). *Children and ESL: Integrating perspectives.* Alexandria, VA: Teachers of English to Speakers of Other Languages (TESOL).

Rivers, W. M. (1983). Learning a sixth language: An adult learner's daily diary. In *Communicating naturally in a second language: Theory and practice in language teaching* (pp. 169–189). Cambridge: Cambridge University Press.

Robeson, P. (1958). *Here I stand.* Boston Beacon Press.

Roberts, C. (1997). Transcribing talk: Issues of representation. *TESOL Quarterly, 31*(1), 167–172.

Rodney, W. (1982). *How Europe underdeveloped Africa*. Washington, DC: Howard University Press.

Rogers, C. R. (1961). *On becoming a person: A therapist's view of psychotherapy*. Boston: Houghton Mifflin.

Rogoff, B. (1990). *Apprenticeship in thinking: Cognitive development in social context*. New York: Oxford University Press.

Ruopp, K., & Wong, S. (1995). *Taking books home: A check-out system for the primary grades.* Instructional Resource No. 9. National Reading Research Center, University of Georgia and the University of Maryland at College Park.

Sadker, M., & Sadker, D. M. (1994). *Failing at fairness: How America's schools cheat girls*. New York: C. Scribner's Sons.

Sagan, C. (1994). *Pale blue dot: A vision of the human future in space.* New York: Random House.

Said, E. (1979). *Orientalism*. New York: Random House.

Salzman, M. (1990). *Iron & silk*. New York: Vintage Departures.

Samway, K. D., & McKeon, D. (1999). *Myths and realities: Best practices for language minority students.* Portsmouth, NH: Heinemann.

Sartre, J. P. (1953). *Being and nothingness: An essay on phenomenological ontology* (H. E. Barnes, Trans.). New York, New York: Washington Square Press.

Sarwar, Z. (2001). Innovations in large classes in Pakistan. *TESOL Quarterly, 35*(3), 497–500.

Saussure, F. (1966). *Course in general linguistics.* New York: McGraw-Hill.

Savignon, S. (1983). *Communicative competence: Theory and classroom practice*. Reading, MA: Addison-Wesley.

Savignon, S. (2002). Communicative language teaching: Linguistic theory and classroom practice. In S. Savignon (Ed.), *Interpreting communicative language teaching: Contexts and concerns in teacher education* (pp. 1–27). New Haven: Yale University Press.

Schreiter, R. J. (1986). *Constructing local theologies.* Maryknoll, NY: Orbis Books.

Schumann, J. (1976). Social distance as a factor in second language acquisition. *Language Learning, 26,* 135–143.

Schumann, J. (1986). Research on the acculturation model for second language acquisition. *Journal for Multilingual and Multicultural Development, 7,* 379–392.

Schurmann, F., & Schell, O. (1967). *Republican China: Nationalism, war and the rise of communism 1911–1949.* New York: Vintage Books.

Scollon, R., & Scollon, S. B. K. (1995). *Intercultural communication: A discourse approach*. Cambridge, MA: Blackwell.

Scollon, S. W. (1997). Metaphors of self and communication: English and Cantonese. *Multilingual, 16*(1), 1–38.

Scribner, S., & Cole, M. (1978). Literacy without schooling: Testing for intellectual effects. *Harvard Educational Review, 48*(4), 448–461.

Selden, S. (1999). *Inheriting shame: The story of eugenics and racism in America*. New York: Teachers College Press.

Serpell, R. (1991). Dialogue: Exaggerating the significance of text. *Curriculum Inquiry, 21*(3), 353–362.

Shamim, F. (1996). In or out of the action zone: Location as a feature of interaction in large ESL classes in Pakistan. In K. M. Bailey & D. Nunan (Eds.), *Voices from the language eclassroom* (pp. 123–144). Cambridge, England: Cambridge University Press.

Shohamy, E. (2000). Argument and entertainment: TESOL as a science. *The Journal of the Imagination in Language Learning, 5,* 10–12.

Shohamy, E. (2001a). Democratic assessment as an alternative. *Language Testing, 18*(4), 373–391.

Shohamy, E. (2001b). *The power of tests: A critical perspective on the uses of language tests*. Harlow, England: Longman, Pearson Education.

Shor, I., & Freire, P. (1987). *A pedagogy for liberation*. South Hadley, MA: Bergin & Garvey.

Simmonds, F. N. (1998). Naming and identity. In D. Cameron (Ed.), *The feminist critique of language: A reader* (pp. 33–38). New York: Routledge.

Skutnabb-Kangas, T. (1988). Multilingualism and the education of minority children. In T. Skutnabb-Kangas & J. Cummins (Eds.), *Minority Education* (pp. 9–44). Clevedon, England: Multilingual Matters.

Skutnabb-Kangas, T. (2000). *Linguistic genocide in education or worldwide diversity and human rights?* Mahwah, NJ: Lawrence Erlbaum Associates.

Skutnabb-Kangas, T., Phillipson, R. (Ed.). (1994). *Linguistic human rights: Overcoming linguistics discrimination*. New York: M. de Gruyter.

Smitherman-Donaldson, G., & van Dijk, T. A. (1988). *Discourse and discrimination*. Detroit, MI: Wayne State University Press.

Snow, E. (1968). *Red star over China*. New York: Grove Press.

Snow, L. (1983). *Edgar Snow's China: A personal account of the Chinese revolution compiled from the writings of Edgar Snow*. New York: Vintage Books.

Snow, M. A., Hyland, J., Kamhi-Stein, _., & Yu, J. (1996). U.S. language minority students: Voices from the junior high classroom. In K. M. Bailey & D. Nunan (Eds.), *Voices from the language eclassroom* (pp. 304–317). Cambridge, England: Cambridge University Press.

Solorzano, D. G., & Ornelas, A. (2002). A critical race analysis of advanced placement classes: A case of educational inequality. *Journal of Latinos and Education, 1*(4), 215–229.

St. Maurice, H. (1987). Clinical supervision and power: Regimes of instructional management. In T. S. Popkewitz (Ed.), *Critical studies in teacher education: Its folklore, theory, and practice* (pp. 242–264). London: Falmer Press.

Starfield, S. (2002). "I'm a second-language English speaker": Negotiating writer identity and authority in sociology one. *Journal of Language, Identity, and Education, 1*(2), 121–140.

Stein, P. (1998). *Reconfiguring the past and the present: Performing literacy histories in a Johannesburg classroom* (Vol. 32).

Stevick, E. W. (1988). *Teaching and learning languages*. Cambridge: Cambridge University Press.

Street, B. (1984). *Literacy in theory and practice*. Cambridge: Cambridge University Press.

Street, B. (1995). *Social literacies: Critical approaches to literacy in development, ethnography and education*. London: Longman.

Sutherland, M. (1997). *Black authenticity: A psychology for liberating people of African descent*. Chicago, IL: Third World Press.

Swain, M. (1985). Communicative competence: Some roles of comprehensive input and comprehensible output in its development. In S. M. Gass, A. & C. E. Madden (Eds.), *Input in second language acquisition* (pp. 235–256). Rowley: MA: Newbury House.

Swain, M. (2000). The output hypothesis and beyond: Mediating acquisition through collaborative dialogue. In J. P. Lantolf (Ed.), *Sociocultural theory and second language learning* (pp. 97–114). Oxford: Oxford University Press.

Sweet, H. (1899). *The practical study of languages: A guide for teachers and learners*. London: Dent.

Takagi, D. Y. (1992). *The retreat from race: Asian American admission and racial politics*. New Brunswick, NJ: Rutgers University Press.

Takaki, R. (1990). *Strangers from a different shore: a history of Asian Americans*. New York: Penguin.

Takaki, R. (1993). *A different mirror: A history of multicultural America*. Boston: Little, Brown and Company.
Tannen, D. (1993). The relativity of linguistic strategies: Rethinking power and solidarity in gender and dominance. In D. Tannen (Ed.), *Gender and conversational interaction* (pp. 165–188). New York: Oxford University Press.
Taylor, C. (1986). Foucault on freedom and truth. In D. C. Hoy (Ed.), Foucault: A critical reader (pp. 64–102). Cambridge, MA: Basil Blackwell.
Tharp, R. G., & Gallimore, R. (1988). *Rousing minds to life : teaching, learning, and schooling in social context*. New York: Cambridge University Press.
Tharp, R. G., & Gallimore, R. (1989). Rousing schools to life. *American Educator: The Professional Journal of the American Federation of Teachers, 13*(2), 20–25, 46–52.
Tharp, R. G., & Educational Resources Information Center (1991). *The instructional conversation teaching and learning in social activity*. Washington, DC: National Center for Research on Cultural Diversity and Second Language Learning; U.S. Department of Education, Office of Educational Research and Improvement, Educational Resources Information Center.
Thomas, W. & Collier, V.P. (1997). *School effectiveness for language minority students*. Washington, DC : National Clearinghouse for Bilingual Education.
Tickoo, M. L. (1991). *Languages and standards: Issues, attitudes, case studies*. Paper presented at the RELC Anthology, Singapore.
Tinker Sachs, G. (2002). Learning Cantonese: Reflections of an EFL teacher educator. In D. C. S. Li (Ed.), *Discourses in search of members: A festschrift in honor of Ron Scollon* (pp. 509–540). New York: University Press of America.
Todorov, T. (1984). *Mikhail Bakhtin: The dialogical principle*. Minneapolis: University of Minnesota Press.
Toh, S. H., & Floresca-Cawagas, V. (2000). Editorial. *International Journal of Curriculum and Instruction, 2*(1).
Tollefson, J. W. (1991). *Planning language, planning inequality: Language policy in the community*. London: Longman.
Tollefson, J. W. (Ed.). (1995). *Power and inequality in language education*. New York: Cambridge University Press.
Toohey, K. (1998). "Breaking them up, Taking them away": ESL students in Grade 1. *TESOL Quarterly, 32*(1), 61–84.
Toohey, K. (2000). *Learning English at school: Identity, social relations, and classroom practice*. Clevedon, England: Multilingual Matters.
Tu, W.-M. (1985). *Confucian thought: Selfhood as creative transformation*. Albany: State University of New York Press.
Tu, W.-M. (1992). Forward. In D. Xu (Ed.), *A comparison of the educational ideas and practices of John Dewey and Mao Zedong in China: Is school society or society school?* (pp. ii–iii). San Francisco: Mellen Research University Press.
Tucker, G. R. (2000). Precision, Elegance and Simplicity: Perspectives on TESOL and art. *Journal of the Imagination in Language Learning, 5*, 24–26.
Tyson, C. A. (1998). A response to "Coloring epistemology: Are our qualitative research epistemologies racially biased?" *Educational Researcher, 27*(9), 21–22.
Urzua, C. (1987). "You stopped too soon": Second language children composing and Revising. *TESOL Quarterly, 21*(2), 279–304.
Valdés, G. (2004). The teaching of academic language to language minority second language learners. In A. F. Ball & S. W. Freedman (Eds.), *Bakhtinian perspectives on language, literacy and learning* (pp. 66–98). Cambridge, England: Cambridge University Press.
Valdez-Pierce, L. (2003). *Assessing English Language Learners*. Washington, DC: National Education Association.

Valli, L. (1992). *Reflective teacher education: Cases and critiques.* Albany: State University of New York Press.
Valli, L. (1995). The dilemma of race: Learning to be color blind and color conscious. *Journal of Teacher Education, 46*(2).
Van Dijk, T. A. (1993). Principles of critical discourse analysis. *Discourse and Society, 4*(2), 249–283.
Vandrick, S. (1997). The role of hidden identities in the postsecondary ESL classroom. *TESOL Quarterly, 31*(1), 153–157.
Vandrick, S. (2002). ESL and the colonial legacy: A teacher faces her "missionary kid" past. In V. a. S. Zamel (Ed.), *Enriching ESOL pedagogy: Readings and activities for engagement, reflection and inquiry* (pp. 411–422). Mahwah, NJ: Lawrence Erlbaum Associates.
van Lier, L. (1994a). Forks and hope: Pursuing understanding in different ways. *Applied Linguistics, 15*(3), 328–346.
van Lier, L. (1994b). Some features of a theory of practice. *TESOL Journal, 4*(1), 6–10.
Vásquez, O. A. (2003). *La Clase Mágica: Imagining optimal possibilities in a bilingual community of learners.* Mahwah, NJ: Lawrence Erlbaum Associates.
Verhoeven, L. (Ed.). (1994). *Functional literacy.* Amsterdam: Benjamins.
Verplaetse, L. S. (2000). Mr. Wonder-ful: Portrait of a dialogic teacher. In J. K. Hall & L. S. Verplaetse (Eds.), *Second and foreign language learning through classroom Interaction* (pp. 221–242). Mahwah, NJ: Lawrence Erlbaum Associates.
Vollmer, H. J. (1997). Strategien der Verstaendinis- und Verstehenssicherung in interkultureller Kommunikation. In U. Rampillion & G. Zimmermann (Eds.), *Strategien and Techniken beim Erwerb Fremder Sprachen* (pp. 216–269). Muenchen: Hueber.
Vollmer, H. J. (1999). From critical discourse awareness to intercultural literacy. In R. Wodak, H. J. Krumm, & R. De-Cellia (Eds.), *Loss of communication in the information Age.* Vienna: Austrian Academy of Sciences.
Vološinov, V. N. (1973). *Marxism and the philosophy of language* (L. Matejka & I. R. Titunik, Trans.). Cambridge, MA: Harvard University Press.
Vygotsky, L. S. (1962). *Thought and language.* Cambridge, MA: MIT Press.
Vygotsky, L. S. (1978). Mind in society: The development of higher psychological processes. Cambridge, MA: Harvard University Press.
Wallerstein, N. (1983). *Language and culture in conflict: Problem posing in the ESL classroom.* Reading, MA: Addison-Wesley.
Walsh, C. E. (1996). *Education reform and social change.* Mahwah, NJ: Lawrence Erlbaum Associates.
Wang, J., Comp. (1984, April). *Entering the mainstream.* Paper presented at the East Coast Asian American Education Conference, Washington, DC.
Weedon, C. (1987). *Feminist practice and poststructualist theory.* London: Blackwell.
Weiler, K. (1988). *Women teaching for change.* South Hadley, MA: Bergin & Garvey.
Weiler, K. (2001). *Feminist engagements: Reading, resisting, and revisioning male theorists in education and cultural studies.* New York: Routledge.
Weinberg, M. (1997). *Asian American education: Historical background and current realities.* Mahwah, NJ: Lawrence Erlbaum Associates.
Weinstein-Shr, G. (1993). Literacy and social process: a community in transition. In B. Street (Ed.), *Cross-cultural approaches to literacy* (pp. 272–293). New York: Cambridge University Press.
Weinstein-Shr, G., & Quintero, E. (Eds.). (1995). *Immigrant learners and their Families: Literacy to connect the generations.* Washington, DC, & McHenry, IL: Center for Applied Linguistics & Delta Systems.
Weis, L., & Fine, M. (Eds.) (1993). *Beyond silenced voices: Class, race and gender in United States schools.* Albany, NY: State University of New York Press.

Welch, S. D. (1985). *Communities of resistance and solidarity: A feminist theology of liberation*. Maryknoll, NY: Orbis.
Wells, G. (1990). Talk about text: Where literacy is learned and taught. *Curriculum Inquiry, 20*(4), 369–405.
Wells, G. (1994). The complementary contributions of Halliday and Vygotsky to a "language-based theory of learning." *Linguistics and Education, 6*, 41–90.
Wells, G. (1999). *Dialogic inquiry: Towards a sociocultural practice and theory of Education*. Cambridge, England: Cambridge University Press.
Wertsch, J. (1985). *Vygotsky and the social formation of mind*. Cambridge, MA: Harvard University Press.
Wertsch, J. (1991). *Voices of the mind*. Cambridge, MA: Harvard University Press.
Whorf, B. L. (1966). *Language, thought, and reality; selected writings*. Cambridge, MA: MIT Press.
Wickeri, P. L. (1984). *Seeking the common ground: Protestant Christianity, the three-self movement and China's united front*. Princeton Theological Seminary, Princeton, NJ.
Widdowson, H. (2000). TESOL: Art and craft. *Journal of the Imagination in Language Learning, 5*, 14–16.
Widdowson, H. G. (1978). *Teaching language as communication*. Oxford: Oxford University Press.
Wiley, T. G. (1996). *Literacy and language diversity in the United States*. Washington, DC, & McHenry, IL: Center for Applied Linguistics & Delta Systems.
Wilkins, D. A. (1976). *Notional syllabuses*. Oxford: Oxford University Press.
Willett, J., Solsken, J., & Wilson-Keenan, J. (1998). The (Im)Possibilities of constructing multicultural language practices in research and pedagogy. *Linguistics and Education, 10*(2), 165–218.
Williams, D. (1996). Christianity and sexism: The challenge of womanist theology. In M. Chapman (Ed.), *Christianity on trial: African American religious thoughts before and after Black power* (pp. 168–180). Maryknoll, NY: Orbis.
Wink, J., & Putney, L. (2002). *A vision of Vygotsky*. Boston, MA: Allyn & Bacon.
Wolfram, W. (1993). Ethical considerations in language awareness programs. *Issues of Applied Linguistics, 4*(2), 225–240.
Wolfram, W., Adger, C. T., & Christian, D. (1999). *Dialects in schools and communities*. Mahwah, NJ: Lawrence Erlbaum Associates.
Wong, K. (1995). Cultural democracy and the revitalization of the U.S. labor movement. In A. Darder (Ed.) *Culture and difference: Critical perspectives on bicultural experience in the United States* (pp. 71–80). Westport, CT: Bergin & Garvey.
Wong, S. (1985). *Do Chinese adult ESL students need survival English?* Unpublished master's thesis. Los Angeles: UCLA.
Wong, S. (1990). *Pilgrimage: An American journey. English as a second language for Chinese theological students*. Unpublished doctoral dissertation, Columbia University, Teachers College, New York.
Wong, S. (1995). Curriculum transformation: A psycholinguistics course for prospective teachers of ESOL K–12. In J. Alatis (Ed.), *Linguistics and the education of second language teachers: Ethnolinguistics, and sociolinguistics aspects* (pp. 471–479). Washington, DC : Georgetown University Press.
Wong, S. (1996). Reflections of a course instructor on a critical incident: Racial conflict and curriculum transformation. *Multiculturalism, 16*(2), 23–26.
Wong, S. (2000). Transforming the politics of schooling in the U.S.: A model for successful academic achievement for language minority students. In J. K. Hall & W.

Eggington (Eds.), *The sociopolitics of English language teaching* (pp. 117–139). Clevedon, UK: Multilingual Matters.

Wong, S., & Grant, R. (1995). Addressing poverty in the Baltimore–Washington metropolitan area: What can teachers do? *Literacy Issues and Practices, 12*, 3–12.

Wong, S., Groth, L., & O'Flahavan, J. (1994). *Characterizing teacher-student interaction in reading recovery lessons.* (No. 17). College Park, MD: National Reading Research Center, University of Georgia and the University of Maryland.

Wong, S., & Teuben-Rowe, S. (1997). Honoring students' home languages and cultures in a multilingual classroom. *Sunshine State TESOL Journal*, 20–26.

Wong-Fillmore, L. (1985). When does teacher talk work as input? In S. Gass & C. G. Madden (Eds.), *Input in second language acquisition* (pp. 17–50). Rowley, MA: Newbury House.

Wong-Fillmore, L. (1993). Learning a language from learners. In C. Kramsch & S. M. Ginet (Eds.), *Text and context* (pp. 46–66). Lexington, MA: D. C. Heath.

Wong-Fillmore, L. (2000). Loss of family languages: Should educators be concerned? *Theory Into Practice, 39*(4), 203–210.

Wright, A. (1984). *1000 Pictures for teachers to copy.* London: Collins ELT & Addison-Wesley.

Wu, L. C. (1986). *Fundamentals of Chinese philosophy.* Lanham. MD: University Press of America.

Wulf-McGraff, R. (2000). Making the difference with reading instruction: Reader's workshop. *Classroom Leadership, 4.*

Xu, D. (1992). *A comparison of the educational ideas and practices of John Dewey and Mao Zedong in China: Is school society or society school?* San Francisco: Mellen Research University Press.

Yamashiro, A. (1996). The "Parfait Effect": Implications of a tracking system on perception of male adolescent language learners. In C. P. Casanave & A. D. Yamashiro (Eds.), *Gender issues in language education* (pp. 82–99). Fujisawa, Japan: Keio University's Shonan Fujisawa Campus (SFC).

Zamel, V. (1983). The composing processes of advanced ESL students: Six case studies. *TESOL Quarterly, 17*(2), 165–187.

Zamel, V. & Spack, R. (Eds.). (1998). *Negotiating academic literacies.* Mahwah, NJ: Lawrence Erlbaum Associates.

Zia, H. (2000). *Asian American dreams: The emergence of an American people.* New York: Farrar Straus and Giroux.

Author Index

Note. Page numbers followed by *n* denotes footnote.

W

X

Y

Z

Subject Index

Note. Page number followed by *n* denotes footnote.